A Guide to Teaching Research Methods in Psychology

Teaching Psychological Science
Series editors: William Buskist and Douglas A. Bernstein

The *Teaching Psychological Science* series focuses on critical aspects of teaching core courses in psychology. The books share ideas, tips, and strategies for effective teaching and offer all the pedagogical tools an instructor needs to plan the course in one handy and concise volume. Written by outstanding teachers and edited by Bill Buskist and Doug Bernstein, who are themselves well-respected authors and teachers, each book provides a wealth of concrete suggestions not found in other volumes, a clear roadmap for teaching and practical, concrete, hands-on tips for novice teachers and experienced instructors alike.

Each book includes:

- Ideas for beginning the course
- Sample lecture outlines for the entire course
- Examples and applications that link the course content to every-day student experience
- Classroom demonstrations and activities with an emphasis on promoting active learning and critical thinking
- Discussion of sensitive and difficult-to-teach topics and ethical issues likely to be encountered throughout the semester
- Course-specific options for evaluating student performance
- A chapter on available resources for teaching the course

Titles in *Teaching Psychological Science* series

A Guide to Teaching Research Methods in Psychology

Bryan K. Saville

BLACKWELL PUBLISHING
350 Main Street, Malden, MA 02148-5020, USA
9600 Garsington Road, Oxford OX4 2DQ, UK
550 Swanston Street, Carlton, Victoria 3053, Australia

First published 2008 by Blackwell Publishing Ltd

1   2008

Library of Congress Cataloging-in-Publication Data

Saville, Bryan K.
   A guide to teaching research methods in psychology / Bryan K. Saville.
      p. cm. — (Teaching psychological science)
   Includes bibliographical references and index.
   ISBN 978–1–4051–5480–2 (hardcover : alk. paper) — ISBN 978–1–4051–5481–9
(pbk. : alk. paper)   1. Psychology—Research—Methodology—Study and
teaching.   I. Title.

   BF76.5.S27 2008
   150.72—dc22

                                                              2007021329

A catalogue record for this title is available from the British Library.

Set in 10.5/13pt Sabon
by Graphicraft Limited, Hong Kong
Printed and bound in Singapore
by Utopia Press Pte Ltd

The publisher's policy is to use permanent paper from mills that operate
a sustainable forestry policy, and which has been manufactured from
pulp processed using acid-free and elementary chlorine-free practices.
Furthermore, the publisher ensures that the text paper and cover board
used have met acceptable environmental accreditation standards.

For further information on
Blackwell Publishing, visit our website:
www.blackwellpublishing.com

Contents

Series Editors' Preface

As the best teachers among us can surely attest, teaching at the college and university level is no easy task. Even psychology, as inherently interesting as it may be, is a difficult subject to teach well. Indeed, being an effective teacher of any discipline requires a steadfast commitment to self-improvement as a scholar, thinker, and communicator over the long haul. No one becomes a master teacher overnight.

Compared to other disciplines, though, psychology has been way ahead of the curve when it comes to taking its teaching seriously. The Society for the Teaching of Psychology (http://teachpsych.org/) was founded in 1946 and continues to be a powerful force in supporting the teaching of psychology in high schools, community colleges, and four-year schools. The annual National Institute on the Teaching of Psychology, or as it is more informally known, NITOP (www.nitop.org), has been featuring an impressive venue of pedagogical presentations since 1978. In addition, several annual regional teaching of psychology conferences offer a variety of talks, workshops, and poster sessions on improving one's teaching.

Psychologists have also led the way in writing books on effective teaching. Perhaps the best known among these texts is McKeachie's (2006) *Teaching Tips*, now in its 12th edition (the first edition was published in 1951). Although McKeachie wrote *Teaching Tips* for all teachers, regardless of discipline, other books focused specifically on teaching psychology have appeared in the past several years (e.g., Buskist & Davis, 2006; Davis & Buskist, 2002; Forsyth, 2003; Goss Lucas & Bernstein, 2005). The common theme across these books is that they offer general advice for teaching any psychology course, and in McKeachie's case, for teaching any college course.

The volumes in Blackwell's *Teaching Psychological Science* series differ from existing books. In one handy and concise source, each book provides everything that instructors need to help them in their courses. Each volume in the series targets a specific course: introductory psychology, developmental psychology, research methods, statistics, behavioral neuroscience, memory and cognition, learning, abnormal behavior, and personality and social psychology. Each book is authored by accomplished, well-respected teachers who share their best strategies for teaching these courses effectively.

Each book in the series also features advice on how to teach particularly difficult topics; how to link course content to everyday student experiences; how to develop and use class presentations, lectures, and active learning ideas; and how to increase student interest in course topics. Each volume ends with a chapter that describes resources for teaching the particular course focused on in that book, as well as an appendix on widely available resources for the teaching of psychology in general.

The *Teaching Psychological Science* series is geared to assist all teachers at all levels to master the teaching of particular courses. Each volume focuses on how to teach specific content as opposed to processes involved in teaching more generally. Thus veteran teachers as well as graduate students and new faculty will likely find these books a useful source of new ideas for teaching their courses.

As editors of this series, we are excited about the prospects these books offer for enhancing the teaching of specific courses within our field. We are delighted that Wiley Blackwell shares our excitement for the series and we wish to thank our editor Christine Cardone and our development project manager Sarah Coleman for their devoted work to help us bring the series to fruition. We hope that you find this book, and all the books in the series, a helpful and welcome addition to your collection of teaching resources.

Douglas A. Bernstein
William Buskist
April 2007

References

Buskist, W., & Davis, S. F. (Eds.). (2006). *Handbook of the teaching of psychology*. Malden, MA: Blackwell.

Davis, S. F., & Buskist, W. (Eds.). (2002). *The teaching of psychology: Essays in honor of Wilbert J. McKeachie and Charles L. Brewer*. Mahwah, NJ: Erlbaum.

Forsyth, D. R. (2003). *The professor's guide to teaching: Psychological principles and practices*. Washington, DC: American Psychological Association.

Goss Lucas, S., & Bernstein, D. A. (2005). *Teaching psychology: A step by step guide*. Mahwah, NJ: Erlbaum.

McKeachie, W. J. (2006). *McKeachie's teaching tips: Strategies, research, and theory for college and university teachers* (12th ed.). Boston: Houghton Mifflin.

Preface

Several years ago, while still in graduate school, I had the opportunity to teach my first research methods course. At the time, I was in the process of applying for academic positions, and I knew that teaching research methods would likely make me a more attractive candidate to potential employers. By then, I had taught a number of different courses, including introductory psychology and social psychology—courses that, for the most part, students enjoy and for which they can easily see how the course material relates to their own lives. As the start of the semester approached, I—an aspiring experimental psychologist, mind you—reveled in the opportunity to teach my students about research methods, a topic that, in my mind, was equally, if not more, important than anything they had learned about in their introductory or social psychology classes. I had no doubt that they would quickly see the importance of research methods in their lives and dive wholeheartedly into the course material.

Boy, was I wrong. I soon learned that teaching research methods was different than teaching many of the other courses that typically make up traditional psychology curricula. Instead of intense classroom discussions about internal validity and shouts of "Yes, of course I understand why statistical regression and factorial designs are important!", I was confronted with looks of apathy—looks that indicated to me that many of my students had simply "checked out." Some were even resentful—resentful that they had to take this class that had "nothing to do with psychology, or our lives, for that matter." In fact, more than once I heard comments such as the following: "I'm going to be a counselor, so I don't need to know about research" or "What does research methods have to do with clinical psychology?" or "I'm not going to graduate school, so this stuff isn't important to me." Most likely, those of you who teach research methods have heard similar comments from your students. At that point, I realized that I had to reassess how I was going to teach the class more effectively—and I've spent the last several years doing just that.

Ultimately, I decided to write this book for one primary reason: Teaching psychological research methods can be difficult. In fact, teaching psychological research methods can be challenging and frustrating—even disheartening at times. For numerous reasons, students frequently enter our research methods courses with a strong distaste for the material and little interest in conducting psychological research—even though few of them know much about the content of research methods in general or the process of conducting research in particular. Thus research methods instructors often face an uphill battle from the minute they enter the classroom, a battle that sometimes continues throughout the semester.

Yet teaching psychological research methods can also be very rewarding. Although not every one of your students will choose a career in which they conduct research—most likely, the large majority won't—many of them, especially with the right amount of encouragement and support, may find themselves more interested in research methods than they ever would have thought possible. And even if your students choose not to pursue research-oriented careers, you nevertheless have the opportunity in your research methods course to affect their lives in other important ways—for example, by teaching them to become better critical thinkers and by teaching them other important skills that will serve them well in a rapidly changing world.

Thus this book is for those of you who understand why it is so important to teach our students about research methods. No doubt there will be times when you will be challenged or when you may become frustrated with how things are going. I hope that the information contained in this book will help lessen the frustration and provide you with strategies that may help you get through the tough times. Stay positive, though. In due time, your students will likely come to appreciate the importance of psychological research methods.

Organization of the Book

This book is divided into six sections. In the first section, made up of Chapters 1 and 2, I discuss general pedagogical issues and issues related to preparing to teach the research methods course. The second section is contained in Chapter 3, where I provide a general overview of science and a discussion of ways in which you can convince your students that psychology is a scientific endeavor. The third section, contained in Chapter 4, focuses on ethical issues in psychology and why researchers must always conduct their research within the context of ethical guidelines. The fourth section, Chapters 5 through 8, focuses on specific research methods concepts (e.g., validity, reliability, experimental and nonexperimental research designs) that are especially challenging to students. Throughout this section, I offer ideas for making these topics easier for your students to understand. In the fifth section, Chapters 9 and 10, I offer a series of suggestions for arranging and teaching the research methods course, and its laboratory component. In the sixth and final section, Chapter 11, I discuss the research methods course from the point of view of someone who wishes to reflect on how the course has gone, and how it can be improved in the future.

Throughout this book, I have focused the discussion on topics that in my mind are some of the most important topics to teach in the research methods course. Some of the chapters are rather focused in nature and center on very specific concepts (e.g., reliability, validity); others are more extensive in their scope and touch on broader issues that may be especially relevant when teaching a challenging course like research methods (e.g., course preparation, using alternative teaching methods to enhance learning). Although you may find discussion of some of these topics scattered about in other places (e.g., instructors' manuals, various teaching handbooks), this book provides the first integrated and comprehensive guide to teaching psychological research methods. From course preparation to reflection and revision, this book is the first integrated teaching resource that focuses specifically on the research methods course. As such, I hope you will find it to be a useful source of information as you prepare and teach your next research methods course.

Bryan K. Saville

Acknowledgments

I would like to thank the following people who reviewed all or part of *A Guide to Teaching Research Methods in Psychology*: Charles Brewer, Barney Beins, and Steve Davis. Their insightful comments and constructive criticism resulted in a greatly improved final product. I would especially like to thank Doug Bernstein, without whom this book may never have seen the light of day. His editorial acumen and continued words of encouragement were invaluable from start to finish.

I would also like to thank my colleagues at James Madison University for their helpful feedback and comments. They selflessly served as a sounding board for many different issues that came to light as I was working on this book. Just as important, however, were my students, past and present, whose enthusiasm consistently reminded me why I enjoy teaching research methods and whose criticism forced me to become a better teacher.

Although they may not know it, Gail Peterson, Bruce Overmier, Tony Marcattilio, and Bill Buskist each played vitally important roles in the production of this book. They taught me much about psychology; more importantly, though, they taught me much about life. It was their influence that ultimately led me to pursue a career I truly love. For that, I am forever in their debt.

I would like to thank my family (Mom, Dad, Brad, Holly, and Braden) for their never-ending support. Without their encouragement over the years, I would not be in the fortunate position I am today. Finally, I would like to thank my wonderful wife Tracy, a dedicated and outstanding teacher in her own right, for her continued support during the time I was writing this book. There were times when the process of writing this book precluded me from spending valuable time with her, but she never once complained. I promise I will make up that missed time with you.

Chapter 1

An Introduction to Psychological Research Methods

As long as psychology has been a recognized discipline, research methods have played an important role in the development of our rapidly evolving field. In a sense, everything psychologists know about behavior, cognition, and emotion—in other words, all they know about psychology—they have gleaned using well-established research methods, some of which have been around as long as science itself and some of which emerged in more recent times. Therefore, it may not be a stretch to claim that the research methods course might be one of the most important courses, if not the single most important course, in the psychology curriculum.

In this chapter I briefly describe several pedagogical issues that you might wish to consider before teaching your research methods course, whether it is for the first or fifth or twenty-fifth time. I also discuss the history and evolution of the research methods course, because your students will probably be unaware of the fact that research methods have played such a crucial role in the history of our discipline.

A Brief History of the Research Methods Course

With the establishment of numerous psychology laboratories in Germany during the late 1800s, most notably and influentially the laboratory of Wilhelm Wundt, curious students from all over the world—including at least 30 from the United States—flocked to Germany in hopes of learning more about, and ultimately earning their degrees in, this new discipline called "psychology" (Benjamin, Durkin, Link, Vestal, & Acord, 1992; Goodwin, 2003).

In contrast to modern-day teaching techniques, which place a heavy emphasis on lecture-based transmission of information (e.g., Benjamin, 2002), students of the new discipline of psychology spent little, if any, time in the classroom, instead learning about their subject matter almost solely by conducting studies in the laboratory. In fact, "the most distinctive characteristic of the German universities was the emphasis placed upon research in all areas of knowledge" (Hilgard, 1987, p. 15). This approach to learning was dominant during the 1800s, a time when academic freedom and an emphasis on research led to an explosion in the number of laboratories using empirical techniques to examine their topics of interest. In step with the prevailing German *zeitgeist*, which emphasized empirical inquiry, Wundt, the "Father of Modern Psychology" and founder of the first psychology laboratory at the University of Leipzig in 1879, set out to examine the human mind using established research methods. In fact, in his classic book *Principles of Physiological Psychology*, Wundt stated that the new discipline of psychology should be a scientific endeavor, rather than purely philosophical in scope (Goodwin, 2005). In essence, then, the history of psychology is really the history of experimental psychology, along with its accompanying methodologies. Your students will probably be unaware of this important fact, so you might want to emphasize it.

After earning their degrees with Wundt in the decade following the opening of his lab in Leipzig, many American students returned to the United States and opened psychology laboratories of their own. Endeavoring to diffuse their new scientific discipline, these psychologists, largely following the model of doctoral training many of them had experienced while studying in Europe, trained other students interested in learning about psychology and the methods it used to examine its subject matter. Although early doctoral education in the United States closely followed the European model of training, there were differences in the way students in Europe and those in the United States learned to be psychologists (Goodwin, 2003). Whereas doctoral training in Germany and other parts of Europe continued to focus mainly on laboratory-based experiences, doctoral training in the United States also included classroom-based experiences, or "drill courses," the primary purpose of which was "[to shape] students to share the values held by those advocating the new scientific psychology" (Goodwin, 2003, p. 19). These drill courses typically included lectures by professors on the process of scientific inquiry and replications by students of "classic" psychology experiments. Although drill courses had their roots in graduate psychology programs, they eventually branched out into undergraduate programs, providing a way for a much larger number of students to learn about the new discipline of psychology.

The presence of drill courses in American psychology programs led to a need for textbooks to serve as guides for both professors and students (Goodwin, 2003). Early textbooks, such as E. B. Titchener's (1901, 1905) monumental four-volume *Experimental Psychology*, were divided into sections, each describing a specific method for studying one of the relatively few psychological phenomena that defined the early years of psychology (e.g., consciousness, perception, reaction time). As the discipline expanded and began to examine other new and interesting topics, so too did the content of psychology textbooks. Yet because psychology was still mostly academic, and thus experimental in nature, the overall format of the books stayed essentially the same (American Psychological Association [APA], 1999). Textbooks such as Woodworth's (1938) *Experimental Psychology* and Stevens's (1951) *Handbook of Experimental Psychology* continued to follow a format in which the authors described topics such as reaction time, attention, emotion, and conditioning, among others, along with the specific research methods for studying each of these topics. Given the emphasis on content in experimental psychology textbooks during the early and middle parts of the 1900s, it is probably safe to assume that courses focusing on research methods followed a similar format.

Beginning in the 1950s and taking hold in the 1960s, the format of experimental psychology textbooks—and presumably the courses in which instructors adopted them—began to change (APA, 1999). As psychology grew, and as psychologists began to study other interesting psychological phenomena, it became impossible to cover each of these topics, along with their accompanying research methods, during a single semester-long course. Additionally, researchers in relatively new areas of psychology (e.g., social and developmental psychology) understood that the methods used by early psychologists, and previously described by Woodworth (1938) and others, were not necessarily unique to certain topics; in fact, researchers could easily adapt these methods to study the phenomena that defined these new domains of psychology. Thus the structure of research methods textbooks changed from one that focused on psychology's content areas (and accompanying methods) to one that instead described the various research methods that psychologists used to examine the vast range of phenomena that now characterized the rapidly expanding discipline. McGuigan's (1960) *Experimental Psychology: A Methodological Approach* was the first methods textbook to adopt this format, marking a shift in the nature of both research methods textbooks and their accompanying courses (APA, 1999; Proctor & Capaldi, 2001). Following McGuigan's lead, most research methods textbooks published in the 1960s and beyond rarely, if ever, contained specific chapters on perception, learning, and attention, for example. Rather, they contained chapters on correlational methods, experimental methods, and other emerging research methods that soon became staples in the field. Along with this change in the general structure of research methods textbooks came a change in the way most instructors taught their research methods courses. Today's research methods course, which one can find in a large majority of undergraduate psychology programs across the country (Perlman & McCann, 1999), has mirrored this tradition and thus has remained relatively stable in its general appearance for well over four decades.

Research Methods in Undergraduate Psychology Curricula

Despite the rapid development of psychology as a discipline over the last several decades, which seems to be reflected in a burgeoning number of course offerings, there are certain courses that have lingered at the forefront of "Top 30" lists for years and that continue to remain vitally important to the expansion of the discipline (Lux & Daniel, 1978; Perlman & McCann, 1999). One such course is research methods (or related courses such as experimental psychology, see, e.g., Messer, Griggs, & Jackson, 1999), a course that, in one form or another, has remained a constant in psychological curricula since the birth of our discipline over 100 years ago (Goodwin, 2003).

It is not surprising, then, that a large majority of psychology departments across the United States include a course, or several courses, on research methodology (Bailey, 2002; Perlman & McCann, 1999). In fact, since the 1950s, various committees charged with examining undergraduate psychology curricula have consistently recommended that a course on research methods be included in undergraduate programs (see Brewer et al., 1993). What's more, Brewer et al. (1993) went so far as to suggest that "The fundamental goal of education in psychology, from which all the others follow, is to teach students to think as scientists about behavior" (p. 169).

In short, the research methods course has been, and will continue to be, one of the most important courses in undergraduate psychology curricula. Not only will this course allow our students to better understand how researchers have studied the different phenomena discussed in other undergraduate psychology courses, it will also allow them to better understand the world in which they live. Given the importance of the research methods course, those of us who teach it have an obligation to do so the best we can. This book is designed to help you do just that.

Changing Trends in Teaching Research Methods

As mentioned earlier, changes in research methods textbooks in the 1960s engendered a change in the way psychology instructors taught their research methods courses. Specifically, prior to 1960, instructors taught content and method simultaneously (e.g., the methods that researchers use to study sensation and perception). Later years, however, saw an increased emphasis on broad methodological issues and less discussion of specific psychological content. The emphasis on methodological issues in research methods courses has continued more or less unabated for over 40 years, but there have been changes in the way instructors structure the course, with hopes of best informing students about psychological research methods. Below I briefly describe some of these more recent trends (see Bailey, 2002, for additional discussion).

Statistics, then methods. The most common trend in teaching research methods has been one in which students first take an introductory course in statistics and then, in a subsequent semester, follow up with a course in research methods. In this way, students (we hope) enter the research methods course with prior knowledge of the statistical concepts that go hand-in-hand with the methodological issues most frequently taught in a research methods course. Because instructors assume that students have preexisting knowledge of statistical issues, instruction in these courses tends to focus most heavily on methodological issues, with only a cursory review of certain statistical concepts. Unfortunately, students' retention of statistical concepts is often less than ideal, meaning that research methods instructors often spend more time than desired reviewing statistical information that is necessary for understanding certain methodological issues.

Statistics and research methods concurrently. One recent approach to combating this problem is to arrange for students to take statistics and research methods courses during the same term. Ideally, students progress through the two courses at approximately the same speed, making it possible for information covered at any given time in the statistics course to be related to information concurrently presented in the research methods course. For example, if all goes as planned in the two courses, students should be discussing *t* tests in statistics at approximately the same time they discuss two-group designs in research methods, and they should be discussing one-way ANOVAs at the same time they are learning about multiple-group designs.

This scenario requires careful planning, especially when different instructors teach the two courses, a common occurrence in many departments. Moreover, despite our best efforts, courses do not always progress as planned. Most instructors, at one time or another, have had to modify their course syllabi in minor or major ways to deal with problems that have thrown into disarray their plans for the semester. As a result, different instructors teaching concurrent statistics and research methods courses might end up presenting information at different times, thus potentially impairing their students' ability to see the relations among important concepts.

Combined statistics and methods. An even more recent trend in teaching research methods is to combine statistics and methods into a single course or series of courses, often taught over two semesters, that integrate statistics and research methods in such a way that students learn about statistical concepts and related methodological concepts at the same time. For example, whereas students in most statistics and methods courses learn about computational and conceptual aspects of *t* tests during one semester and then focus more on two-group designs the following semester, students in an integrated course learn about these ideas together, thus enhancing their ability to see how researchers use t tests to examine differences between two groups.

The increasing popularity of integrated statistics and methods courses has led to a need for textbooks that integrate these topics as well. Fortunately, several authors have tried to meet this need (e.g., Davis & Smith, 2005; Furlong, Lovelace, & Lovelace, 2000; Heiman, 2001). The emergence of a number of textbooks that integrate statistics and methods has eased the burden for instructors, who otherwise would need to seek out supplementary materials that do an adequate job of combining statistical and methodological information, or, worse yet—at least in the minds of students— require students to buy more than one textbook.

Clearly, there are costs and benefits to structuring your research methods course in each of the preceding ways. Whereas teaching statistics and research methods in a sequence might be easier from an administrative point of view, such a format may not be optimal for students' retention of material. Teaching the topics together in a two-sequence course might improve learning and retention, but there are practical issues that might make such a course offering less feasible. For example, if students transfer to your institution after having completed a statistics course, will you require them to take the entire sequence? You will likely need to consider factors both internal and external to your course before deciding which format best suits your needs as well as the needs of your department and your students.

Difficulties and Rewards of Teaching Research Methods

For many students, the thought of taking research methods is over-whelming, producing feelings of trepidation, torpidity, and torment— often all at the same time. During their statistics courses, many students probably heard the following statement from their instructors: "Don't worry. You'll learn more about this material next semester, in research methods . . . ." Unfortunately, such declarations often do little to enhance students' enthusiasm for their subsequent research methods courses. More often than not, they are thinking, and some-times even saying, "Oh great, I get to study this stuff again. I can hardly wait!" Such is the life of a research methods instructor and hence the reason why the very thought of teaching research methods sometimes produces for both neophyte and veteran instructor alike feelings of trepidation, torpidity, and torment—often all at the same time. Yes, teaching research methods can be difficult and, at times, more than a little frustrating. At the same time, however, it can also be incredibly rewarding. Let's consider some of the difficulties that make research methods a tough class to teach, as well as some of the rewards that come with teaching research methods, rewards that often show up unannounced and usually when we least expect them.

Difficulties

Quite possibly the greatest barrier to overcome when teaching research methods is the fact that many, if not most, undergraduate students become psychology majors in hopes of pursuing careers in something having to do with counseling or clinical psychology. Later, after students have had more courses, many switch gears slightly, choosing instead to pursue careers in another area of applied psychology, such as school psychology, industrial/organizational psychology, or forensic psychology (although many are unaware of what forensic psychology actually entails; see, e.g., Huss, 2001).

Because of their interest in applied psychology, many of our students are under the mistaken impression that knowledge of research methods is not pertinent to them, simply because they are not going to be "doing research," and especially if they know they are not going to pursue graduate training in psychology or a related field. Even if our students understand, and maybe even appreciate, why knowledge of research methods might be an important goal for some, they feel they would be better served spending their time learning more about abnormal psychology, personality, and other more "interesting" topics that will help them become effective clinicians and counselors.

Unfortunately, our students often underestimate the importance of research methods in helping them pursue their postbaccalaureate goals, whether those goals ultimately include employment or graduate school. Briihl (2001), for example, found that although undergraduate students viewed as important such objective criteria as grade point average for obtaining a job or getting into graduate school, they downplayed the relative importance of research experience and other skills (e.g., analytical skills) often acquired in research methods courses. Regrettably, some of our talented students may have trouble getting into graduate school or obtaining employment simply because they failed to see the importance of research methods in helping them pursue future endeavors (sec, e.g., Keith-Spiegel, Tabachnick, & Spiegel, 1994).

A second reason why teaching research methods can be rather difficult is because students often find the material less interesting than the material they cover in their other psychology courses. I am confident, and I presume many of you would agree with me, that undergraduate students become psychology majors because they are interested in topics such as depression, schizophrenia, personality, and the like—topics they likely know something about or have some experience with—and not in topics such as random assignment, control techniques, threats to internal validity, and factorial designs. Consequently, getting students engaged in the subject matter may take more cajoling than might normally be the case.

A final reason why teaching research methods can be difficult concerns the fact that students often enter our courses with misconceptions about science in general and misconceptions about psychology as a science in particular (e.g., Brems, 1994). These misconceptions likely interfere with our ability to teach students about the importance of research methods in our discipline. Consequently, teaching research methods may be difficult not because students find the material unimportant or uninteresting, but because many of them do not see psychology as a scientific discipline and simply want to move on and learn more about what psychologists "really do."

Rewards

Just as there are difficulties that often come with teaching psychological research methods—possibly more difficulties than we like to acknowledge—so too are there significant rewards. Most likely, the rewards that come with teaching this course are quite variable and, in many cases, specific to each individual. Yet conversations with my colleagues suggest that there are some common rewards that many research methods instructors experience either during or after teaching their courses.

Arguably the most rewarding aspect of teaching research methods is watching our students come to appreciate the importance of research methods in psychology. As mentioned earlier, it is rather common for students to enter our research methods courses either uninterested in, or already detesting, the material they have yet to learn. Slowly, but surely, many of these students come to realize that the research methods course is not the "evil" course they thought it would be and that knowledge of research methods can be both useful and interesting.

A second reward comes when students begin to think both scientifically and critically about issues they may not have considered very deeply before. With additional exposure to the scientific method, they begin to realize that much of the information they encounter in the "real world" is based on tenuous arguments and that faulty conclusions regarding all types of research (e.g., causation inferred from correlational studies) are alarmingly commonplace (Brewer et al., 1993). Critical thinking will serve them well not only in the research methods course, but also in their subsequent courses and, maybe even more importantly, as they venture outside the protective walls of academia.

Finally, as perhaps you have discovered yourself, it can be very rewarding when students, who at the beginning of the semester showed a strong dislike of research methods, approach you later and inquire about possible research opportunities they might pursue. Not only have these students come to understand the importance of research methods in psychology, they have become motivated to put into practice what they have learned in your course. Quite often, students' negative opinions about research methods melt away once they have the opportunity to use the knowledge they gained in the course to examine some psychological phenomenon that is of interest to them. If their experiences go well, some of these students might even consider careers as research psychologists and academicians.

In sum, there are both difficulties and rewards that you can expect to encounter when teaching research methods, and sometimes the difficulties may outnumber the rewards. However, the satisfaction that occurs when students "see the light" more than outweighs the effort and frustration that often accompany the teaching of this vitally important course.

Course Content and Sequence

As research methods have become more sophisticated over the last several decades, those who teach the research methods course have felt compelled to include an increasing number of topics. For example, the last 30 years have witnessed a sizeable increase in the use of qualitative research methods in psychology (Rennie, Watson, & Monteiro, 2002). Consequently, some research methods instructors have started to devote a good amount of class time to such topics as grounded theory, participatory action research, ethnography, and discourse analysis, topics that past research methods instructors rarely, or barely, discussed in their courses. Similarly, with an increased emphasis on effect size (e.g., Cohen, 1992), instructors now frequently spend a good portion of their classes discussing with students how various research methods accomplish the feat of increasing effect size.

Unfortunately, an increase in the length of college and university semesters has not accompanied the increase in the number of topics that research methods instructors feel inclined, or may even be required, to cover in their courses. As a result, many of us who teach research methods frequently feel as though we are attempting to cram an ever-increasing number of important topics into what sometimes feels like a shorter and shorter period of time. Consequently, we are often left asking ourselves, "What content do I absolutely have to cover this semester?"

Perhaps you have spent some time discussing with colleagues what topics they typically cover when teaching research methods; you may have also examined numerous research methods textbooks to see if there is any consistency in the topics they include. In both cases, you may have found, as I have, that there is considerable variability in the topics that research methods instructors include in their courses and that methods textbooks contain. Nevertheless, I believe there are certain topics that all instructors should include in their courses if they wish to provide their students with a relatively thorough understanding of research methods. Below I briefly discuss each of these topics. In addition, I have listed these topics in the approximate sequence that seems to maximize both learning and retention of the material.

History of research methods. As mentioned earlier, you may wish to include only a brief discussion of this topic, but introducing the history of research methods in psychology will put the rest of your course in context, thus giving your students a better understanding of course content and how the discipline has evolved since its humble beginnings (e.g., Goodwin, 2003).

Characteristics of science. Ideally, your students will remember from their introductory courses that psychology is a science. Nevertheless, you may wish to discuss with them the characteristics of science and why psychology constitutes "science" just as much as so-called "hard" sciences (e.g., physics, chemistry). You would also do well to discuss with them how the scientific analysis of psychological phenomena differs from pseudoscientific approaches (see Stanovich, 2001). In doing so, your students will likely obtain a better understanding of why psychology is scientific in nature and how researchers are able to study topics such as love, self-esteem, and intelligence, phenomena that some consider to be beyond the scope of scientific analysis. Your students will also see how the research methods you discuss later in the semester are central to the scientific method and how these methods help psychologists gain a better understanding of the phenomena that constitute our discipline.

Ethics. As with any scientific endeavor, there are ethical considerations that guide, as well as constrain, the practices of psychologists. Because ethical considerations pervade the work of all psychologists— instructors, researchers, and practitioners—your students should be aware of the principles that serve as a beacon for psychologists who are confronted with the foggy murk of ethical dilemmas. During your coverage of ethical considerations, you should especially focus your discussion on those guidelines that directly affect the practices of psychological researchers (see APA, 2002).

Reliability and validity. As two of the most importance concepts in psychological research, reliability and validity should remain at the forefront of your discussions throughout the semester. Early in the semester, you should introduce your students to the ideas of reliability and validity as well as to related topics such as (a) operational definitions; (b) measurement, including variables, scales of measurement, and sources of measurement error; and (c) how each of the preceding topics is related to reliability and validity. As the semester progresses, you should introduce different types of reliability (e.g., interobserver reliability) and validity (e.g., internal validity) when you discuss related topics.

Research design and statistical analysis. Your students likely received exposure to this topic in statistics, but now is the perfect time to reinforce their understanding of the relation between research design and statistical analysis. However, rather than presenting this material in full prior to subsequent course material, you may want to introduce early in the semester the general idea of statistical analysis—including null hypothesis significance testing, an idea with which they should be at least vaguely familiar—and then discuss in more detail later in the semester the specific hypotheses and statistical analyses that go with each design. In my experience, students really come to understand the relation between research design and statistical analysis once they encounter the information typically covered in the research methods course.

Nonexperimental research methods. Some instructors choose to skim over these topics, which are also known as descriptive research methods. However, given their omnipresence in our field, you would do well to spend considerable time discussing correlational studies, *ex post facto* designs (including predictor and criterion variables), and naturalistic observations. Not only will your students become familiar with the wide range of methods that psychologists use, they will also have the opportunity to compare and contrast these methods with experimental methods, which will likely improve their understanding of both.

Experimental research methods. Most researchers view experiments as the *crème de la crème* of research methods, because of their ability to show cause-and-effect relations between variables. Coverage of experimental methods should include extensive discussion of independent, dependent, and extraneous variables; threats to internal validity; techniques for controlling threats to internal validity; different types of experimental designs, including two-group designs, multiple-group designs, and factorial designs; and the use of control groups.

Large-N vs. small-N designs. Although most textbooks provide extensive coverage of large-N (between-groups) designs, they seldom contain more than minimal coverage of small-N (single-subject) designs. Because small-N designs provide a useful way to study causal relations with one or a small number of subjects, and because they are important in psychology's history (Saville & Buskist, 2003), discussion of these designs might be of interest to students who wish to pursue careers as practitioners, in which they will most likely be working closely with individual clients.

Writing research reports. Once your students have an understanding of how the research process works, they should learn how to write APA-style papers in which they report the results of their research. Writing these reports will allow your students to synthesize much of the material they covered during the semester and will serve them well in their subsequent courses, many of which will require APA-style papers. Although many instructors wait until the end of the semester to discuss APA-style papers, presumably because their students then have the requisite knowledge to write the papers more effectively, you might also wish to introduce this information early in the semester, so students can work on multiple drafts throughout the semester, as they are learning about the research process (see Chapter 9).

Conclusion

As mentioned earlier, teaching research methods can be both diffi-cult and rewarding. Although many students enter our classrooms with feelings of disinterest, dislike, or even fear, we can take steps to assuage their initial concerns and turn the course into one that students find both useful and interesting. In this chapter, I have addressed general pedagogical issues that you should consider as you prepare for your next research methods course. In the chapters that follow, I turn in more detail to many of the topics that you will likely discuss in your course and attempt to delineate ways to teach these topics more effectively. With concerted effort, research methods can be a course that students look forward to taking, rather than a course that produces apprehensiveness and antipathy.

References

American Psychological Association. (1999). The evolution of experimental psychology. *APA Monitor Online*, *30*(11). Retrieved September 6, 2006, from www.apa.org/monitor/dec99/ss5.html

American Psychological Association. (2002). Ethical principles of psycholo-gists and code of conduct. *American Psychologist*, *57*, 1060–1073.

Bailey, S. A. (2002). Teaching statistics and research methods. In S. F. Davis & W. Buskist (Eds.), *The teaching of psychology: Essays in honor of Wilbert J. McKeachie and Charles L. Brewer* (pp. 369–377). Mahwah, NJ: Erlbaum.

Benjamin, L. T., Jr. (2002). Lecturing. In S. F. Davis & W. Buskist (Eds.), *The teaching of psychology: Essays in honor of Wilbert J. McKeachie and Charles L. Brewer* (pp. 57–67). Mahwah, NJ: Erlbaum.

Benjamin, L. T., Jr., Durkin, M., Link, M., Vestal, M., & Acord, J. (1992). Wundt's American doctoral students. *American Psychologist, 47*, 123–131.

Brems, C. (1994). Taking the fear out of research: A gentle approach to teaching an appreciation for research. *Teaching of Psychology, 21*, 241–243.

Brewer, C. L., Hopkins, J. R., Kimble, G. A., Matlin, M. W., McCann, L. I., McNeil, O. V., et al. (1993). Curriculum. In T. V. McGovern (Ed.), *Handbook for enhancing undergraduate education in psychology* (pp. 161–182). Washington, DC: American Psychological Association.

Briihl, D. S. (2001). Life after college: Psychology students' perceptions of salary, business hiring criteria, and graduate admission criteria. *North American Journal of Psychology, 3*, 321–330.

Cohen, J. (1992). Statistical power analysis. *Current Directions in Psychological Science, 1*, 98–101.

Davis, S. F., & Smith, R. A. (2005). *An introduction to statistics and research methods: Becoming a psychological detective.* Upper Saddle River, NJ: Prentice Hall.

Furlong, N. E., Lovelace, E. A., & Lovelace, K. L. (2000). *Research methods and statistics: An integrated approach.* Belmont, CA: Thomson.

Goodwin, C. J. (2003). Psychology's experimental foundations. In S. F. Davis (Ed.), *Handbook of research methods in experimental psychology* (pp. 3–23). Malden, MA: Blackwell.

Goodwin, C. J. (2005). *A history of modern psychology* (2nd ed.). Hoboken, NJ: Wiley.

Heiman, G. W. (2001). *Understanding research methods and statistics: An integrated introduction for psychology* (2nd ed.). Boston: Houghton Mifflin.

Hilgard, E. R. (1987). *Psychology in America: A historical survey.* Orlando, FL: Harcourt Brace Jovanovich.

Huss, M. T. (2001). What is forensic psychology? It's not Silence of the Lambs! *Eye on Psi Chi, 5*, 25–27.

Keith-Spiegel, P., Tabachnick, B. G., & Spiegel, G. B. (1994). When demand exceeds supply: Second-order criteria used by graduate school selection committees. *Teaching of Psychology, 21*, 79–81.

Lux, D. F., & Daniel, R. S. (1978). Which courses are most frequently listed by psychology departments? *Teaching of Psychology, 5*, 13–16.

McGuigan, F. J. (1960). *Experimental psychology: A methodological approach.* Englewood Cliffs, NJ: Prentice Hall.

Messer, W. S., Griggs, R. A., & Jackson, S. L. (1999). A national survey of undergraduate psychology degree options and major requirements. *Teaching of Psychology, 26*, 164–171.

Perlman, B., & McCann, L. I. (1999). The structure of the psychology undergraduate curriculum. *Teaching of Psychology, 26,* 171–176.

Proctor, R. W., & Capaldi, E. J. (2001). Improving the science education of psychology students: Better teaching of methodology. *Teaching of Psychology, 28,* 173–181.

Rennie, D. L., Watson, K. D., & Monteiro, A. M. (2002). The rise of qualitative research in psychology. *Canadian Psychology, 43,* 179–189.

Saville, B. K., & Buskist, W. (2003). Traditional idiographic approaches: Small-N research designs. In S. F. Davis (Ed.), *Handbook of research methods in experimental psychology* (pp. 66–82). Malden, MA: Blackwell.

Stanovich, K. E. (2001). *How to think straight about psychology* (6th ed.). Boston: Allyn & Bacon.

Stevens, S. S. (1951). *Handbook of experimental psychology.* New York: Wiley.

Titchener, E. B. (1901). *Experimental psychology: A manual of laboratory practice. Vol. 1: Qualitative experiments. Part 1: Student's manual; part 2: Instructor's manual.* New York: Macmillan.

Titchener, E. B. (1905). *Experimental psychology: A manual of laboratory practice. Vol. 2: Quantitative experiments. Part 1: Student's manual; part 2: Instructor's manual.* New York: Macmillan.

Woodworth, R. S. (1938). *Experimental psychology.* New York: Holt.

Chapter 2

Getting Ready to Teach

Teaching research methods in psychology can be rewarding but, as discussed in Chapter 1, teaching the course for the first time can be daunting. Nevertheless, once you have agreed to do so, there eventually comes a time when you have to prepare your course. In this chapter, I will discuss some of the items you may need to consider. As in planning other courses, there is a lot to do: You'll have to construct a syllabus, prepare lecture notes, come up with interesting demonstrations, think about lab activities, and write exams. Where do you start? The obvious answer is "at the beginning," meaning that you first work on the syllabus, then the lectures notes, then the exams, and so on. But course preparation isn't always so linear. Often, it follows a "two steps forward, one step back" process, in which things you think about later in the planning process may prompt you to go back and modify earlier steps (McKeachie, 2002).

Course Objectives

The most important step in the planning process is identifying your course objectives, because what you hope to achieve in your research methods course will affect everything else you do throughout the semester. So prior to constructing a syllabus, preparing lecture notes, or anything else, you would do well to spend some time thinking about what you hope to accomplish during your course. For example, do you want your students to have a firm grasp of APA style when the semester is over? Do you want them to understand the relation between research design and statistical analysis? Do you want them to understand the ethics of conducting psychological research? The answers you give to questions like these will help you identify your specific course objectives. The goals you have for your course will depend, too, on a number of other factors, some of which may be beyond your control, such as whether you have a teaching assistant who can help you with certain parts of the course.

You may wish to keep in mind two general pieces of information as you develop (or revise) your course. First, the primary goal for any course should be *"to facilitate student learning and thinking"* (McKeachie, 2002, p. 11, italics in original), not simply to introduce course content. This exhortation seems especially important in the research methods course. Because students often enter this course with little interest in, and consequently little motivation to *learn* about, the research process, they may choose to "go through the motions," simply memorizing information as best they can, rather than truly attempting to understand how these ideas pertain to the scientific process of learning about the phenomena psychologists study. As you develop your objectives, consider including those that will engage students to a greater degree and serve to facilitate student learning. Second, be aware that others have already suggested some of the major objectives for undergraduate psychology courses (e.g., McGovern, 1993; McGovern & Reich, 1996). In general, those objectives include (a) acquiring general knowledge about psychology, including knowledge of research methods; (b) acquiring intellectual skills, including the ability to think critically and communicate effectively; and (c) acquiring practical skills, including the ability to apply psychological ideas to one's own life (Forsyth, 2003). Consider including these among your own course objectives.

Constructing and Presenting a Syllabus

When it is time to develop a syllabus for your course, remember that a syllabus serves as a contract between you and your students, stating in exact terms the responsibilities that each of you must fulfill during the course. There are many sources of useful information about what to include in your syllabus (e.g., Appleby, 1999; Davis, 1993; Forsyth, 2003; McKeachie, 2002; Suddreth & Galloway, 2006), so I will not discuss that information here. I would, however, like to suggest a way of constructing your syllabus that could potentially have a positive effect on how your students view your research methods course.

In his recent book *What the Best College Teachers Do*, Ken Bain (2004) reported that the best college instructors tend to engage in similar practices, both in and out of the classroom. For example, Bain found that exceptional college instructors worked hard to build trust with their students, to reduce the student–instructor power differential, and to invite, rather than require, students to engage in the learning process. Many of these instructors began to communicate these ideas on the first day of class, through wording in their course syllabi that promised to help their students set and realize ambitious goals. Bain dubbed this type of syllabus the "promising syllabus" and suggested that such syllabi typically contain three major parts (see also Lang, 2006). First, promising syllabi highlight the opportunities that students will have in a course or, put another way, the information that the instructor promises to make available. For example, a research methods syllabus might promise that students will have the opportunity to learn how knowledge of research methods will help them become better applied practitioners or better consumers of information.

Second, a promising syllabus contains information about what students will have to *do* to realize the benefits of the opportunities presented in the course. So the syllabus might state that developing and carrying out an experiment will help students better understand how they can use research methods at a later time to determine, for example, if a certain therapy is effective in reducing depression in college-aged individuals. According to Bain, by replacing the demand-oriented language of course requirements with information about how students can seize on the opportunities presented to them, students will be more likely to believe that they can strongly affect their own learning.

Finally, the promising syllabus contains information about how the instructor and the students will determine whether students are learning what they need to learn in order to realize the opportunities that the instructor has promised them. Most of us view this information as a statement of grading policies, but Bain found that exceptional instructors view it as "the beginning of a dialogue in which both students and instructors explored how they would understand learning, so they could both make adjustments as they went and evaluate the nature of the learning by the end of the term" (p. 75). As such, a promising syllabus encourages instructors to discuss with their students ways they might evaluate whether students have learned important course information. For example, allowing students to have some input on how you structure your labs and what types of assignment might pique their interest in research methods could have a profound effect on their motivation to learn more about important course content (see Benjamin, 2005, for a discussion of how you might involve your students in the planning process). It is probably not a good idea to put grading policy decisions in your students' hands, but at least having a discussion with them about why you constructed your course the way you did will likely set the stage for a mutually respectful instructor–student relation.

Some version of a promising syllabus might be especially useful in research methods for the following interrelated reasons. First, the way you frame your course could have an impact on how your students feel about their time in your classroom. For example, simply informing your students on the first day of class that you will *require* them to take three essay exams over different research methods and write two APA-style papers over a lab project may not provide a context in which students feel a burning desire to learn more about the importance and practicality of research methods. Likewise, not providing students with a rationale for using alternative teaching methods (see Chapter 10) may lead some of them to conclude that you don't care about teaching, because it might appear that you don't "teach" that much. Second, given that some students might be especially apprehensive about a research methods course, framing it as a set of opportunities rather than as a series of requirements, might help assuage some of their fears. Finally, students who view their courses as a set of opportunities rather than a set of requirements, and their instructors as individuals who are willing to help them benefit from these opportunities, may be more likely to feel some degree of control over their education. They may realize that, if they work hard and perform the activities that will help them realize the opportunities they have in your course, they can succeed.

You may be wondering exactly how much information to include in your syllabus. I would suggest that too much information is better than too little. For one thing, a brief syllabus may signal to your students that you are not all that interested in the course or in their learning (McKeachie, 2002). Further, as already mentioned, your syllabus serves as a contract between you and your students. As such, syllabi that contain extensive and specific information about your course policies and procedures can have great value if students violate those policies and procedures or later question the way you handled some aspect of the class. For example, if you fail to note on your syllabus that late papers will receive a 5-point penalty, students may (legitimately) argue that it is unfair to assess such penalties. Similarly, if your syllabus does not include a statement of your right to change the course syllabus if necessary (and within reason, of course), any changes you subsequently make, such as changing the date of an exam, may result in a coterie of disgruntled students.

Once you have constructed your syllabus, you may be tempted simply to distribute it, talk briefly about it on the first day of class, and then trust that your students will treat it as a sacred document, reading it religiously throughout the semester. However, Becker and Calhoon (1999) found that students in an introductory psychology course reported that they typically pay relatively little attention to even important syllabus items, such as policies regarding academic dishonesty.

In reality, the likelihood that students will pay attention to your syllabus may depend on whether there are consequences for *not* doing so. For example, if students can simply ask you for reminders about exam dates or course features or policies, they will quickly learn that reading the syllabus isn't necessary. One way to get your students to attend to important information is by incorporating a syllabus quiz into your course. Raymark and Connor-Greene (2002) found that giving students a take-home syllabus quiz increased their understanding of important course information. However, they also found that many students still answered certain questions incorrectly, even though they had access to the answers by reading the syllabus. Consequently, they suggested that it may be necessary to introduce an additional contingency that will increase students' motivation to read the syllabus more carefully. For example, instructors could make extra credit contingent on answering all syllabus quiz questions correctly, or they could factor students' syllabus quiz scores into their overall course grades. A system for assuring that students read the course syllabus will likely save both you and your students the frustrations that result when they fail to do so. Some of your students might complain that being given syllabus quizzes makes them feel "immature" (they may even use a different descriptor), but if you explain *why* you do so—namely that you want to save them frustration later on and help them succeed in the course—they will more likely accept the value of this policy.

Choosing a Textbook

Just as there are numerous resources that will help you identify the types of information to include in your course syllabus, so too are there numerous resources that will help you identify the types of question to ask when you are choosing a research methods textbook (e.g., Davis, 1993; Dewey, 1999; Forsyth, 2003; McKeachie, 2002; Morris 1977). Because these resources are readily available, I will not consider this topic in detail, but I would like to offer some brief pointers.

First and foremost, you should always attempt to link your textbook choice back to your course objectives. Does the textbook do a nice job of explaining the concepts that you feel are especially important with regard to your course objectives? Similarly, do *you* feel comfortable with the way a certain book describes important course material, and do you feel it can help you meet your course objectives? If not, you may want to consider another textbook, regardless of how well the book is written, how many pedagogical aids it contains, and so on. The more your course objectives jibe with the textbook, the more likely both you and your students will find the textbook to be an important learning tool.

Second, be sure to consider the following criteria when choosing a research methods textbook (Dewey, 1999; Forsyth, 2003; McKeachie, 2002):

1. *How difficult is the text?* As with most psychology textbooks, research methods textbooks come in varying degrees of difficulty. Although lower-level textbooks may appeal to students, simply because they may seem "easier," these books may not contain the in-depth coverage that you might want, meaning that using one of them may make it harder for you to meet your course objectives.
2. *Does the text "grab" your attention?* Certain textbooks seem to have the ability to draw the reader in, resulting in faster and

clearer comprehension of course material. Although some of your students may argue that no research methods textbook has this ability, you would do well to consider carefully which of your book options seems most likely to capture your students' attention.

3. *Is the text clearly written?* As I mentioned above, although certain textbooks may contain lots of fun "bells and whistles," clarity will determine whether your students feel that the book is worth reading.

4. *How is the text organized?* In general, most research methods textbooks contain similar sorts of information. However, the way in which these textbooks are organized may vary considerably (Jackson, Lugo, & Griggs, 2001). If the organization of a certain textbook does not match the order in which you like to cover course material, that textbook may not be for you, especially if its chapters build on each other in a fixed sequence that makes it difficult or impossible to assign chapters in your own preferred sequence.

Third, read the texts on your list of adoption possibilities. Although you may be able initially to discard some textbooks simply on the basis of their more objective features (e.g., number of pedagogical aids; see Jackson et al., 2001, for a comparative review of recent research methods textbooks), ultimately, "there is no substitute for detailed review of the competing texts for the course you are teaching" (McKeachie, 2002, p. 14).

Using Supplementary Materials

In addition to using a standard research methods textbook, you may want to consider using supplementary materials in your course. Because your students will most certainly be writing one or more APA-style papers, you would do well to have them purchase the *Publication Manual of the American Psychological Association* (APA, 2001). Alternatively, depending on your course objectives and your students' long-term goals, you may want them to purchase one of APA's other style guides (see www.apastyle.org). Either way, you should not ask your students to rely solely on their textbooks for information on APA style. In a recent study, Ernst and Michel (2006) examined 29 research methods textbooks published between

2001 and 2005 and found that sample APA papers in the textbooks contained a number of formatting errors. Although the very thought of perusing the hefty *Publication Manual* might seem a daunting task for many of your students, it may be a better alternative for assuring that they learn correct APA format. In addition, owning APA's *Publication Manual* or another style guide will likely serve your students well, not only in your research methods course, but also in subsequent courses that will require the writing of APA-style papers.

You might also consider assigning other books that focus on writing style or critical thinking, both of which are vitally important in research methods courses. For example, Strunk and White's (2000) classic *The Elements of Style* and Pyrczak and Bruce's (2007) *Writing Empirical Research Reports* can be especially useful to students (and faculty) who need help not only with APA style, but with writing style in general. Similarly, I have found Stanovich's (2007) *How to Think Straight about Psychology* and Ruscio's (2006) *Critical Thinking in Psychology* to be useful supplements that teach students to think critically about the scientific method and to appreciate the conclusions that one can draw from different types of research.

Finally, you might consider supplementing your course with primary readings from the psychological research literature. Though your textbook will serve as the core reading for your students, it may also be a good idea to ask them to read research articles and identify important course concepts within those articles. I have found that although students can grasp these concepts by reading their textbooks or engaging in a class discussion, they tend to have a more difficult time recognizing how researchers apply those same concepts unless they have a chance to see them in action in research reports. Having students read research literature is also valuable because they will no doubt have to become more familiar with that literature in their upper-level courses. When choosing primary articles for your students to read, you may want to seek out articles that possess the following characteristics (see Banyard & Grayson, 1999, for more discussion on using primary articles in your course):

1. Use articles that are well-known. Although you could quite easily find articles in which the authors employed certain research methods, your students may be more interested in learning about research methods if you ask them to review

articles they might have already heard about or, at least, should be familiar with. For example, when discussing ethics, you might ask your students to read Milgram's (1963) classic article on obedience to authority, or when teaching matched pair research designs, you might assign Bandura, Ross, and Ross's (1961) classic "Bobo doll" study.

2. Use articles that will stimulate discussion. Although any number of articles may be adequate for illustrating certain course concepts, those that stimulate discussion will probably increase your students' interest in research methods. For example, in addition to assigning Milgram's paper, I often ask my students to read the Stanford Prison Experiment (Haney, Banks, & Zimbardo, 1973) and identify which common control technique the authors used (random assignment). After reading Haney et al.'s conclusions—that situational variables were responsible for the dramatic behavioral changes observed in both the guards and prisoners—someone inevitably asks, "How do you know the guards weren't mean to begin with?" At this point, we are able to discuss random assignment in more depth and how the use of this control technique allowed Haney et al. to reach the conclusions they did.

3. Use articles that have contemporary or personal relevance. As you are well aware, students tend to view course material as more interesting if they can relate it to something that is happening in the world around them or something that has relevance in their own lives (Buskist, Sikorski, Buckley, & Saville, 2002). So when choosing articles for your students to read, consider current events and your students' personal goals. For example, research on terrorists and terrorism might be of interest, as should articles in clinical psychology, forensic psychology, developmental psychology, or other subfields that many of your students might want to pursue.

4. Use articles that are neither too difficult nor too easy to read and understand. Remember that most of your students are receiving their first exposure to research methods, and most will have little, if any, experience in reading the primary literature. So although you will want to choose articles that require your students to think a bit, be careful not to assign readings that require a knowledge base that they don't yet have. Trying to read such difficult articles is far more likely to elicit feelings of frustration rather than a sense of excitement and motivation. ·

Your students may struggle a bit when first reading the primary research articles you assign, but if you choose the articles carefully, their comfort should quickly increase as they become more familiar with this genre. Indeed, asking your students to read and critique primary research may be one of the best ways to teach them about research methods.

Conclusion

As daunting as it might initially seem, preparing your research methods course can also be quite enjoyable. And although thinking of new and exciting ways to stimulate your students' interest in research methods can be time-consuming and effortful, it can also be challenging and fun. Ultimately, there is nothing like the pleasure of seeing your efforts rewarded as your students come to understand the importance of research methods in psychology.

References

American Psychological Association. (2001). *Publication manual of the American Psychological Association* (5th ed.). Washington, DC: Author.

Appleby, D. C. (1999). How to improve your teaching with the course syllabus. In B. Perlman, L. I. McCann, & S. H. McFadden (Eds.), *Lessons learned: Practical advice for the teaching of psychology* (pp. 19–24). Washington, DC: American Psychological Association.

Bain, K. (2004). *What the best college teachers do.* Cambridge, MA: Harvard University Press.

Bandura, A., Ross, D., & Ross, S. A. (1961). Transmission of aggression through imitation of aggressive models. *Journal of Abnormal and Social Psychology, 63,* 575–582.

Banyard, P., & Grayson, A. (1999). Teaching with original sources. In B. Perlman, L. I. McCann, & S. H. McFadden (Eds.), *Lessons learned: Practical advice for the teaching of psychology* (pp. 29–35). Washington, DC: American Psychological Society.

Becker, A. H., & Calhoon, S. K. (1999). What introductory psychology students attend to on a course syllabus. *Teaching of Psychology, 26,* 6–11.

Benjamin, L. T., Jr. (2005). Setting course goals: Privileges and responsibilities in a world of ideas. *Teaching of Psychology, 32,* 146–149.

Buskist, W., Sikorski, J., Buckley, T., & Saville, B. K. (2002). Elements of master teaching. In S. F. Davis & W. Buskist (Eds.), *The teaching of psychology: Essays in honor of Wilbert J. McKeachie and Charles L. Brewer* (pp. 27–39). Mahwah, NJ: Erlbaum.

Davis, B. G. (1993). *Tools for teaching*. San Francisco: Jossey-Bass.

Dewey, R. A. (1999). Finding the right introductory psychology textbook. In B. Perlman, L. I. McCann, & S. H. McFadden (Eds.), *Lessons learned: Practical advice for the teaching of psychology* (pp. 25–28). Washington, DC: American Psychological Society.

Ernst, K., & Michel, L. (2006). Deviations from APA style in textbook sample manuscripts. *Teaching of Psychology, 33,* 57–59.

Forsyth, D. R. (2003). *The professor's guide to teaching: Psychological principles and practices*. Washington, DC: American Psychological Association.

Haney, C., Banks, C., & Zimbardo, P. (1973). Interpersonal dynamics in a simulated prison. *International Journal of Criminology and Penology, 1,* 69–97.

Jackson, S. L., Lugo, S. M., & Griggs, R. A. (2001). Research methods textbooks: An objective analysis. *Teaching of Psychology, 28,* 282–288.

Lang, J. M. (2006). The promising syllabus [Electronic version]. *The Chronicle of Higher Education, 53*(2), C2.

McGovern, T. V. (Ed.). (1993). *Handbook for enhancing undergraduate education in psychology*. Washington, DC: American Psychological Association.

McGovern, T. V., & Reich, J. (1996). A comment on the quality principles. *American Psychologist, 51,* 252–255.

McKeachie, W. J. (2002). *McKeachie's teaching tips: Strategies, research, and theory for college and university teachers* (11th ed.). Boston: Houghton Mifflin.

Milgram, S. (1963). Behavioral study of obedience. *Journal of Abnormal and Social Psychology, 67,* 371–378.

Morris, C. J. (1977). Choosing a text for the introductory course. *Teaching of Psychology, 4,* 21–24.

Pyrczak, F., & Bruce, R. R. (2007). *Writing empirical research reports: A basic guide for students of the social and behavioral sciences* (6th ed.). Glendale, CA: Pyrczak Publishing.

Raymark, P. H., & Connor-Greene, P. A. (2002). The syllabus quiz. *Teaching of Psychology, 29,* 286–288.

Ruscio, J. (2006). *Critical thinking in psychology: Separating sense from nonsense* (2nd ed.). Belmont, CA: Thomson Wadsworth.

Stanovich, K. E. (2007). *How to think straight about psychology* (8th ed.). Boston: Allyn & Bacon.

Strunk, W. Jr., & White, E. B. (2000). *The elements of style* (4th ed.). New York: Longman.

Suddreth, A-M., & Galloway, A. T. (2006). Options for planning a course and developing a syllabus. In W. Buskist, & S. F. Davis (Eds.), *Handbook of the teaching of psychology* (pp. 31–35). Malden, MA: Blackwell.

Chapter 3

Teaching Psychology as a Science

"Psychology occupies a unique position as a discipline, addressing basic questions of meaning and value normally associated with the humanities but approaching the study of thought and behavior from the methodological perspective of the natural sciences" (Friedrich, 1996, p. 6).

No doubt, a large number of students in our psychology courses, especially those in introductory courses who may have had little exposure to the discipline, agree steadfastly with the view of "psychology as humanity." And although most people have a positive view of psychology, they know considerably less about the ways in which our discipline is scientific in nature (Webb & Speer, 1985; Wood, Jones, & Benjamin, 1986). Fortunately, we have in our research methods courses a wonderful opportunity to inform our students about what psychologists do and how these endeavors are well-grounded in the scientific method. By taking certain steps, which I will discuss momentarily, we can hopefully convince our students that psychology is a science and "that science, done right, *is* one of the humanities" (Daniel Dennett, quoting his high school physics teacher, 1995, p. 263, italics in original).

Psychology as Science

Open any introductory psychology textbook and the first chapter will likely contain a definition of psychology that reads something like this: "Psychology is the scientific study of behavior and mental processes." Although this definition is usually followed by a brief discussion of "the scientific method" and "research methods," such an epigrammatic discussion of science is unlikely to inform our students of what science entails and how psychology fits the bill as a scientific discipline. Similarly, although most research methods textbooks contain some discussion of science, the treatment is often relatively brief and does not delve into particulars, thus leaving our students with only a vague understanding of science in general and how the research methods we discuss later in the course serve as the particular "tools" of the scientific method. If we want our students to appreciate the fact that psychology is scientific and that research methods serve as an important piece in the scientific puzzle, we must preface our presentation of research methods with a discussion of what we mean by science, and how scientific knowledge differs from knowledge acquired via tenacity, authority, experience, and so on (see Smith & Davis, 2007).

What is Science?

Unfortunately, science is not a concept that one can easily define. Consider the following definitions chosen at random from various sources:

"The study and theoretical explanation of natural phenomena" (Webster, 1996, p. 608);
"A body of knowledge, particularly that which has resulted from the systematic application of the scientific method" (Reber, 1985, p. 670);
"A branch of knowledge or study dealing with a body of facts or truths systematically arranged and showing the operation of general laws" (http://dictionary.reference.com/browse/science);
"Any system of knowledge attained by verifiable means" (http://en.wikipedia.org/wiki/Portal:Science).

Clearly, there is variability in how people define science, and asking 10 different people to say what science is will likely result in

10 different answers. However, on closer analysis, one will notice that different definitions, including those listed above, contain certain common characteristics that most scientists will agree generally define science. These include:

Falsifiability. For an idea to have scientific value, it must be falsifiable. In other words, there must be some empirical test that allows researchers to show that a particular idea is either true or false. For example, some have argued that Freud's notion of the unconscious mind is not scientific because there is no empirical test that can falsify his ideas, rendering them beyond the reach of science (e.g., Popper, 1963, 1998; Stanovich, 2001). Similarly, one cannot currently examine supernatural phenomena empirically. Hence, they do not fall within the realm of science (e.g., Lilienfeld, 2005).

In short, falsifiability is arguably the most important characteristic of science and scientific thinking. Once your students understand the concept of falsifiability, it should be easier for them to realize why it is necessary for researchers to discard falsified ideas. The ability to do so, even when it means discarding cherished views based on deeply rooted assumptions and personal experience, is a vital part of learning to be a critical thinker, one who is capable of changing his or her mind after encountering valid contradictory evidence.

Objectivity. Another characteristic of science is objectivity, a reliance on evidence that at least two observers can independently verify. For example, if a researcher claims to have seen pigs fly, others should also be able to verify the presence of pigs overhead. Psychological researchers build objectivity into their research partly by providing operational definitions for the phenomena they study (see Chapter 5). For example, although studying "self-esteem" may seem somewhat difficult—simply because it is a "fuzzy" term that carries different meanings for different people—operationally defining it as "a person's score on the Rosenberg Self-Esteem Scale" helps remove subjective bias and allows others to verify a researcher's observations. One way to increase the likelihood of objectivity in science is through the use of peer review, a process by which experts scrutinize the validity of certain knowledge claims, check for mistakes, and, in general, determine if a piece of research is useful to the scientific community. Ultimately, by emphasizing objectivity, researchers can be more certain that the claims they make are valid.

Replicability. Closely related to falsifiability and objectivity is the concept of replicability. One of the first steps necessary for evaluating the reliability and validity of a phenomenon is to determine if others can replicate, or reproduce, a set of findings. The possibility of doing so, of course, depends on whether previous researchers operationally defined the phenomenon of interest and provided a falsifiable hypothesis. In essence, replication allows researchers to test certain knowledge claims and determine whether these claims accurately represent nature or whether they are the result of some artifact, confound, or other misleading factor. For example, some researchers have suggested that listening to music by Wolfgang Amadeus Mozart temporarily increases certain cognitive abilities (e.g., Rauscher, Shaw, & Ky, 1993, 1995). However, because other researchers were unable to replicate these early studies, they were able to show that the "Mozart effect" was not a reliable phenomenon (see Steele, Bass, & Crook, 1999).

Self-correction. In general, researchers tend to be of the "show me" variety, typically choosing healthy skepticism over blind acceptance of knowledge claims. In other words, researchers tend to be wary of knowledge claims until additional studies have replicated earlier findings. For example, when researchers could not reproduce the Mozart effect, scientists' views of it changed, thus illustrating another important characteristic of science: It is self-correcting. Because researchers have the ability to replicate other studies and verify whether the knowledge claims that resulted from those studies are valid, they also help correct any errors or faulty conclusions that emerged from previous research. Thus science is an ever-evolving enterprise, producing results, replicating earlier research, and correcting any mistakes that emerged along the way.

Systematic. Finally, science is systematic; that is, it tends to approach problems in a methodical way. Most often, researchers start by identifying a problem that is in need of examination. Once they have identified a problem, researchers typically collect data in an attempt to identify relations among variables. When distinct patterns emerge, researchers may produce more general statements (i.e., theories) that describe these relations. (By the way, many of your students may have misconceptions about the meaning of "theory." Thus you would do well to explain to them that a scientific theory is not "just a guess" or "a random hunch." Rather, a theory is a coherent statement or set of statements, derived from empirical observations, that describes, and makes predictions about, some phenomenon.) Because theories also make predictions, researchers typically deduce additional hypotheses that test these predictions. If subsequent data support the theory, it is strengthened, and additional studies continue to test its veracity. However, if enough data contradict the theory, researchers either discard or revise it, whereupon additional hypotheses test the newly revised theory.

Once you have introduced your students to the general characteristics of science, you may then wish to discuss how these characteristics define psychology as well. Ideally, by focusing on the characteristics of science and how they pertain to psychology, your students will come to see that psychology is not only a humanistic discipline, concerned with helping people, but also a scientific discipline.

What is Pseudoscience?

One way to enhance your students' understanding of science is by contrasting it with activities that have the trappings of science but do not incorporate its core characteristics. In other words, you may want to consider teaching your students the difference between science and pseudoscience. Pseudoscience, like science, is not a concept that one can easily define, and distinguishing the two can be tricky at times (Lilienfeld, 2005; Ziman, 1998). Nevertheless, Shermer (1997) provided a nice starting point for understanding what characterizes a statement as pseudoscientific in nature: Pseudoscience refers to "claims presented so that they appear scientific even though they lack supporting evidence and plausibility" (p. 33). By comparing and contrasting science and pseudoscience, your students will most likely be in a better position to evaluate certain scientific and pseudoscientific claims they may subsequently encounter (Lilienfeld, 2005; Lilienfeld, Lohr, & Morier, 2001; Ruscio, 2006).

As with science, the characteristics of pseudoscience may vary depending on the source. However, I have found the following characteristics of pseudoscience to be useful when discussing this topic with my students (Ruscio, 2006):

1. *Scientific appearance.* Although the use of scientific language may provide a guise for pseudoscientific topics, the "substance" of these topics does not contain the characteristics of science

mentioned above. For example, although astrology may have a certain scientific air about it—in fact, an astrology Web site defines it as "the science of the stars" (www.astrologycom.com/glossary.html)—astrology has little or no scientific support. Lilienfeld and his colleagues (e.g., Lilienfeld et al., 2001) have provided additional examples of topics that appear scientific but, upon closer analysis, fail to meet the criteria that characterize science (e.g., extrasensory perception, polygraph testing).

2. *Absence of peer review.* For the scientific community to accept an idea, researchers must subject their ideas to peer review. Without peer review, however, one should view knowledge claims with a wary eye. Take, for example, the claims made by Kathy Kolbe, described in one of her books as "the world's leading authority on human instincts" (Kolbe, 2004) and on her Web site (www.kolbe.com) as a "well-known and highly honored author and theorist" (www.kolbe.com/the_kolbe_concept/the_kolbe_concept.cfm). Kolbe has developed a system that purportedly helps people "identify the nature of creative instincts and [enables them] to unleash the boundless power of their own natural instincts" (www.kolbe.com/the_kolbe_concept/what_is_conation.cfm). By answering questions on the Kolbe A Index, touted on Kolbe's Web site as "the only validated method of measuring instinct-based actions" (which, based on my review of their available materials, is a rather dubious claim), respondents can learn more about their instinctive strengths and how they can use them to be more successful in various areas of their lives. Although the Kolbe Web site contains numerous testimonials, results derived from "over 500,000 case studies," and links to several popular press articles, a search of several academic databases (e.g., PsycINFO, ERIC) yielded only one Kolbe-authored, peer-reviewed publication, the focus of which was an unrelated topic (Kolbe, Shemberg, & Leventhal, 1985). If, in fact, Kolbe's system produces the effects she claims it does, researchers and clinicians would have embraced it long ago and subjected it to rigorous peer review.

3. *Anecdotal evidence.* Although anecdotes and testimonials can provide tentative insight into various psychological phenomena, they cannot take the place of controlled experimentation when it comes to discovering how nature "works." For example, although some of your students may swear that they learn best by listening to lectures and using rote memory techniques,

numerous experiments suggest that lecture-based courses tend to be less effective than courses that employ alternative teaching methods (see Chapter 10) and that rote memory tends to be worse than other types of memory. Because your students likely have a rich history of using anecdotal evidence to make decisions, you may need to spend some time discussing why anecdote and personal experience are insufficient substitutes for rigorous empirical analysis.

4. *Absence of rigorous testing.* Another characteristic of scientific endeavors is a willingness to subject hypotheses to rigorous testing—testing that may ultimately prove a hypothesis false. In contrast, pseudoscientists often attempt to avoid rigorous testing altogether, knowing that subjecting their ideas to empirical analysis will likely result in findings that do not support their assertions.

5. *Supernatural explanations.* Whereas scientific endeavors focus on natural explanations (i.e., explanations grounded in natural principles), pseudoscience often retreats to supernatural explanations of the phenomena it studies, which are untestable using current scientific methods. For example, there has been much recent debate in the popular press about the so-called "controversy" between evolutionary theory and intelligent design (see, e.g., Forrest & Gross, 2004). Although proponents of intelligent design suggest that it is a viable alternative to evolutionary theory (e.g., Behe, 1996; Dembski, 2002; Johnson, 1991), their focus on a supernatural designer whose presence is not falsifiable is but one reason why many view their ideas as pseudoscience (Shermer, 2005).

6. *Tolerating inconsistencies.* One hallmark of science is its distaste for contradiction. When different studies produce knowledge statements that conflict with one another, scientists assume that both statements cannot accurately describe nature (e.g., "Opposites attract" *and* "Birds of a feather flock together"). Accordingly, they take steps via replication to determine which of the two statements is more accurate, or to understand the conditions under which each of them might be accurate. In contrast, one characteristic of pseudoscience is its willingness to tolerate such inconsistencies, perhaps describing them as mysteries that are beyond understanding (Lilienfeld, 2005).

7. *Appeals to authority.* Whereas science invokes empirical data when making knowledge statements, pseudoscience tends to

focus on anecdotal evidence (see above), often delivered by so-called "authorities," in an attempt to convince people of the validity of their statements. For example, advertisers routinely appeal to authorities in an attempt to hock their wares. How often have you seen a commercial on TV in which a medical doctor endorses a product and encourages viewers to buy it if they want to improve their lives in some way? Such occurrences are probably more common than any of us would like to admit.

8. *Grandiose claims.* Yet another characteristic of pseudoscience is its ostentatious, often highly flamboyant, claims. For example, just a few years ago, a popular television "infomercial" featuring recent *New York Times* best-selling author Kevin Trudeau (author of *Natural Cures "They" Don't Want You to Know About*) and Dr. Robert Barefoot, a supposed health authority, claimed that consuming large quantities of coral calcium was the cure for cancer, heart disease, and a host of other degenerative diseases. In reality, Barefoot was not a doctor, coral calcium was not the cure-all Trudeau and Barefoot claimed it was, and the Federal Trade Commission eventually investigated Trudeau for making false claims about a product's efficacy (see www. quackwatch.org/01QuackeryRelatedTopics/DSH/coral.html). Yes, consuming calcium does have numerous health benefits. Nevertheless, such grandiose statements—for example, that consuming calcium can cure cancer—are often a sure sign of pseudoscience.

9. *Stagnation.* A leisurely trip through your institution's library will likely convince you that there is a lot of scientific activity going on. Clearly, science is a rapidly changing endeavor—ever evolving, never stagnant. In contrast, pseudoscience tends to be inert—never evolving, ever stagnant. As a recent example, let's again consider the intelligent design movement. Although proponents of intelligent design have vigorously promoted their ideas (often through mainstream venues where they can avoid skeptical peer review), the American Association for the Advancement of Science has asserted that intelligent design proponents "have yet to propose meaningful tests for their claims, there are no reports of current research on these hypotheses at relevant scientific society meetings, and there is no body of research on these hypotheses published in relevant scientific journals" (www. aaas.org/news/press_room/evolution/qanda.shtml). This lack of scientific activity is, once again, a sign of pseudoscience.

As you can see, there are many characteristics that define a knowledge statement as pseudoscientific. Ultimately, though, "what renders these claims largely or entirely pseudoscientific is not that they are necessarily incorrect, but rather that their proponents have typically insisted that they are correct, despite compelling evidence to the contrary" (Lilienfeld et al., 2001, p. 183).

Unfortunately, simply telling your students about science and pseudoscience—for example, by discussing the information provided above—may be insufficient to modify their beliefs and attitudes about psychology. As Miller, Wozniak, Rust, Miller, and Slezak (1996) stated:

> When students arrive on the first day of class with a preconceived notion about the content of the class, instructors cannot assume that simply laying out the facts will cause them to change their minds. In fact, students will more likely persevere in their false beliefs than readily renounce them, even when confronted with disconfirming evidence. (pp. 215–216)

Thus you may need to take special steps to help your students examine and alter erroneous beliefs about psychology as a science and about the importance of research methods in psychology.

Hands-on Tip

To help you to do this, you may want to incorporate in your course some version of a "counterattitudinal advocacy" activity. In the original version of this activity (Miller et al., 1996), students first read several declarative statements about various psychological phenomena, some of which were true and some of which were false (e.g., "Under hypnosis, people have the ability to perform feats that they would otherwise find impossible"), and then rated on a Likert-type scale the extent to which they agreed with each of the statements. Based on how students responded to each statement, Miller et al. had them either (a) write a supportive essay that countered their stated belief (e.g., write an essay explaining why people under hypnosis *cannot* perform impossible feats), (b) read an essay written by another student that supported the opposite of their stated belief, or (c) neither (i.e., a control condition). After writing their essays, students responded once again to the initial set of declarative statements.

Miller et al. (1996) observed that students who wrote counter-attitudinal essays showed a greater reduction in erroneous beliefs than students who read another student's essay or neither wrote nor read an essay. In fact, students who read another student's essay showed the least change in erroneous beliefs. Miller et al. suggested that students who wrote essays experienced cognitive dissonance because their original beliefs were at odds with the act of writing a counterattitudinal essay. Only when they changed their original beliefs was the dissonance reduced.

So after discussing the characteristics of science and pseudoscience in your course, you might ask your students to write a short essay explaining why psychology fits the bill as a scientific discipline. For example, because many of your students may view psychology as primarily a "helping" discipline and less as a "research" discipline, you could ask them to discuss ways in which clinical, school, and counseling psychology are scientific in nature. You could also use the same activity to change your students' views on the importance of understanding research methods. For example, after your students have acquired some general knowledge about research methods, you could ask them to write a short essay describing the importance of research methods as it relates to their future goals. To ensure this activity has the expected effect, you should tailor the essay to individual students by allowing them to choose the specific topic they discuss (e.g., students interested in counseling can explain why knowledge of research methods is important to counselors). Research on cognitive dissonance suggests that your students—especially those who hold erroneous beliefs about psychology's scientific status or who have negative attitudes toward research methods—should have a different view of these topics once they complete the activity. In addition, Lilienfeld et al. (2001) outlined a model syllabus for those interested in teaching a course on science and pseudoscience; they also discussed how instructors could incorporate the resources they provided into a research methods course.

Conclusion

Undoubtedly, one of the primary goals of any methods course should be to teach students the particulars of conducting research. However, many, if not most, of the students who enter our courses have little to no interest in conducting (and sometimes even learning about) psychological research, preferring instead to focus on psychology's humanistic side. Unfortunately, without knowledge of science and research methods, students may be susceptible to the very pseudoscientific claims we want them to question. Hence it is important to discuss with your students what science is and how it contrasts with pseudoscience. By discussing these topics, your students will eventually realize that knowledge of science can be a boon, regardless of the personal and professional paths they ultimately choose to follow.

References

Behe, M. J. (1996). *Darwin's black box: The biochemical challenge to evolution*. New York: Simon & Schuster.

Dembski, W. A. (2002). *No free lunch: Why specified complexity cannot be purchased without intelligence*. Lanham, MD: Rowman & Littlefield.

Dennett, D. C. (1995). *Darwin's dangerous idea: Evolution and the meanings of life*. New York: Touchstone.

Forrest, B. C., & Gross, P. R. (2004). *Creationism's Trojan horse: The wedge of intelligent design*. New York: Oxford University Press.

Friedrich, J. (1996). Assessing students' perceptions of psychology as a science: Validation of a self-report measure. *Teaching of Psychology, 23*, 6–13.

Johnson, P. E. (1991). *Darwin on trial*. Lanham, MD: Regnery Gateway.

Kolbe, K. (2004). *Powered by instinct: 5 rules for trusting your guts*. Phoenix, AZ: Monumentus Press.

Kolbe, K., Shemberg, K., & Leventhal, D. (1985). University training in psychodiagnostics and psychotherapy. *The Clinical Psychologist, 38*, 59–61.

Lilienfeld, S. O. (2005). Teaching psychology students to distinguish science from pseudoscience: Pitfalls and rewards. In B. K. Saville, T. E. Zinn, & V. W. Hevern (Eds.), *Essays from excellence in teaching, 2004* (Chap. 6). Retrieved October 16, 2006, from the Society for the Teaching of Psychology Web site: http://teachpsych.org/resources/e-books/eit2004/eit04-06.pdf

Lilienfeld, S. O., Lohr, M., & Morier, D. (2001). The teaching of courses in the science and pseudoscience of psychology. *Teaching of Psychology, 28*, 182–191.

Miller, R. L., Wozniak, W. J., Rust, M. R., Miller, B. R., & Slezak, J. (1996). Counterattitudinal advocacy as a means of enhancing instructional effectiveness: How to teach students what they do not want to know. *Teaching of Psychology, 23*, 215–219.

Popper, K. R. (1963). *Conjectures and refutations*. New York: Harper & Row.

Popper, K. R. (1998). Science: Conjectures and refutations. In E. D. Klemke, R. Hollinger, & D. W. Rudge (Eds.), *Introductory readings in the philosophy of science* (3rd ed.) (pp. 38–47). Amherst, NY: Prometheus.

Rauscher, F. H., Shaw, G. L., & Ky, K. N. (1993). Music and spatial task performance. *Nature, 365,* 611.

Rauscher, F. H., Shaw, G. L., & Ky, K. N. (1995). Listening to Mozart enhances spatial-temporal reasoning: Towards a neurophysiological basis. *Neuroscience Letters, 185,* 44–47.

Reber, A. S. (1985). *The Penguin dictionary of psychology.* New York: Penguin.

Ruscio, J. (2006). *Critical thinking in psychology: Separating sense from nonsense* (2nd ed.). Belmont, CA: Thomson Wadsworth.

Shermer, M. (1997). *Why people believe weird things: Pseudoscience, superstition, and other confusions of our time.* New York: Freeman.

Shermer, M. (2005). *Science friction: Where the known meets the unknown.* New York: Holt.

Smith, R. A., & Davis, S. F. (2007). *The psychologist as detective: An introduction to conducting research in psychology* (4th ed.). Upper Saddle River, NJ: Prentice Hall.

Stanovich, K. E. (2001). *How to think straight about psychology* (6th ed.). Boston: Allyn & Bacon.

Steele, K. M., Bass, K. E., & Crook, M. D. (1999). The mystery of the Mozart effect: Failure to replicate. *Psychological Science, 10,* 366–369.

Webb, A. R., & Speer, J. R. (1985). The public image of psychologists. *American Psychologist, 40,* 1063–1064.

Webster's II new riverside dictionary (revised ed.). (1996). Boston: Houghton Mifflin.

Wood, W., Jones, M., & Benjamin, L. T., Jr. (1986). Surveying psychology's public image. *American Psychologist, 41,* 947–953.

Ziman, J. (1998). What is science? In E. D. Klemke, R. Hollinger, & D. W. Rudge (Eds.), *Introductory readings in the philosophy of science* (3rd ed.) (pp. 48–53). Amherst, NY: Prometheus.

Chapter 4

Ethical Considerations in Psychological Research: Teaching Issues

Research methods have played—and will continue to play—an enormous role in the continued pursuit of knowledge about human and nonhuman behavior, cognition, and emotion. However, the process of gathering data on interesting psychological phenomena is always subject to important ethical considerations that all researchers will eventually face. Ignoring these considerations would leave researchers at risk for doing harm to their participants, other researchers (whose work could be constrained by a colleague's ethical lapse), members of society who depend on science to guide decisions and policies, and the reputation of science itself (R. L. Miller, 2003). It is vital, then, that we inform our students about the centrality of ethical considerations in all research endeavors and, more specifically, why over the past 50 years these considerations have played an increasingly important role in the field of psychology.

In the paragraphs that follow, I briefly discuss the history of ethics in psychological research and why it is important to discuss this history with your students. I then turn to various ethical considerations of which your students should be aware as they learn about research methods. In addition, I describe several simple activities that you can use to inform your students of the importance of ethical considerations in psychological research.

Teaching the History of Ethical Issues in Psychological Research

The knowledge most students have about research ethics usually relates to issues of participant harm—presumably because of their brief exposure in introductory psychology to Stanley Milgram's (1963) classic obedience study. Indeed, because there is relatively little coverage of ethical issues in most introductory psychology courses (Fisher & Kuther, 1997; Korn, 1984)—or in many other undergraduate psychology courses, for that matter—research methods instructors can safely assume that typical students enter their course with little or no knowledge of the myriad ethical issues that psychological researchers face. Thus the onus of teaching our students about important ethical issues, as well as the murkiness that sometimes surrounds the process of deciding how to deal with different ethical dilemmas, falls squarely on those of us who teach the research methods course.

Some instructors begin—and end—their discussion of ethics by introducing their students to the American Psychological Association's (APA) list of ethical standards and code of conduct (APA, 2002), and how these standards affect those conducting research in psychology. Instead of taking this minimalist approach, you might consider beginning your discussion of ethics with some historical background on the events that led to APA's codification of its first set of ethical guidelines.

Your students will likely be interested to know that early psychological researchers did not operate under the same set of ethical guidelines that affects today's researchers. In fact, it may intrigue your students to discover that the first set of ethical guidelines for practicing psychologists was not discussed until the mid-20th century (Hobbs, 1948) and that explicit guidelines for conducting research with both humans and nonhumans did not emerge until the early 1970s (APA, 1971, 1973). Once introduced to this information, students can begin to understand how Milgram was able to carry out his controversial obedience studies without having to answer to an Institutional Review Board (IRB).

Additional information might provide an even broader sociocultural context in which to discuss present-day ethical standards. Accordingly, you might consider spending some additional classroom time discussing other important events that occurred outside the walls of our discipline but that subsequently had an impact on the development of the ethical guidelines that affect psychological researchers today (Goodwin, 2005; R. L. Miller, 2003). For example, it may be easier for students to appreciate why early (and some present-day) psychologists conducted research with nonhuman subjects when they learn about the impact that Charles Darwin's (1859) theory of evolution (which suggests continuity among species) was having in the late 1800s and early 1900s. And it may be easier for them to see why psychologists in the early 1900s became interested in applying their laboratory findings when one understands that, at that time, "Americans were becoming accustomed to the idea that science should be used to improve their lives . . . [and for] psychology to gain public support, it needed to produce useful results" (Goodwin, 2005, p. 211). Finally, it may be easier for your students to understand and appreciate the history of ethics in psychology, as well as the importance of ethics in present-day psychological research, if you tell them about some of the events outside psychology that greatly affected practices within the discipline.

For example, you might point out that the codification of ethical guidelines in psychology emerged partly because of at least three events that occurred outside the field during the early and middle parts of the 20th century. First, horrific "research" on Jewish prisoners by Nazi scientists in concentration camp experiments during World War II led to the adoption of the Nuremberg Code, a set of principles and guidelines regarding the treatment of research participants. This Code greatly influenced APA's first code of ethics.

A second event that ultimately affected the treatment of research participants took place in Tuskegee, Alabama. From 1932 to 1972, the Public Health Service Syphilis Study (now known as the Tuskegee Syphilis Study) recruited poor African American men for health check-ups. Researchers found that approximately 400 of their participants were syphilitic but did not inform them of their diagnosis. Rather, they simply told these participants that they had "bad blood." Keeping the participants ignorant about their condition allowed researchers to study the untreated progression of the disease. Moreover, although the researchers promised "free treatment" to the infected men if they remained in the study, the researchers did not obtain informed consent or allow the infected men to seek treatment elsewhere. Eventually the unethical aspects of this study became public and resulted in a series of actions that ultimately led to the creation of the various research review boards, including the ubiquitous IRB, that now play a prominent role in the conduct of psychological research.

A third event that affected guidelines for the ethical treatment of research participants—especially in closed institutions—occurred following a study conducted in the mid-1960s at Willowbrook State School, a facility for mentally retarded children on Staten Island, New York. In this study, researchers purposely infected a small percentage of otherwise physically healthy children with mild strains of hepatitis and used them as test cases in research on the effectiveness of various treatments for combating the virus. Although many of these children's parents were aware of the study and actually agreed to let their children be tested, many later reported feeling pressure to provide consent. When the study became public, protests led to its discontinuation. Moreover, subsequent investigations found the living conditions at Willowbrook to be detestable, which led to further laws regarding the rights of research participants and institutionalized individuals.

You might also want to tell your students about events within the field of psychology that led to the introduction of ethical guidelines for working with humans and nonhumans. I often describe two psychological studies that serve to introduce subsequent discussion of research ethics. The first of these is Milgram's (1963) obedience study, a classic example with which, as mentioned earlier, your students are likely to be familiar. The second is the equally controversial Stanford Prison Experiment in which Philip Zimbardo and his colleagues (Haney, Banks, & Zimbardo, 1973) randomly assigned "normal" male participants to be either "prisoners" or "guards" in a mock jail setting constructed in the basement of Stanford University's psychology building. Although Zimbardo and his colleagues initially planned to conduct the study for 2 weeks, they decided to terminate it after only 6 days, due to degrading behavior on the part of prison guards and emotional disturbances experienced by several prisoners.

These studies, along with many others (see, e.g., Rosnow, 1990), provide you with numerous opportunities to discuss with your students various ethical issues that confront psychological researchers. Regardless of which studies you choose as a prologue to your discussion of ethics, they will provide your students with historical context in which they can better grasp the rise of ethical issues in psychology and the importance of engaging in ethical behavior when conducting psychological research.

Teaching Ethical Considerations:
Human Participants

With a bit of historical context now in place, the time has come to introduce your students to some of the most fundamental issues that psychologists face when conducting research with human participants. Because there are many ethical considerations—some blatantly obvious, others more subtle—that psychological researchers encounter (see APA, 2002), I have found it useful first to provide my students with a simple organizational structure that helps them better remember the primary questions psychologists typically address when conducting research with human participants. By presenting the following steps (or questions), and incorporating additional information where relevant and when needed, you can be fairly certain that your students will understand the issues most germane to conducting ethically sound research. Moreover, by organizing these issues into a smaller number of general ideas, your students will likely have an easier time learning and retaining this important information. The research steps I highlight include (a) gaining approval from an IRB, (b) recruiting participants and obtaining informed consent, (c) describing any risks that participants might incur during a study, (d) informing participants that any data they provide will be treated with confidentiality, (e) informing participants of their right to withdraw from the study at any time, and (f) debriefing participants upon their completion of the study.

Institutional Review Board Approval

Once researchers have identified a potential research problem, the first question they must ask with regard to ethical considerations is: Is this study ethical? Quite possibly the easiest way for researchers to determine whether their study is ethical is by consulting the APA's (2002) *Ethical Principles of Psychologists and Code of Conduct*, which bases its more specific guidelines on five general principles: (a) beneficence and nonmaleficence, (b) fidelity and responsibility, (c) integrity, (d) justice, and (e) respect for people's rights and dignity.

Your students should know that although APA's principles and ethical standards provide researchers with specific information regarding the ethical treatment of human participants, researchers are not solely responsible for determining the ethicality of their studies. Rather, all researchers must obtain the approval of their institution's IRB, or other equivalent review boards, before they initiate any research with human participants.

Hands-on Tip

Students should understand that the job of these review boards is to determine whether researchers plan to conduct their studies in an ethical manner, not whether the studies have scientific merit (Smith & Davis, 2007). To help make this point, you may find it useful to show your students an example of an IRB proposal (or similar form) from your institution. Showing these forms may also help students understand the amount of detail that goes into conducting an ethical study and the issues that review boards typically discuss when deciding if the conduct of a study adheres to ethical standards.

Recruitment and Informed Consent

Your students should also understand that there are several important guidelines regarding the recruitment of research participants (e.g., advertising, exaggeration of research goals; see R. L. Miller, 2003), and that it is of particular importance that researchers do not coerce participants to take part in their studies. Minimizing coercion is especially important when (a) researchers use monetary incentives to compensate participants for their time (R. L. Miller, 2003) and (b) research is being conducted in university settings, where the emphasis on research—and the faulty belief that research participation may be linked to grades—may lead some students to feel pressure to participate (e.g., Leak, 1981). Because many psychology departments require their students to participate in research or, alternatively, complete some other specified activity (see APA, 2002), your students will probably be particularly interested in learning about issues surrounding participant recruitment.

I suggest placing even heavier emphasis on what is arguably the most important step in conducting ethical research: obtaining informed consent. It is important to point out that informed consent serves as a contract between researchers and participants, providing participants with important information regarding their involvement in the study (APA, 2002).

Hands-on Tip

Again, you may wish to show some examples of consent forms to illustrate that these forms typically disclose to participants the general purpose of the study (although certain studies may require deception and thus may preclude complete disclosure), how long the study will last, and what activities the participant will perform.

Explain, too, that informed consent notifies participants that the researcher will treat them with respect and do everything possible to keep them out of harm's way. Finally, point out that informed consent also serves as a guarantee that a participant has agreed to endure any procedures that occur during the course of the study (R. L. Miller, 2003).

Your students should also know that obtaining informed consent in most research is mandatory if participants (a) will experience anything more than minimal risk (see below), and (b) are under the age of 18 years (in university settings, participants under 18 must have the option of completing an alternate activity if participating in research is part of a course requirement) or otherwise unable to provide consent themselves (e.g., if participants are developmentally disabled). Finally, it is important to tell your students that informed consent is *not* mandatory in studies where researchers (a) will not be exposing participants to anything more than minimal risk; (b) will be examining pedagogical practices in classroom, or other educational, settings; (c) will be using anonymous questionnaires or examining archival data; or (d) will be collecting data using naturalistic observations (APA, 2002).

Describing Risks Involved

The next important step in conducting ethically sound research, which your students should know, concerns describing to participants any potential risks associated with the study. I like to point out that although researchers must take steps to minimize possible risks, participants sometimes incur more than minimal risks when participating in psychological research. Thus your students should know that research participants often fall into two categories: participants at risk and participants at minimal risk. Participants at risk are participants who may incur some type of psychological stress during the course of the study. For example, studies that have examined the effects of exercise on various measures of health (e.g., Fitterling, Martin, Gramling, Cole, & Milan, 1988) usually include more than minimal risk because of the potential stressors participants may experience while exercising. Similarly, researchers who study anxiety disorders sometimes must induce mild to moderate anxiety in their participants to learn more about the etiology and development of these often debilitating disorders (e.g., McGlynn, Karg, & Lawyer, 2003). In contrast, participants at minimal risk are those who are not expected to incur any risks greater than what they might experience during the course of their everyday activities, for example, completing innocuous computer tasks or filling out nonintrusive questionnaires.

Although I have listed "describing risks" as a separate step in conducting ethical research, I always inform my students that researchers often accomplish this step by including a brief statement in the consent form.

Hands-on Tip

Again, showing your students a sample consent form at this time might help them better understand the notion of risk in psychological research.

Maintaining Confidentiality

Students should appreciate that researchers must inform participants that any data they provide during a study will be completely confidential. Typically, this requires researchers to (a) tell their participants that only individuals connected to the study (e.g., assistants bound by the same ethical standards as the primary researcher) will have access to their data; (b) code all data so others cannot connect participants with their responses; and (c) store the data in a secure location, such as a locked filing cabinet. As with describing any risks involved in a study, you may wish to tell your students that one way to inform participants about confidentiality is to include a detailed statement in the consent form.

Finally, you may find it useful to explain to your students the difference between anonymous data and confidential data. Anonymity suggests that researchers are obtaining no data, such as participants' names, that would allow them or others to determine the identity of a participant. In contrast, confidentiality implies that researchers are obtaining identifiable data (e.g., participants' names) but are taking steps to maintain the privacy of their participants. Whereas researchers can conduct certain studies under conditions of total anonymity, and thus may not require informed consent (see APA, 2002), other studies—for example, studies on the efficacy of certain clinical treatments that require follow-ups—typically necessitate the collection of identifiable data and, consequently, always require the obtainment of informed consent.

Right to Withdraw at Any Time

Your students should also know that before participants begin any study, they must understand that they have the right to withdraw from the study at any time, with no questions asked and with no penalties for early withdrawal. It is important to explain this point because research participants—especially those participating in a university setting as part of a course requirement—often feel pressure to complete the studies in which they participate.

Debriefing

The final step in conducting ethical research concerns the debriefing of participants upon completion of a study. You should tell your students that the APA (2002) guidelines require researchers to provide participants with immediate and accurate information regarding the true purpose of a study, especially if deception was involved. Highlight, too, that debriefing provides an opportunity for participants to ask questions they might have about the study, such as why it included a certain activity or what the researcher hopes to find by conducting the study. Explain that, in general, debriefing should occur immediately upon completion of a study, but that it can be delayed as long as the researcher takes reasonable measures to reduce any risk that might result from withholding this information (APA, 2002). In essence, the reason for completely—and, if possible, immediately—debriefing participants on the nature of a study is to ensure that they leave a study in the same psychological state of mind they were in when they arrived. Remind your students that debriefing serves to inform participants about the purpose of the study and remove any psychological harm they may have experienced while participating; it also serves as a way for researchers to obtain relatively immediate feedback regarding the overall conduct of the study (Smith & Davis, 2007).

Describing for your students the six research steps listed here may help them to better understand the important ethical issues that confront psychological researchers. However, as McMinn (1988) pointed out, "Memorizing the [APA guidelines] is not the same as learning to be ethical" (p. 100). Thus you should make it exceptionally clear to students that the steps presented above serve only as a starting point and that conducting ethical research often requires psychological researchers to weigh the potential costs and benefits of different courses of action (see below), each of which may provide a reasonable answer to a challenging ethical dilemma.

Other Considerations with Human Participants

In addition to the ethical considerations discussed above, there are other issues that may pique the interest of your students and increase their motivation to learn more about the many ethical issues related to conducting research with human participants. I describe two of these issues below.

Deception. The first issue you would do well to discuss with your students concerns the use of deception in psychological research. As you know, deception refers to the practice of shielding research participants from the true purpose of a study. Most often, researchers resort to deception because fully informing their participants would possibly alter their behavior in light of the study's purpose, thus resulting in outcomes that might not be valid (see Chapter 5). For example, although Milgram (1963) has been the recipient of considerable criticism for his use of deception, one might argue that his participants would likely not have behaved the way they did if they knew the true purpose of the study. One might also argue, however, that Milgram's use of deception ultimately resulted in a study that tiptoed the end lines of ethicality. For this reason, the use of deception in psychological research continues to be the focus of much debate.

Hands-on Tip

To help your students further understand the sometimes necessary use of deception in psychological research, you may wish to include the following activity in your course (see also Beins, 1993). Fernald and Fernald (1990) told students they were going to participate in a demonstration of graphology (the analysis of personality through handwriting) and then instructed them to write the following sentence: The quick brown fox jumps over the lazy dog. They told students it was necessary to examine the same sentence for everyone, because analyzing different sentences from different people might in itself provide insights into their personality characteristics. Fernald and Fernald also had students write the sentence on the same type of paper with the same type of pen (which the authors provided), along with a unique number (e.g., student ID number) at the top of the sheet—both of which, Fernald and Fernald told their students, would allow them to conduct unbiased graphological analyses (and to lend credibility to the exercise). During the next class period, Fernald and Fernald gave the students a supposedly individualized personality analysis, which in reality consisted of the same set of 12 vague statements taken from an astrological source (e.g., "You have a strong need for other people to like you and for them to admire you"). The students then rated each statement on a five-point scale as to how accurately it described their own personality. (The students did not know they each received the same analysis, because Fernald and Fernald told them not to look at each other's papers.) Finally, Fernald and Fernald asked several students to read their personality assessment aloud. After students realized they had all received the same assessment, the class discussed the ethics of deception and why researchers sometimes use deception as a way to learn more about human behavior. In conclusion, Fernald and Fernald suggested that this experiential learning exercise might help students understand what it feels like to be deceived and why deception may be important in some studies.

Clinical research. Assuming that many of your students have interests pertaining to clinical or counseling psychology, you may also wish to discuss with them an ethical issue that continues to capture the attention of researchers in psychology as well as in other disciplines: the use of no-treatment control groups in clinical research. As we know, the simplest way to determine if an independent variable effected changes in a dependent variable is to randomly assign participants to either an experimental group or a control group and compare their average levels of responding at the end of the study. Although this idea seems relatively straightforward, it raises ethical issues when the use of a control group means that some participants may not receive a treatment (e.g., medication, psychotherapy) that could potentially have a dramatic effect on their physical or psychological well-being. Although some students might question the ethicality of research that withholds from some participants a potentially beneficial treatment, other researchers (e.g., Charney, 2000; F. G. Miller, 2000) have argued that the use of control groups is vital to identifying therapies that may potentially benefit a greater number of people in the future. Moreover, when examining the efficacy of a clinical treatment, many researchers address this highly controversial issue by clearly stating in their consent forms that participants initially assigned to a control group will receive treatment—either the new treatment, if it is shown to be effective, or another effective treatment—upon completion of the study. Nevertheless, it is important to discuss with your students the continued debate that psychological researchers are having regarding the initial omission of treatment for some participants in clinical studies of treatment efficacy.

Teaching Ethical Considerations: Nonhuman Subjects

Few students enter our research methods courses with more than minimal awareness of the ethical issues involved in conducting research with human participants; even fewer understand the ethical issues that surround the use of nonhuman subjects in psychological research. Those who are aware that psychological researchers sometimes study nonhuman subjects are probably familiar only with the research of Ivan Pavlov, B. F. Skinner, Harry Harlow, and the few other psychologists whose research they encountered in their introductory psychology textbooks. Further, those students who are familiar with the use of nonhuman subjects in psychological research are often ill-informed regarding the treatment of those subjects (N. E. Miller, 1985). Given that research with nonhumans has been, and most likely will continue to be, vitally important in psychology (N. E. Miller, 1985), our students need to be at the very least aware of (a) the general ethical issues that surround the use of nonhuman subjects in psychological research and (b) the steps that researchers take to maximize the ethical treatment of nonhuman subjects.

Why is it important to spend time discussing the ethics involved in conducting research with nonhuman subjects? After all, the majority of research studies conducted in psychology involve human participants. Indeed, some research methods instructors tend not to spend much time discussing ethical issues related to nonhumans, but I think there are several important reasons why you should at least introduce your students to the topic. First, some of your students, like other members of the lay public, tend to hold firm misconceptions regarding psychological research with nonhuman subjects (N. E. Miller, 1985). Second, some of your students may already be familiar with, or may eventually learn about, numerous important psychological phenomena that researchers have discovered using nonhuman subjects. They should at least be aware of the ethics that guided that research. Finally, some psychology courses (e.g., biopsychology, learning) include a laboratory component in which students conduct projects using nonhuman subjects. If this is the case at your institution, your students will likely receive additional instruction on the ethical treatment of nonhuman subjects, but an early discussion of ethical issues in research with nonhumans will provide a valuable foundation.

Ethical Debate About the Use of Nonhuman Subjects in Research

No presentation on the ethics of research would be complete without a discussion of the debate that has raged for the past several decades over the ethicality and morality of using nonhuman subjects in scientific research of any kind. It is a good idea to frame the debate by pointing out that whereas some people see research with nonhuman subjects as acceptable under most, if not all, conditions, others believe that any kind of nonhuman research is unwarranted, unnecessary, and unethical. Most people fall somewhere between these extremes, and, as Rowan (1997) stated, "believe some form of cost-benefit analysis should be performed to determine whether the use of animals is acceptable" (p. 79).

In organizing your classroom presentation, consider using Kantowitz, Roediger, and Elmes's (1997) summary of three issues that separate opponents and proponents of research with nonhuman subjects. First, opponents of research with nonhuman subjects argue that because humans and nonhumans both feel pain, both have moral standing, which affords them certain rights of protection, for example, protection from pain (see also Gluck & Bell, 2003; Regan, 1997). Because ethical (and moral) standards do not allow researchers to inflict pain or suffering on human participants or use them in research against their will, neither should researchers engage in similar practices with nonhumans. In response, proponents of research with nonhuman subjects argue that, by law, they must treat their subjects humanely and that the care their subjects receive is often considerably better than the "treatment" they would receive in the wild (e.g., Epling, 1989; Herzog, 1988). In addition, proponents argue that only a few studies involve painful stimulation and that in those studies, researchers take care to create the least amount of pain possible, with the fewest number of subjects necessary. Proponents argue, too, that research of this kind proceeds only when there are no alternatives and, even then, only after a very careful examination of the potential costs and benefits of conducting the study (see below), not only by the researchers themselves, but also by the appropriate review boards, who carefully evaluate the ethicality of the study.

The second issue involves the argument by opponents of research with nonhumans that any type of research that harms or destroys life, in whatever form, ultimately "dehumanizes" the researcher responsible for the harm or destruction, and thus should be minimized or eliminated. In rebuttal, proponents of research with nonhuman subjects assert that this argument carries with it repercussions that reach far beyond the realm of scientific research—many of which even the staunchest advocates of eliminating research with nonhumans would find largely impractical. For example, if research with nonhuman subjects is "dehumanizing," so too should be the consumption of any products derived from such research, for example, many common medicinal products and certain types of psychotherapeutic interventions (e.g., systematic desensitization).

Third, opponents of research with nonhuman subjects argue that conducting certain types of research on nonhumans, but not humans, amounts to "speciesism," or neglect of certain species, in the same way that the neglect of certain groups of people amounts to racism or sexism (Singer, 1975). In response, proponents of research with nonhuman subjects point to the many benefits their research has had not only for humans, but also for members of other species (see N. E. Miller, 1985, for examples).

The Ethical Treatment of Nonhuman Subjects in Psychological Research

Ultimately, your students will need to make their own decisions regarding the use of nonhuman subjects in psychological research. Presenting both sides of the issue should help them to do so.

Once you have discussed the ethical debate about using nonhuman subjects in research, it is time to introduce your students to the ethical guidelines that direct the conduct of that research. Fortunately, many of the standards that guide research with human participants also guide research with nonhuman subjects, thus making it easier for you to teach—and your students to learn and remember—these guidelines.

Point out that, as is the case when working with human participants, psychologists who conduct research with nonhuman subjects are expected to treat those subjects humanely, following the APA's (2002) general principles of beneficence and nonmaleficence, fidelity and responsibility, integrity, justice, and respect for subjects' rights and dignity. Explain that researchers who conduct studies with nonhuman subjects must first gain approval of an appropriate review panel, such as the Institutional Animal Care and Use Committee (IACUC), whose job it is to evaluate research proposals and make sure the researchers will conduct their studies in accordance with established ethical guidelines. Mention that the APA (2002) also requires that researchers working with nonhuman subjects must take steps to minimize any discomfort or pain subjects might experience during the course of a study—which is, of course, analogous to minimizing any risks that human participants might experience during a study. Furthermore, as stated above, researchers can inflict pain or stress on their subjects *only* if there are no alternative ways to study the topic of interest—and then, only if the ends justify the means (i.e., if the potential knowledge gained is far greater than any harm experienced by the subjects).

After covering these general guidelines, describe the guidelines that are more specific to research with nonhuman subjects (see APA, 2002). First, any study that uses nonhuman subjects must involve supervision by someone trained in research methods and knowledgeable about issues regarding the care of animals. Second, researchers using nonhuman subjects must ensure that any students working with them receive training in the care and handling of animals and that the students' responsibilities are commensurate with their level of experience. (Together, the preceding guidelines state that experienced researchers are ultimately responsible for the care and treatment of their nonhuman subjects, regardless of whether the lead researcher is actually responsible for their day-to-day care.) Finally, in situations where researchers must end an animal's life, whether because of old age or for other reasons, they must take steps to minimize pain for the animal.

Other Issues in the Teaching of Ethical Considerations

In addition to the ethical issues that one must consider when conducting research with humans and nonhumans, there are several other important considerations that are of vital importance to psychological researchers and, consequently, that you should discuss with your students. Two of the most important of these issues are plagiarism and the fabrication of data.

Plagiarism

Unfortunately, for those of us who teach research methods, plagiarism is an issue with which we often have to deal. More common than we probably wish to admit is the APA-style paper that contains plagiarized information—sometimes intentional, sometimes not. In fact, studies of academic dishonesty in general (e.g., Davis, Grover, Becker, & McGregor, 1992; McCabe & Trevino, 1993) have found that a majority of college students (i.e., often well over 50%) self-report having engaged in some form of cheating. Studies on plagiarism in college students in particular have observed similar high rates of occurrence. Although cautious in his conclusions, Hale (1987), for example, suspected that in any given class, there is likely at least one, if not more, instance of plagiarism. In contrast, however, Roig (1997) found that over one-half of his participants could not correctly identify more subtle forms of plagiarism, for example, using a direct quote without quotation marks but including a correct citation (see also Froese, Boswell, Garcia, Koehn, & Nelson, 1995). Clearly, plagiarism is an issue we will continue to confront in our research methods courses, so it is important that we (a) educate our students on exactly what plagiarism is and (b) take steps to reduce it in our courses, most of which require students to write APA-style papers.

What is plagiarism? The first step in effectively teaching your students about the ethicality—or lack thereof—of plagiarism is to define plagiarism for them. Although plagiarism may come in many different forms, in general, it refers to "using someone else's words, thoughts, or work without giving proper credit" (Mitchell & Jolley, 2004, p. 456). Although some of your students may be able to identify blatant instances of plagiarism (e.g., Hale, 1987), more common is the student who has a general grasp on the concept of plagiarism but fails to understand more nuanced instances (Roig, 1997). The relatively high incidence of plagiarism in college courses likely stems from the fact that many of our students either (a) have not learned the specifics of plagiarism in the past or (b) have plagiarized material in the past—sometimes knowingly, sometimes unknowingly—and gotten away with it.

How to reduce plagiarism

Hands-on Tip

Landau, Druen, and Arcuri (2002) described an effective activity that you can implement in your courses to reduce, and maybe even eliminate, the prevalence of plagiarism. Landau et al. first gave students a brief passage from the scientific literature, six rewritten versions of the same passage, and instructions to identify which of the rewritten versions were instances of plagiarism (see also Roig, 1997). Landau et al. then provided feedback or additional examples of plagiarism to some of the students. Next, students examined a different passage (along with accompanying rewrites) and again attempted to determine whether each rewrite constituted an instance of plagiarism. Finally, students examined a third scientific passage and attempted to paraphrase the passage in their own words. Landau et al. found that students given feedback and additional examples of plagiarism detected more instances of plagiarism in the second passage and did a better job of rewriting the third passage than students in a control group. Thus a relatively simple way to teach your students to avoid instances of plagiarism would be to (a) discuss first exactly what constitutes plagiarism, (b) give your students practice examining passages for instances of plagiarism, (c) provide your students with feedback for their answers along with additional examples of plagiarized material, and (d) give your students additional practice (and feedback) rewriting material from the scientific literature.

Fabrication of Data

A second issue you should spend time discussing with your students concerns the fabrication of data. Although we would like to assume that our students understand why it is unethical—and potentially damaging—to fabricate data, research suggests that students are quite likely to engage in various forms of academic dishonesty (e.g., Davis et al., 1992). We can probably assume that at least some of these cases have involved the fabrication of data on class research projects. In fact, some of you may have had an experience similar to the one I had not so long ago. A few years ago, I asked students in my research methods course to complete small projects. One student decided to examine if there was a relation between students' self-esteem and grade point average. Two weeks later, the student came to my office, asking if I could help with data analysis. Upon viewing the data—which, the student reported, came from a sample consisting of 10 friends—we observed a correlation coefficient for self-esteem and grade point average that was well over .90. Knowing that few studies on the relation between self-esteem and grade point average—or few studies on the relation between *any* variables, for that matter—have found such a strong relation (e.g., Demo & Parker, 2001; Griffore, Kallen, Popovich, & Powell, 1990; Grzegorek, Slaney, Franze, & Rice, 2004), especially with a sample size of 10, I was certain the results were not "real" and questioned the student about the authenticity of the data.

Most likely, fabricating data on a small research methods project, as in the preceding example, will not have a negative, long-term impact on psychology as a whole. Nevertheless, you should explain to your students why data fabrication—even on supposedly "small" research methods projects—is unethical and possibly detrimental to our discipline. To introduce the topic of data fabrication to your students, you may wish to discuss with them some well-known case studies of data fabrication.

One well-known case of data fabrication involved the British psychologist Cyril Burt (see Tucker, 1997, for a review). Burt, who died in 1971, published in the mid-1900s data from several twin studies suggesting that IQ was largely determined by genetic factors. Shortly after Burt's death, psychologist Leon Kamin (1974) reanalyzed several of Burt's publications and found that much of the data, which were supposedly from different studies and thus published in different outlets, were strikingly similar. For example, Kamin found that several of the correlation coefficients that Burt reported in different studies were identical up to several decimal places, even though the studies included different sample sizes. Consequently, Kamin and others (e.g., Hearnshaw, 1979; Jensen, 1974) suggested that Burt had fabricated his data. However, because Burt died before Kamin reported his findings, other researchers were unable to examine Burt's original data or ask him for clarification (Jensen, 1974). Since that time, psychologists have argued fervently about the authenticity of Burt's data, with some suggesting that he engaged in fraudulent practices and others suggesting that he was simply careless and did not set out to deceive others (cf. Joynson, 2003; Mackintosh, 1995).

Once again, because your students may better understand the particulars of the Burt case with some knowledge of sociocultural context, you may wish to explain to them how many psychologists in the 1950s and 1960s were retaliating to what they felt was an overemphasis on the influence of environment rather than heredity on human development. As a consequence, many researchers were in search of data that purported to show a strong genetic basis for various psychological phenomena, including intelligence.

Hopefully, your students will recognize the potentially damaging effects that Burt's fabricated data could have had on the discipline of psychology as well as on the numerous individuals whose lives are affected by such scientific findings. Regardless of whether you choose to include the preceding case or other cases of data fabrication in your courses (see Bechtel & Pearson, 1985, for additional examples), once you have introduced your students to the specifics of these cases, you would do well to discuss with them in more detail reasons why data fabrication is not only unethical, but also potentially damaging to our discipline and to those whose lives may be affected by the implications of our research. When doing so, you might also discuss with your students APA's (2002) ethical guidelines for reporting and publishing data, which state that "Psychologists do not fabricate data," and "If psychologists discover significant errors in their published data, they take reasonable steps to correct such errors" (p. 1070). In addition, because students sometimes wonder why anyone would risk his or her career to publish falsified data, you may want to discuss the possible reasons why researchers engage in such fraudulent practices (e.g., pressure to publish, recognition).

Finally, because of the prevalence of academic dishonesty in college courses—again, some of which likely includes data fabrication on class research projects—you would do well to address with your students some of the reasons why other students choose this avenue of recourse. Although some instructors might simply argue that students fabricate data because of certain dispositional factors (e.g., "They are lazy"), I have not necessarily found this to be true. Instead, when discussing the potential confluence of factors that might lead a student to fabricate data, I believe there is one important factor that often gets overlooked.

During their time in our statistics and research methods courses (and in subsequent courses they take), our students are bombarded with the idea that "significance" is the holy grail of psychological research. We teach them what significance means, we show them how to identify significant differences in their data, we instruct them how to design studies in ways that increase the likelihood that they will obtain significant results ("You need to use more participants"), and we sometimes even mention to them that many psychology journals do not publish studies with nonsignificant findings. Moreover, we frequently have our students read journal articles, the majority of which interpret findings based on what Loftus (1996) called "The Artificial 'Effects/Non-Effects' Dichotomy" (p. 163), which implicitly sends the message that only significant findings are worth discussing. In his paper on the downfalls of null hypothesis significance testing, Loftus (1996) argued that because "people prefer simple, strong decisions . . . investigators, journal editors, reviewers, and scientific consumers often . . . behave as if the .05 cutoff were somehow real rather than arbitrary" (pp. 163–164).

In essence, we are teaching our students not only the distinction between "significant" and "nonsignificant" but also, implicitly, that "significant" equals "good" and "nonsignificant" equals "bad." As a result, our students on occasion, if not more frequently, come to the mistaken conclusion that their definitive goal should be to conduct a study that yields significant results. In fact, quite common in my experience, and possibly in yours, too, are the students who, upon completing their data collection, enthusiastically analyze their data, only to find, quite disappointingly, that their results are not significant (i.e., $p > .05$). Quite often, these "disappointing" revelations are followed by comments such as, "I was really hoping I'd get significant results" or "My study didn't turn out very good." Our students have come to believe that obtaining nonsignificant results will somehow affect their performance in our courses. Thus many feel it is better to fabricate data than risk getting a poorer grade because of a "bad" study.

We need to impress upon our students that significant and nonsignificant do not mean "effects" and "no effects," respectively (see Loftus, 1996), nor are they equivalent with "good" and "bad" research. Rather, our students should know that p values, for example, simply provide information—information that is potentially useful, regardless of the level of significance obtained. Although nonsignificant findings may provide information regarding the overall conduct of a study, our students need to know that nonsignificant findings sometimes simply reflect the true state of nature—and studies that accurately reflect nature are, in fact, good.

Cost–Benefit Analysis and the Ethics of Research

Conducting ethical research in psychology often boils down to an analysis of the costs incurred by participants in a study and the benefits or advances in knowledge that may come from conducting a particular study. For example, because of the extreme emotional distress experienced by some participants in Milgram's (1963) classic study, many researchers today—along with most, if not all, review boards—would conclude that the risks involved in similar studies would likely exceed the potential benefits. Consequently, most researchers—along with most, if not all, review boards— would reject these studies outright on ethical grounds. Similarly, review boards typically reject on comparable grounds any studies that require participants to incur excessive mental, emotional, or physical distress.

Not all ethical dilemmas, however, are this unambiguous. Because ethical decision making often requires more than simply following a short list of clear-cut guidelines, you would do well to expose your students to the idea of cost–benefit analysis and allow them to examine some of the subtle difficulties that psychological researchers sometimes encounter when confronted with an ethical dilemma.

Hands-on Tip

Rosnow (1990) described a relatively simple activity that might help your students "develop an appreciation of the subtleties of research ethics" (p. 179; see also Bragger & Freeman, 1999; Strohmetz & Skleder, 1992). First, following a review of textbook material on ethical considerations, Rosnow asked his students to discuss a case study that posed a potential ethical dilemma (see Rosnow, 1990, for examples). In class, your students could discuss a case in which mentally ill participants, assigned to a control condition in a study of treatment efficacy, did not receive a potentially beneficial treatment. Another possibility would be to have them discuss a case in which control participants received a placebo instead of a much-needed medication. In lieu of case studies, you might wish instead to discuss well-known psychological studies that posed certain ethical dilemmas, for example, Milgram's (1963) obedience study, Rosenthal and Jacobson's (1966) early work on the Pygmalion (or Rosenthal) effect, the Stanford Prison Experiment (Haney et al., 1973), or even Jane Elliott's influential "blue eyes/ brown eyes" study (Peters, 1987), to name but a few.

Rosnow next introduced his students to APA's guidelines for the ethical treatment of research participants and assigned each student the task of identifying a recent journal article that included, in the student's opinion, an unethical manipulation or some other questionable practice. After students reconvened and discussed each article as a group, Rosnow required his students to role-play the part of the author in the articles they had identified, defending their "unethical" practices and addressing questions and criticisms from other members of the class. After completing the role-play portion of the activity, students rated on a 100-point scale the studies' ethical costs and theoretical, or practical, benefits (i.e., utilities). (To see if defending their studies affects students' cost-benefit ratings, you may want to collect ratings both before and after the role-play; see Strohmetz & Skleder, 1992). A quick examination of the students' individual and average responses allowed Rosnow and his class to discuss reasons that there were discrepancies among students' ratings as well as the types of question that researchers often ask themselves when contemplating possible recourse following the introduction of an ethical dilemma. For example, should researchers conduct a study if both the ethical costs and practical benefits are relatively high? What if the costs are low but so are the benefits? Might there be potentially negative consequences if a certain study is *not* carried out?

Although Rosnow's (1990) activity may be easier to carry out in smaller classes (e.g., fewer than 20 students), you might still find it useful in larger classes if you conduct the activity in small groups or in separate lab sections. Regardless, the questions that will likely arise as a result of this activity will not only give your students some sense of the issues that IRBs must consider when reviewing research proposals, but also the opportunity to grapple with the ambiguities that often arise when considering ethical issues in psychological research.

Conclusion

As instructors of research methods, we are largely responsible for teaching our students about the particulars of conducting scientifically sound research; we are also largely responsible for teaching them about the ethical standards and guidelines that guide psychologists' research practices. However, whereas teaching our students what research methods will allow them to state with certainty that there was a meaningful relation between their variables or that their independent variables affected their dependent variables, teaching them the best course of action to take when confronted with a particular ethical dilemma is not quite so clear-cut. In short, ethics is a tricky business. What might qualify as a good ethical decision in some cases might not be the best ethical decision in others. It is our job, therefore, to arm our students with knowledge regarding what steps they can take to maximize the ethical treatment of their research participants; it is also our job to provide them with critical thinking skills, so they can resolve in an ethical manner any ethical dilemmas they might encounter in the future and so they can feel good about their decisions, knowing full well they behaved in accordance with extant ethical standards.

References

American Psychological Association. (1971). *Principles for the care and use of animals*. Washington, DC: Author.

American Psychological Association. (1973). *Ethical principles in the conduct of research with human subjects*. Washington, DC: Author.

American Psychological Association. (2002). Ethical principles of psychologists and code of conduct. *American Psychologist, 57*, 1060–1073.

Bechtel, H. K., Jr., & Pearson, W., Jr. (1985). Deviant scientists and scientific deviance. *Deviant Behavior, 6,* 237–252.

Beins, B. C. (1993). Using the Barnum Effect to teach about ethics and deception in research. *Teaching of Psychology, 20,* 33–35.

Bragger, J. D., & Freeman, M. A. (1999). Using a cost-benefit analysis to teach ethics and statistics. *Teaching of Psychology, 26,* 34–36.

Charney, D. S. (2000). The use of placebos in randomized clinical trials of mood disorders: Well justified, but improvements in design are indicated. *Biological Psychiatry, 47,* 687–688.

Darwin, C. (1859). *On the origin of species by means of natural selection.* London: Murray.

Davis, S. F., Grover, C. A., Becker, A. H., & McGregor, L. N. (1992). Academic dishonesty: Prevalence, determinants, techniques, and punishments. *Teaching of Psychology, 19,* 16–20.

Demo, D. H., & Parker, K. D. (2001). Academic achievement and self-esteem among Black and White college students. *The Journal of Social Psychology, 127,* 345–355.

Epling, W. (1989). Rats. *The Behavior Analyst, 12,* 251–253.

Fernald, P. S., & Fernald, L. D. (1990). Ethical principles and dilemmas in the practice of psychology. In V. P. Makosky, C. C. Sileo, L. G. Whittemore, C. P. Landry, & M. L. Skutley (Eds.), *Activities handbook for the teaching of psychology, Vol. 3* (pp. 271–274). Washington, DC: American Psychological Association.

Fisher, C. B., & Kuther, T. (1997). Integrating research ethics into the introductory psychology course curriculum. *Teaching of Psychology, 24,* 172–175.

Fitterling, J. M., Martin, J. E., Gramling, S., Cole, P., & Milan, M. A. (1988). Behavioral management of exercise training in vascular headache patients: An investigation of exercise adherence and headache activity. *Journal of Applied Behavior Analysis, 21,* 9–19.

Froese, A. D., Boswell, K. L., Garcia, E. D., Koehn, L. J., & Nelson, J. M. (1995). Citing secondary sources: Can we correct what students do not know? *Teaching of Psychology, 22,* 235–238.

Gluck, J. P., & Bell, J. (2003). Ethical issues in the use of animals in biomedical and psychopharmacological research. *Psychopharmacology, 171,* 6–12.

Goodwin, C. J. (2005). *A history of modern psychology* (2nd ed.). Hoboken, NJ: Wiley.

Griffore, R., Kallen, D., Popovich, S., & Powell, V. (1990). Gender differences in correlates of college students' self-esteem. *College Student Journal, 24,* 287–291.

Grzegorek, J. L., Slaney, R. B., Franze, S., & Rice, K. G. (2004). Self-criticism, dependency, self-esteem, and grade point average satisfaction among clusters of perfectionists and nonperfectionists. *Journal of Counseling Psychology*, 51, 192–200.

Hale, J. L. (1987). Plagiarism in classroom settings. *Communication Research Reports*, 4, 66–70.

Haney, C., Banks, C., & Zimbardo, P. (1973). Interpersonal dynamics in a simulated prison. *International Journal of Criminology and Penology*, 1, 69–97.

Hearnshaw, L. S. (1979). *Cyril Burt: Psychologist*. London: Hodder & Stoughton.

Herzog, H. (1988). The moral status of mice. *American Psychologist*, 43, 473–474.

Hobbs, N. (1948). The development of a code of ethical standards for psychology. *American Psychologist*, 3, 80–84.

Jensen, A. R. (1974). Kinship correlations reported by Sir Cyril Burt. *Behavior Genetics*, 4, 1–28.

Joynson, R. B. (2003). Selective interest and psychological practice: A new interpretation of the Burt affair. *British Journal of Psychology*, 94, 409–426.

Kamin, L. (1974). *The science and politics of IQ*. New York: Wiley.

Kantowitz, B. H., Roediger, H. L., III, & Elmes, D. G. (1997). *Experimental psychology: Understanding psychological research* (6th ed.). St. Paul, MN: West.

Korn, J. H. (1984). Coverage of research ethics in introductory and social psychology textbooks. *Teaching of Psychology*, 11, 146–149.

Landau, J. D., Druen, P. B., & Arcuri, J. A. (2002). Methods for helping students avoid plagiarism. *Teaching of Psychology*, 29, 112–115.

Leak, G. K. (1981). Student perception of coercion and value from participation in psychological research. *Teaching of Psychology*, 8, 146–149.

Loftus, G. R. (1996). Psychology will be a much better science when we change the way we analyze data. *Current Directions in Psychological Science*, 5, 161–171.

Mackintosh, N. J. (Ed.). (1995). *Cyril Burt: Fraud or framed?* Oxford: Oxford University Press.

McCabe, D. L., & Trevino, L. K. (1993). Academic dishonesty: Honor codes and other contextual influences. *Journal of Higher Education*, 64, 522–538.

McGlynn, F. D., Karg, R. S., & Lawyer, S. R. (2003). Fear responses to mock magnetic resonance imaging among college students: Toward a prototype experiment. *Journal of Anxiety Disorders*, 16, 165–173.

McMinn, M. R. (1988). Ethics case-study simulation: A generic tool for psychology teachers. *Teaching of Psychology*, 15, 100–101.

Milgram, S. (1963). Behavioral study of obedience. *Journal of Abnormal and Social Psychology*, 67, 371–378.

Miller, F. G. (2000). Placebo-controlled trials in psychiatric research: An ethical perspective. *Biological Psychiatry, 47,* 707–716.

Miller, N. E. (1985). The value of behavioral research on animals. *American Psychologist, 40,* 423–440.

Miller, R. L. (2003). Ethical issues in psychological research with human participants. In S. F. Davis (Ed.), *Handbook of research methods in experimental psychology* (pp. 127–150). Malden, MA: Blackwell.

Mitchell, M. L., & Jolley, J. M. (2004). *Research design explained.* Belmont, CA: Thomson Wadsworth.

Peters, W. (1987). *A class divided: Then and now.* New Haven, CT: Yale University Press.

Regan, T. (1997). The rights of humans and other animals. *Ethics & Behavior, 7,* 103–111.

Roig, M. (1997). Can undergraduate students determine whether text has been plagiarized? *The Psychological Record, 47,* 113–122.

Rosenthal, R., & Jacobson, L. (1966). Teachers' expectancies: Determinants of pupils' IQ gains. *Psychological Reports, 19,* 115–118.

Rosnow, R. L. (1990). Teaching research ethics through role-play and discussion. *Teaching of Psychology, 17,* 179–181.

Rowan, A. N. (1997). The benefits and ethics of animal research. *Scientific American, 276*(2), 79.

Singer, P. (1975). *Animal liberation.* New York: Avon Books.

Smith, R. A., & Davis, S. F. (2007). *The psychologist as detective: An introduction to conducting research in psychology* (4th ed.). Upper Saddle River, NJ: Prentice Hall.

Strohmetz, D. B., & Skleder, A. A. (1992). The use of role-play in teaching research ethics: A validation study. *Teaching of Psychology, 19,* 106–108.

Tucker, W. H. (1997). Re-considering Burt: Beyond a reasonable doubt. *Journal of the History of the Behavioral Sciences, 33,* 145–162.

Chapter 5

Teaching Reliability and Validity

Imagine a researcher is interested in studying the effects of exercise on health in adults (e.g., Fitterling, Martin, Gramling, Cole, & Milan, 1988; Sherman, Cherkin, Erro, Miglioretti, & Deyo, 2005). To determine with some degree of certainty whether exercise affects health, our researcher could, for example, (a) require some participants to exercise for 8 weeks (whereas other participants would not exercise during that same time period); (b) attempt to control the differential effects of other nonmanipulated (i.e., extraneous) variables, such as weekly alcohol consumption, that could potentially affect adults' health; and (c) measure the health of each participant after 8 weeks to see if there is an average difference in health between the groups. Although this experiment might seem relatively straightforward, it becomes trickier when one starts to ask certain questions:

1. There are many different types of exercise—e.g., walking, swimming, rollerblading, weight lifting. What do you mean by *exercise*?
2. *Health* could mean many different things as well. How are you going to measure health?
3. And what exactly do you mean by *alcohol consumption*? Does that mean drinking a glass of wine each night, or does it mean binge drinking several times a week?

Clearly, before our researcher can conduct the experiment, she or he needs to explain how each of these variables is going to be defined and measured. Furthermore, our researcher needs to be sure that the way these variables are defined and measured is going to provide relatively accurate information regarding the relation between exercise and health.

These ideas are at the heart of two of the most important concepts in all of science, as well as two of the most difficult concepts to teach effectively: reliability and validity. In fact, no discussion of research methods would be complete without extensive discussion of these two highly important topics. Therefore, this chapter will briefly describe each of these topics and then discuss ways to teach them most effectively; it will also discuss several simple but effective activities you may wish to include when teaching your students about reliability and validity.

Operational Definitions and Measurement

Before introducing the concepts of reliability and validity, it might be useful first to discuss two related topics: *operational definitions* and *measurement*. Specifically, you should inform your students that the reliability and validity of any study depend greatly on how researchers define their variables of interest. For example, without knowing that other researchers previously defined self-esteem as "the number of positive self-statements a person makes each day," it may be difficult to compare findings across studies. Moreover, because precise definitions help to inform researchers of how they are going to measure the phenomena they wish to study, operational definitions become vital to obtaining reliable and valid data.

Operational Definitions

Open nearly any psychology textbook, and you will likely find discussion of one, or several, of the following oft-studied, but hard to define, topics: *learning*, *memory*, *motivation*, *personality*, *depression*, and *consciousness*. Although our everyday conversations about such topics do not require us to provide definitions of them, your students should know that psychological researchers do not have the luxury of such imprecision. Rather, for researchers to study and discuss these somewhat abstract concepts more efficiently, they must define them in such a way that communication with other researchers is less cumbersome.

S. S. Stevens, taking his cue from the Nobel-prize winning Harvard University physicist Percy Bridgeman, suggested in 1935 that psychologists should define their variables in terms of the operations needed to produce them. Such definitions are *operational definitions*. For example, although it is possible in everyday discourse for students to talk about self-esteem as "how good they feel about themselves" and love as "a feeling of deep affection for someone," these definitions likely do not provide the accuracy needed by researchers wishing to study these topics more systematically. Instead, psychological researchers take steps to spell out their variables in such a way that others interested in studying the same topics could easily replicate earlier studies. Thus a researcher might define "self-esteem" as "the score a person obtains by filling out the Rosenberg Self-Esteem Scale" (e.g., Rosenberg, 1965), "happiness" as "the [self-reported] mean frequency of positive-mood adjectives minus the [self-reported] mean frequency of negative-mood adjectives across an individual's [daily] reports" (Diener & Seligman, 2002, p. 81), and "reinforcement" as "3-sec access to 0.1 cc sweetened multi-vitamin supplemented with condensed milk" (Brown, 1963, p. 395). Such operational definitions make variables more concrete and allow researchers to communicate more clearly about them. Finally, as the preceding definitions suggest, operational definitions can be of two varieties: experimental and measured (Kerlinger & Lee, 2000). Whereas experimental definitions describe the ways a researcher will *manipulate* different independent variables within a study (e.g., the preceding definition of "reinforcement"), measured definitions describe the way a researcher will *measure* the dependent variables of interest (e.g., the preceding definition of "happiness").

When first discussing operational definitions with your students, do not be surprised if they have trouble providing good operational definitions. They may not understand initially what it means to say that variables "should be defined in terms of the operations needed to produce them." For example, I often ask my students to operationally define "love" and receive responses such as the following: "how much you care for someone" and "your feelings toward someone." One useful way to circumvent this problem is by explaining to your students that operational definitions typically require researchers to state in *behavioral* (and sometimes *physiological*) terms what exactly the researchers or participants need to *do* for the researchers to know they have observed the phenomenon of interest. For example, when discussing operational definitions of love, I might ask students the following question: How exactly would two people need to *behave* toward each other for you to say they love one another? This question usually prompts responses such as, "They would need to hold hands" and "They would need to say 'I love you' to one another." A useful operational definition of love, then, might be, "the number of times a couple holds hands each week." I then tell them that these are the beginnings of operational definitions—definitions that are objective, easily measured, and behavioral (or physiological) in nature.

Vandervert (1988) provided a useful analogy in suggesting that psychological constructs, such as memory, depression, and intelligence, are related to operational definitions in the same way that "cake" is related to "recipe." Just as easy-to-follow recipes allow other people to know how different cooks made their cakes, clear operational definitions allow others to know exactly how researchers measured the variables in their studies. Vandervert's analogy also helps to inform students that operational definitions are not "set in stone." Rather, just as adding ingredients to a recipe may ultimately result in a better cake, researchers may ultimately find better ways to define and measure the constructs in which they are interested.

Considerable evidence suggests that students often need much practice to acquire new skills and then transfer those skills to new settings (e.g., Halpern & Hakel, 2003). Learning how to operationally define concepts is no exception, and you should give your students as much practice as possible after introducing this topic.

Hands-on Tip

Herringer (2000) described an activity that might help your students better understand operational definitions (see also Vandervert, 1988). Herringer asked his students to develop research hypotheses regarding personality differences between Captain James T. Kirk from the original *Star Trek* television series and Captain Jean-Luc Picard from *Star Trek: The Next Generation*. First, the students watched one episode each of *Star Trek* and *Star Trek: The Next Generation*. Next, teams of students each identified a personality trait (e.g., extraversion) on which they believed the two captains differed. After constructing a research hypothesis about the perceived personality differences (e.g., We hypothesize that Captain Kirk will be more extraverted than Captain Picard, as measured by the number of times each speaks during an episode), teams of students "operationally defined their traits in terms of concrete, observable, and behavioral indicators (e.g., number of words spoken or number of people spoken to)" and "discussed the importance of indicators that were reliable, objective, and sensitive to variance" (Herringer, 2000, p. 51). After operationally defining their constructs, team members independently watched one episode of each show, recorded the number of behavioral indicators for each captain, and then compared their observations. Herringer reported that most of his students were unable to confirm their hypotheses of personality differences between Kirk and Picard. He also reported that most students viewed the activity as helpful in teaching the idea of operational definitions. Finally, although Herringer chose to use fictional *Star Trek* characters in his study, you could obviously use a variety of other television shows and a variety of characters in this exercise.

Measurement

Once your students have a good understanding of operational definitions, it is then useful to discuss with them the relation between operational definitions and measurement. Specifically, the way researchers define their variables affects how they ultimately measure those variables. For example, imagine that a researcher was measuring *social anxiety*. He or she might define social anxiety in a number of ways: (a) as the self-reported presence or absence of anxiety (i.e., participants verbally report whether or not they were anxious); (b) as participants' responses on a Likert-type scale (e.g., participants indicate whether they experienced "no," "some," or "a lot" of anxiety); or (c) as the increase in heart rate participants experienced when they engaged in some anxiety-provoking activity. Each of these definitions would require the researcher to measure social anxiety in quite different ways, and knowing how that researcher measured social anxiety would be useful to other researchers studying the same phenomenon. As your students will see shortly, measurement—and hence operational definitions—is vitally important to the reliability and validity of a study.

An important first step in teaching the idea of measurement involves telling students exactly what measurement is. In its most elementary form, measurement refers to the process of assigning arbitrary symbols, according to a predetermined set of rules, to different events or objects (Kerlinger & Lee, 2000). Although researchers can feasibly use any symbols in this process of assignment, they typically use numbers. This is because numbers allow researchers to assign quantitative meaning to different types of events (e.g., "Mary ate *one* cupcake, and Johnny ate *two* cupcakes" vs. "Mary ate @ cupcake, and Johnny ate * cupcakes"). Once researchers have decided on which symbols, or numbers, to assign to a set of events, they then must determine which set of rules to follow when assigning these symbols. For example, when attempting to determine what kinds of furniture are in a room, a researcher might assign numbers according to the following rule: "If an object is a desk, assign 1; if an object is a chair, assign 2; and if an object is a sofa, assign 3." Similarly, if one is observing a race and wants to determine who ran the fastest, one might use the following rule: "Whoever crosses the finish line first, assign 1; whoever crosses the finish line next, assign 2; whoever crosses the finish line next, assign 3, and so on." When discussing these rules of assignment, it is also important to inform your students that the measurement of any set of events requires the set to contain at least two, and often more (see below), different types of event. In other words, at the very least, a researcher must be able to separate the objects or events into "something" and "not something." For example, when assigning numbers to personality characteristics, researchers must be able at the very least to separate people into *extroverted* and *not extroverted* (i.e., *introverted*), or *neurotic* and *not neurotic* (i.e., emotionally stable). It might also be helpful at this point to revisit with your students the concept of a variable (see Chapter 6). By definition, a variable contains at least two different categories of objects or events, which allows researchers to measure changes in that variable.

Once students understand the general idea of measurement, you can then introduce a slightly more circumscribed topic: *scales of measurement*. After discussing the concept of measurement and its importance with regard to research methods, you may want to inform your students that psychologists have historically used a special set of rules to assign numbers to different observations (Stevens, 1946). This special set of rules resulted in four distinct ways of assigning symbols, or numbers, to different types of observations, and these distinct methods of assignment define the four different scales of measurement we typically discuss with our students: nominal, ordinal, interval, and ratio.

Although most research methods textbooks spend at least some time discussing the different scales of measurement, it has been my experience that students still struggle when it comes to identifying them. When teaching students the different scales of measurement, I have found it most effective simply to present the scales in the common order in which they are typically presented in most research methods textbooks (i.e., nominal, ordinal, etc.) and then give students mountains of practice identifying them. The strongest argument for introducing the scales this way comes from the fact that scales of measurement build on one another: Along with a new property, each scale contains the properties of the preceding scales. In other words, ordinal scales contain the properties of nominal scales, interval scales contain the properties of both ordinal and nominal scales, and so on. Moreover, along with each new property comes an increase in the amount of information that each scale conveys (Kantowitz, Roediger, & Elmes, 1997). Thus introducing scales in this fashion allows instructors to capitalize on students' existing knowledge, a factor that tends to improve learning and retention (e.g., Bain, 2004; Halpern & Hakel, 2003).

It may also be worth mentioning to your students, however, that there is still disagreement regarding the different scales of measurement, the relation between scales of measurement and statistical analysis (see below), and whether scales of measurement are even useful when conducting research (see, e.g., Lord, 1953; Velleman & Wilkinson, 1993). For example, some researchers have suggested that Likert-type scales are inherently ordinal in nature, because one never knows the exact distance between adjacent events represented by the scale (e.g., how much more than "agree" is "strongly agree"?). Conversely, others have argued that as long as Likert-type scales contain enough response options (e.g., at least seven points), they take on many of the properties of intervals scales of measurement and should be treated as such. Nevertheless, it is probably a good idea to inform students of the continued debate among researchers regarding scales of measurement but insist they learn the difference between the scales anyway.

Finally, your students should know that the way researchers measure their variables is important for one additional reason: It helps determine which statistical procedures they will use to analyze their data. At this point, it might be helpful to give students some examples of how two studies, each examining the same psychological phenomenon, would require different statistical analyses depending on how the researchers defined their variables. You might also wish to inform your students that interval and ratio scales of measurement require the same statistical analyses (e.g., *t* test or one-way ANOVA). This tends to alleviate some of the frustration that students experience when attempting to differentiate between these two scales.

Once you have spent some time discussing operational definitions and measurement, you can now turn your attention to the central topics of this chapter: reliability and validity.

Reliability

In the context of research methods, reliability refers to the extent to which a certain set of findings is reproducible. However, in truth, researchers discuss the concept of reliability in at least two different ways. The first definition of reliability refers to the most common conception of reliability: the extent to which the study of some phenomenon yields approximately the same results across repeated trials. In essence, this notion of reliability refers to re-plicability or reproducibility (i.e., are researchers able to replicate the findings from a study?). Again I find it useful to start discussion of this topic with an example that seems fairly obvious: If an instructor measures the average size of his or her students' feet today and again in 2 weeks, will the results be approximately the same? Most often, students quickly answer in the affirmative and begin to see what researchers mean when they speak of reliability. You might then wish to discuss examples of psychological research that have proven reliable, as well as studies for which the outcomes have been less reliable.

For example, I often discuss Milgram's (1963) classic study on obedience to authority and how he was able to replicate these early results under many different conditions (Milgram, 1974). I also discuss studies on the so-called "Mozart Effect," which suggested that playing the music of Wolfgang Amadeus Mozart shortly before an IQ test temporarily enhanced spatial reasoning skills (Rauscher, Shaw, & Ky, 1993, 1995). Subsequent studies, however, failed to reproduce this effect (i.e., they were not reliable; see Steele, Bass, & Crook, 1999).

The second, more precise, way to discuss reliability—one that is related to our first definition and one that students sometimes have more difficulty understanding—concerns the notion of *measurement error*. Specifically, in this case, "reliability can be defined as the relative absence of errors of measurement" (Kerlinger & Lee, 2000, p. 643). Whereas our first definition of reliability referred generally to reproducibility of data, this definition refers more specifically to errors in the way researchers measure their variables.

Measurement error can be of two forms, systematic or random (Kerlinger & Lee, 2000; Mitchell & Jolley, 2004), both of which you should spend some time explaining to your students. Systematic measurement errors are known more colloquially as *bias*. For example, if a researcher believes that one group of children will perform better on a test than another group, this belief may systematically affect the way the researcher measures the children's behavior, thus influencing his or her results (e.g., Rosenthal & Jacobson, 1966). These types of bias function as extraneous variables. Consequently, researchers should take steps to remove these variables from a study, if at all possible.

In contrast, measurement error can also vary randomly. When errors vary randomly, they *should* be distributed in such a way that they do not contribute to systematic differences between groups. If these random errors are relatively small or nonexistent, a measuring instrument will be reliable; in contrast, if these errors are large, a measuring instrument will be less reliable, which may increase within-groups variance and blur our ability to identify significant differences between groups. Finally, students should know that random errors in measurement (our second definition of reliability) may affect the reliability of data across studies (our first definition of reliability). In other words, measurement error may affect the reproducibility of outcomes across studies.

Hands-on Tip

Camac and Camac (1993) described a useful activity to teach students about reliability. Students first learned about the construct "sensation seeking" and that it consists of four dimensions: (a) thrill and adventure seeking, which refers to an interest in risky physical activities; (b) experience seeking, which entails an interest in novel sensual or intellectual experiences; (c) disinhibition, which consists of tendencies toward activities such as getting high, drinking, and enjoying varied sexual experiences; and (d) boredom susceptibility, which is the degree to which people are bothered by sameness (Camac & Camac, 1993, p. 102).

Next, each student constructed two items that attempted to measure one of these dimensions. The following week, the class reviewed each item, provided feedback to one another, and decided which items to include on their Activities and Preferences Scale (APS). After agreeing on 47 different items, each student administered the APS to two respondents who were not members of the class. One week later, the same respondents completed the APS once again, along with several additional questionnaires. Finally, students compared respondents' answers on both administrations of the APS and examined the extent to which the responses were reliable. Camac and Camac reported that the APS was reliable and that students found the activity to be enjoyable.

At this point, your students should have a relatively good understanding of what researchers generally mean when they speak of "reliability." Next, you should spend some time discussing the different ways that researchers assess reliability.

Types of Reliability

Reliability, as mentioned earlier, refers to reproducibility of data, and is inversely related to measurement error (i.e., high reliability usually accompanies low measurement error and vice versa). Below I discuss some of the different types of reliability and how they attempt to minimize measurement error. I also describe some activities you might wish to use when discussing these concepts with your students.

Test–retest Reliability

To begin a discussion of different types of reliability, it is often sufficient to ask students how they might assess whether a certain measure produces consistent results across time (i.e., it is reproducible). Most often, I have found that students quickly identify what is quite possibly the easiest way to assess the absence of random measurement error: test–retest reliability. Researchers usually measure test–retest reliability by giving subjects a psychological test at two different points in time and measuring the correspondence between the scores (typically by obtaining a correlation coefficient). Assuming stability in other conditions that could affect test scores, if scores result in a large coefficient, there is high test–retest reliability (i.e., differences in scores are not due to random measurement error); if scores produce a small coefficient, there is low test–retest reliability (i.e., differences in scores are likely due to random measurement error). Moreover, although measures of test–retest reliability refer to the *total* amount of variability that is due to measurement error, they do not inform you of the different sources of that error (see below).

Hands-on Tip

A simple way to teach students about test–retest reliability would be to have them either take, or administer, a psychological inventory twice during the semester and calculate the correlation between resulting scores (e.g., Camac & Camac, 1993).

After discussing test–retest reliability with your students, it is useful to discuss what factors might produce random measurement error and, consequently, contribute to overall test–retest reliability—or lack thereof. In general, random measurement error can come from two different sources: observers and participants.

Sources of measurement error: observers. One of the most common sources of measurement error is simple error on the part of human observers who are measuring the behavior of interest, and one way to assess this source of measurement error is by calculating *interobserver reliability.* Interobserver reliability refers to a method in which two individuals observe some event independently of one another and then measure the extent to which they agree the event did or did not occur. For example, imagine that a researcher wanted to know if two different teaching methods produced significantly different exam scores. In one such study, Saville, Zinn, Neef, Van Norman, and Ferreri (2006) exposed students either to traditional lectures or to a new method of classroom instruction called interteaching (see Chapter 10). After each unit of information, students from both conditions took the same exams. To obtain a measure of interobserver reliability, two teaching assistants each graded several of the exams independently of one another. Saville et al. observed a high level of agreement between the assistants in the way they graded the exams. In other words, they found a high level of interobserver reliability in their study.

In general, I have found that students have little trouble understanding the rationale for collecting interobserver reliability data. They see relatively quickly that using two independent observers and measuring the extent to which those observers agree that some event did or did not happen increases researchers' confidence in their measuring instrument and that their data are "believable" (Johnston & Pennypacker, 1993). What students often do not understand—or at least do not realize at first—is how difficult it can be to obtain high interobserver reliability, especially in psychology studies where the variables of interest are sometimes hard to define. One way to combat this problem is by introducing simple classroom activities that give students the opportunity to collect their own interobserver reliability data. I describe two of these activities later in this chapter.

There is one other issue, however, that complicates matters somewhat when teaching about interobserver reliability. An informal sampling of several research methods textbooks suggests that different authors often conflate the terms interobserver reliability and *interobserver agreement*. Although some textbooks suggest, or at least imply, that these two concepts refer to the same process of calculating observer agreement, other textbooks clearly differentiate between the two, suggesting they are related but different concepts.

Although interobserver reliability and interobserver agreement both produce indices of agreement between two independent observers, they do so in slightly different ways. Technically, interobserver reliability is "an index of the degree to which different raters give the same behavior similar ratings" (Mitchell & Jolley, 2004, p. 555). This method typically involves calculating a correlation coefficient between observers' ratings and then squaring the resulting value. For example, imagine that two teaching assistants independently graded ten 100-point exams and produced the following grades:

	Assistant 1	Assistant 2
Exam 1	97	97
Exam 2	77	80
Exam 3	84	84
Exam 4	62	69
Exam 5	88	90
Exam 6	84	88
Exam 7	100	100
Exam 8	74	76
Exam 9	79	81
Exam 10	72	75

Calculating a Pearson correlation coefficient would produce $r = .99$ and an interobserver reliability coefficient (r^2) of approximately .98. As with regular correlation coefficients, higher values mean higher levels of interobserver agreement.

Whereas interobserver reliability produces a correlation coefficient, interobserver agreement simply refers to "the *percentage* of times the raters agree" (Mitchell & Jolley, 2004, p. 99, my italics). Although there are several different ways to calculate interobserver agreement (see Cooper, Heron, & Heward, 1987), the following formula is most common: the number of agreements divided by the number of agreements *and* the number of disagreements (i.e., the total number of opportunities to agree) multiplied by 100.

$$\frac{\text{agreements}}{\text{agreements} + \text{disagreements}} \times 100\% = \% \text{ of agreement}$$

To illustrate, imagine that two researchers were observing college students to see if they dressed nicely when going to their classes. The researchers might sit outside a classroom, observe every student who enters the classroom, and, based on their operational definition of "well-dressed," mark down the number of students who met those criteria. During the course of the day, imagine that our researchers rated 100 college students and agreed on 75 of their observations. Their level of interobserver agreement would be

$$\frac{75}{75 + 25} \times 100\% = 75\% \text{ agreement}$$

At present, there are no formal rules for deciding what constitutes an acceptable level of agreement. However, convention seems to suggest that observers should agree a minimum of 80% to 85% of the time. It is worth telling your students, however, that this number may be more or less acceptable depending on the purpose of the study and complexity of the phenomenon being observed (Cooper et al., 1987).

Hands-on Tip

Although it is relatively easy to think of activities that would allow students to measure interobserver reliability or interobserver agreement, one published activity seems especially effective at teaching these ideas (see also Becker, 1999). In this activity, described by Carr, Taylor, and Austin (1995), students form groups of three and measure the number of times each student blinks his or her eyes during a 2-minute interval. Specifically, two students take turns independently counting the number of times the third student blinks. After each student has served as "counter" and "blinker," students then calculate interobserver agreement by "dividing the smaller number by the larger number and multiplying by 100% . . . For example, if two students [record] the third student's eye-blinks as 40 and 50, the interobserver agreement [will] be 80% [(40 ÷ 50)100%]" (p. 143). Carr et al. reported that their students found the activity to be very helpful for learning about interobserver agreement. In addition, because several groups did not obtain agreement measures that met or exceeded the 80% minimum that is standard in experimental psychology, students were able to discuss why they did not obtain high levels of agreement (e.g., poor operational definitions of "eye-blink," observer drift, reactivity).

If you are interested in incorporating this activity into your classes, you could easily modify it to teach students the subtle difference between interobserver reliability and interobserver agreement. For example, you could ask your students to note the number of times their partners blinked during 10 successive 30-second intervals. They could then calculate the reliability coefficient to determine the extent to which they agreed.

Finally, it is important for your students to know that all measures of reliability are prone to certain problems. For example, when calculating interobserver reliability, it is possible to obtain a relatively high reliability coefficient when, in fact, the observers did not agree on many of their observations. In the example given earlier, our fictional teaching assistants only agreed on 3 of the 10 exams they scored. Yet because there was a systematic relation between the scores, we obtained a high reliability coefficient. In addition, you probably noticed that Assistant 1 consistently produced lower scores than Assistant 2 (i.e., either Assistant 1 or Assistant 2 was biased in his or her grading). Although closer examination of the data would reveal this bias, simply reporting the reliability coefficient would not necessarily yield this information.

Similarly, when calculating interobserver agreement, it is possible for two observers to obtain a high percentage of agreement when, in fact, they actually observed different events. Imagine that two researchers, Sigmund and Burrhus, are observing whether students on a college campus are well-dressed. Prior to initiating their observations, our researchers have agreed to assess the first 20 students who pass by.

Now imagine that, for some reason, Sigmund missed the first student who walked by, whereas Burrhus did not, and thus made his observations for a slightly different set of 20 students (i.e., Sigmund and Burrhus did not observe the same first and last person). Sigmund and Burrhus could still obtain a high level of interobserver agreement, especially if a majority of students were either well-dressed or poorly dressed, even though their agreement score was based on slightly different observations. In addition, the number of observations a pair of researchers makes can affect the level of interobserver agreement. If two observers make only four observations but disagree on one of them, their score will be 75%, which is below conventional standards. Conversely, if two observers make 10 observations and disagree on 1 of them, their agreement score will be 90%, an acceptable level of agreement. Thus the level of agreement may in part be a function of how many observations two researchers have available to them. Requiring extensive training of observers should help to obviate these problems to some extent (Cooper et al., 1987).

Sources of measurement error: participants. Although low measures of interobserver reliability (or agreement) between trained observers likely implies low test–retest reliability, the converse is not necessarily true: High levels of interobserver reliability do not necessarily imply high test–retest reliability. Specifically, it is possible that researchers might obtain a high level of agreement in their observations but still find that overall test–retest reliability is relatively low. This finding suggests that some other source of measurement error is reducing overall test–retest reliability. At this point, it is useful to discuss with students another possible source of measurement error: participants.

Imagine that you have developed an aggression inventory on which participants answer 50 questions regarding their aggressive tendencies (e.g., "How often do you strike inanimate objects when you are angry?"). To assess its test–retest reliability, you asked participants to complete the inventory again, 2 months later. In order to identify possible sources of measurement error, you also asked two of your research assistants to obtain a reliability coefficient, from which they ascertained a high level of agreement. Nevertheless, you still observed that the overall level of test–retest reliability was fairly low. Most likely, minor (or even major) changes in the way your participants behaved during the second administration of the inventory— for example, they were tired, hungry, or recently experienced a string of good luck, all of which may have affected aggression—possibly contributed to low test–retest reliability.

Your students might once again understand relatively quickly that high interobserver reliability (or agreement) may not be a sign of high test–retest reliability. Nevertheless, a follow-up question might result in a bit more perplexity: How might researchers go about assessing if their participants are to "blame" for errors in measurement? More often than not, students suggest a way of examining changes in the participants (e.g., "Ask if they are more tired than they were the first time they took the test"). Paradoxically, however, researchers typically examine the extent to which participants are contributing to measurement error in their studies by examining their measurement instruments.

Once your students have recovered from the utter shock—or mild surprise, at least—of hearing that researchers control their participants' contributions to measurement error by examining a study's measurement instruments, you will want to inform them just how researchers accomplish this goal. Psychological researchers typically modify their measurement instruments, and consequently random measurement error on the part of their participants, by employing one (or both) of the following methods. The first method entails increasing the number of times that participants must respond. For example, if participants are filling out a questionnaire, researchers might simply increase the number of questions. Or if participants are completing a memory task in which they attempt to recall words from a previously presented list (e.g., Roediger & McDermott, 1995), researchers might simply increase the number of trials. This practice, in effect, should function the same way random assignment does when placing subjects in different treatment conditions: With enough test items or trials, any random variations in responding should eventually balance out.

Hands-on Tip

To illustrate this point, it might even be useful to construct a short multiple-choice quiz (e.g., 25 questions), for which your students likely do not know the answers and thus have to guess. After each question, you can simply ask how many students have answered all of the questions correctly so far. As the number of questions increases, you will likely see a decrease in the number of students who answer in the affirmative, which will allow them to see how increasing the number of test questions reduces overall participant variability as a source of measurement error.

A second method that researchers often use to reduce participant variability requires them to examine more closely the items they have decided to include on a test or questionnaire. More specifically, researchers attempt to reduce participants' contribution to measurement error by improving the *internal consistency* of a test or inventory, which is a measure of the relation *between* test items (Mitchell & Jolley, 2004). Instead of simply increasing the number of questions on a test or inventory, in hopes that random measurement error will "average out," researchers focusing on internal consistency make a concerted effort to create homogeneous questions. For example, if each question on the Rosenberg Self-Esteem Scale (RSES) truly "taps into" self-esteem, then there should be little change in the way participants complete the scale across administrations, and there should be a strong relation between items on the scale. Most often, researchers measure internal consistency either by calculating split-half reliability (e.g., finding the correlation between answers on odd and even items) or by calculating a coefficient alpha, such as Cronbach's alpha (Cronbach, 1951).

Hands-on Tip

A relatively easy way to teach your students about measurement error that results from changes in the way participants respond is by having them administer some already established test or inventory, such as the 10-item RSES. When your students have finished, ask them to calculate internal consistency using either the split-half method or by calculating Cronbach's alpha. If you have the time, however, it might be a good idea to have them administer their own assessment instrument along with an already established one, such as the RSES. This way, they would be able to compare the internal consistency of the RSES, for example, which has well-established reliability, with their own assessment, which may not have a similar level of internal consistency (see Camac & Camac, 1993).

Validity

As you know, in its most general form, validity refers to the extent to which a knowledge claim about some phenomenon is truthful or accurate. As you also know, measures of validity typically attempt to answer the following general question: Are we studying what we think we're studying?

Hands-on Tip

To explain this idea more effectively, I have found it useful to start out with an example that is ridiculously obvious. To accomplish this, I often ask my students the following question: If a researcher were attempting to study "intelligence" in college students, would the size of the participants' feet be an appropriate measure of their intellects? More often than not, students respond in the negative, asking what foot size has to do with intelligence. I then follow up by asking them to tell me how our researcher might more accurately measure intelligence in college students. Often, students mention college grade point averages, scores on a particular exam, scores on an IQ test, and the like. Similarly, I might ask my students if running speed would provide a researcher with a valid measure of depression in elderly adults (e.g., the slower the runner, the more depressed the person is). Again, students often mention other measures of depression, such as self-reported data on the number of times that elderly adults cried during a 2-week period or a person's scores on the Beck Depression Inventory (BDI). Exposing students to examples that contain such obvious shortcomings seems to improve students' initial comprehension of these ideas and increases the likelihood they will understand more difficult examples that follow (e.g., Chew, 2005).

Although the answers to the preceding questions might seem obvious to your students, you may also wish to let them know that such answers are not always so forthcoming and that such questions still occupy the time of many psychologists. For example, researchers have spent much time and effort attempting to validate certain personality assessments. As a result, psychologists have questioned whether certain personality tests such as the Myers–Briggs Type Indicator (MBTI), Thematic Apperception Test (TAT), and Rorschach Inkblot Test allow psychologists to "tap into" personality in the same way that a valid and reliable assessment such as the revised Minnesota Multiphasic Personality Inventory (MMPI-2) does (e.g., Lilienfeld, Wood, & Garb, 2000; Meyer & Archer, 2001; Wood, Nezworski, Lilienfeld, & Garb, 2003).

Types of Validity

After you have introduced students to the general concept of validity, it becomes important to inform them that there are in fact several different subtypes of validity, each of which allows researchers to assess the extent to which they are studying what they think they are studying. Campbell and his colleagues (Campbell & Stanley, 1963; Cook & Campbell, 1979) suggested that four types of validity are of utmost importance to researchers: construct validity, statistical conclusion validity, internal validity, and external validity. Although it is very difficult to obtain high levels of each type of validity in a single study (e.g., high internal validity may preclude high external validity), by assessing each of them—both within and across studies —researchers can make accurate claims regarding the various psychological phenomena they study. Given the importance of validity in psychological research, you should spend ample time discussing these critical concepts with your students.

Construct Validity

Construct validity is "the degree to which [a] study measures and manipulates the underlying psychological elements that the researcher claims to be measuring and manipulating" (Mitchell & Jolley, 2004, p. 19; see also Cronbach & Meehl, 1955). Many psychological researchers consider construct validity to be the most important type of validity in science (Kerlinger & Lee, 2000), because it embraces all other types of validity. In other words, before researchers can assess other types of validity, they need to be sure they are in fact manipulating and measuring the psychological variables they claim to be manipulating and measuring.

Before discussing construct validity with your students, you might wish to discuss with them exactly what the term "construct" means. A construct is an abstract psychological phenomenon that researchers infer from observable behavior, "deliberately and consciously invented or adopted for a special scientific purpose" (Kerlinger & Lee, 2000, p. 40). Common constructs in the psychological literature include personality, love, aggression, intelligence, motivation, and depression. For example, a researcher might observe dogs failing to jump over a barrier to avoid shock (e.g., Seligman & Maier, 1967) and infer some level of "learned helplessness." Thus the number of times a dog fails to jump over a barrier to avoid shock is not only an operational definition, but also an *indicant* of the underlying construct of learned helplessness (Kerlinger & Lee, 2000).

Now that your students are familiar with constructs, they will likely have an easier time understanding construct validity. To introduce this type of validity, I often ask my students to imagine that a researcher is studying depression in college-age students. Some measures of depression, such as the BDI, tend to have high construct validity; in other words, psychologists believe they "tap into," or measure, depression accurately (Richter et al., 1997; Schotte, Maes, Cluydts, de Doncker, & Cosyns, 1997; Steer, Rissmiller, & Beck, 2000). In contrast, although the RSES is a valid and reliable measure of self-esteem—which in fact may be related to depression (e.g., Crocker & Wolfe, 2001)—it is not an instrument that would accurately measure depression. In other words, it would have low construct validity for depression.

Once you feel that your students have a good understanding of construct validity, it is then time to inform them that psychological researchers do not assess construct validity directly. Rather, they measure other types of validity, each of which provides indirect evidence that the researchers are manipulating and measuring the underlying psychological phenomena they claim to be manipulating and measuring. Although there are in fact many different subtypes of validity, you should spend your time discussing those that are most vital to evaluating construct validity: content validity, convergent validity, and discriminant validity.

Content validity. The first type of validity that provides support for construct validity is *content validity*, or the extent to which items on a test, questionnaire, or inventory adequately measure the construct they are supposed to measure. For example, if you are attempting to measure your students' "understanding" of construct validity on one of your tests, the items should provide a representative sample from the possible population of items that would *theoretically* measure "understanding" (Kerlinger & Lee, 2000). Although drawing a representative sample of items can sometimes be difficult, researchers can assess the adequacy of their sample (i.e., content validity) by calculating an index of agreement known as *interrater reliability*. Although similar in scope to interobserver reliability and interobserver agreement, interrater reliability is a measure of the extent to which two researchers agree that a *test or survey item* represents a specific construct. In contrast, interobserver reliability and interobserver agreement tend to focus on observable behavior rather than on test items.

Hands-on Tip

One effective way to teach students about content validity and interrater reliability is to reintroduce Camac and Camac's (1993) activity (or a variation of it), which I described earlier in the chapter. As you work your way through the activity, remind your students that the development of any test questions should follow from established definitions of the construct you choose to examine. For example, before developing a self-esteem inventory, students should review accepted definitions of self-esteem. Next, ask your students to create questions they think will accurately measure the construct. After students have come up with different questions, ask them to discuss as a group if the questions accurately represent the different dimensions of the construct they are studying. At this point, you would do well to introduce interrater reliability to your students and discuss how it relates to content validity. Moreover, it is worth telling them that although interrater reliability does not guarantee high content validity—because the content validity of test items is somewhat subjective—agreement between raters does increase the likelihood that test items accurately measure the different dimensions of the construct they purportedly measure.

Convergent and discriminant validity. Two additional types of validity that, along with content validity, provide support for construct validity are *convergent validity* and *discriminant validity*. Whereas convergent validity refers to "the extent to which [a] measure correlates with other indicators of [a] construct" (Mitchell & Jolley, 2004, p. 110), discriminant validity measures the extent to which a measure *does not* correlate with other measures that *do not* measure the construct of interest. For example, if one were constructing a questionnaire to measure self-esteem, scores on the questionnaire should correlate highly with scores on the RSES, which would demonstrate convergent validity (i.e., they converge on the same construct). Conversely, if one were constructing a test to measure self-esteem, scores on the test should not correlate highly with scores on an IQ test, which would demonstrate discriminant validity (i.e., the two measures *discriminate* between different constructs).

Hands-on Tip

Again, Camac and Camac's (1993) test construction activity provides a nice way to discuss these types of validity. By comparing scores on the student-constructed scale with, for example, (a) other measures of sensation seeking (e.g., Zuckerman, Eysenck, & Eysenck, 1978) and (b) measures that should not correlate with sensation seeking (e.g., the RSES), students can see how convergent and discriminant validity provide indirect support for construct validity.

Statistical Conclusion Validity

Hopefully, at this point, your students are starting to understand exactly what validity is and why it is of the utmost importance to psychological researchers. Assuming that your students now have a grasp on construct validity, as well as a handle on the different ways that researchers attempt to measure construct validity, you can introduce to them a second type of validity that provides additional information regarding the veracity of a knowledge claim: statistical conclusion validity.

Once researchers have collected their data, their typical *modus operandi* is to use statistical analyses to determine if there are meaningful relations between their variables (although see Ch. 8 for a discussion of designs that do not historically employ statistical analysis). More specifically, if researchers took care when designing their studies, these statistical analyses should help them determine if there is a meaningful relation between their variables (Cook & Campbell, 1979). Statistical conclusion validity, then, asks the following question: Can the results of your statistical analyses help you determine whether there is a "real" relation between your variables? Without high statistical conclusion validity, researchers might incorrectly conclude that there were (or were not) relations between their variables, which, in turn, might decrease the accuracy of the statements they make about various psychological phenomena.

Cook and Campbell (1979) identified several factors that influence statistical conclusion validity: (a) committing Type I (incorrectly rejecting the null hypothesis) and Type II (incorrectly failing to reject the null hypothesis) errors; (b) using inappropriate statistical tests (i.e., using a certain statistical test that is inappropriate for a given set of data); (c) employing variables that are not reliable; and

(d) using heterogeneous participants, which increases the amount of participant variability in a study and, consequently, can make it difficult to identify true relations between variables.

Most likely, as you read the preceding list of "some major threats to statistical conclusion validity" (Cook & Campbell, 1979, p. 41), you recognized many, if not most, of these threats. You probably also realized that you already discuss many, if not most, of them in your research methods courses. However, an informal survey of my colleagues suggests that fewer research methods instructors discuss these threats within the context of statistical conclusion validity specifically and validity in general. Because validity is a concept you likely revisit throughout the course of the semester, you may find it useful to introduce the notion of statistical conclusion validity when you first introduce the concept of validity to your students and then revisit it more specifically as you introduce different topics that require discussion of Cook and Campbell's "threats." Although this type of validity is less common in research methods textbooks, discussing statistical conclusion validity in relation to validity *and* statistical analysis will likely help your students link together some important— and seemingly discrepant—course topics.

Internal Validity

A third type of validity, one that you probably spend a good amount of time discussing in your research methods course, is internal validity. A quick glance at nearly any research methods textbook should make it abundantly clear that internal validity and its related topics (e.g., control techniques, threats to internal validity) are very important concepts. As well they should be: It is this type of validity that allows researchers to state with some degree of certainty that they have identified *causal* relations between their variables of interest. Whereas statistical conclusion validity is concerned simply with identifying relations between variables, internal validity, in contrast, asks the following question: Was the independent variable the sole cause of changes in the dependent variable? When researchers conduct experiments, they want to be able to state with some certainty that changes in their dependent variable(s) were produced by changes in their independent variable(s) and not by other uncontrolled factors (Cook & Campbell, 1979; Ruscio, 2006). When researchers have taken steps to control for extraneous variables, they can be relatively confident that changes in the dependent variable were a function of changes in the independent variable—and thus their experiment had high internal validity. In contrast, when changes in the dependent variable were likely due to uncontrolled changes in one or more extraneous variables, an experiment has low internal validity.

At this point, your students will likely be ready to discuss factors that hinder researchers' ability to state with certainty that their independent variable affected their dependent variable—or, in other words, that their study had high internal validity. In their classic text on experimental design, Campbell and Stanley (1963) identified eight factors that can jeopardize the internal validity of a study: *history, maturation, testing, statistical regression, selection, instrumentation, mortality,* and *selection-maturation interaction* (or *interaction with selection*). Some textbooks (e.g., Smith & Davis, 2007) include a ninth factor as well: *diffusion of treatments.* Although I will not discuss each of these in detail, suffice it to say that you should provide your students ample opportunity to practice identifying examples of these threats, as well as constructing their own examples of each.

External Validity

When teaching psychological research methods, it is often easy to spend an inordinate amount of time discussing the preceding types of validity and why they are so important with regard to furthering our understanding of various psychological phenomena. Unfortunately, excessive discussion of the preceding types of validity may come with a price: Students may wonder if psychological researchers care at all whether their highly controlled, laboratory-based studies have any relevance to "real life." For example, it is not uncommon for students to ask questions like the following: "Can you explain to me how a lab-based study examining when and why dogs fail to jump over a barrier to avoid a shock [Seligman & Maier, 1967] has any relevance to my life?" In essence, our students—probably unknowingly—are asking questions about *external validity.*

Assessing external validity allows researchers to determine the extent to which the results of a certain study generalize to other participants, settings, or times. To illustrate, imagine that a highly controlled, laboratory-based study has shown that a new teaching method is more effective at promoting long-term retention than other traditional methods of instruction (e.g., Saville, Zinn, & Elliott, 2005). External validity would assess the extent to which the new teaching method would produce similar results if implemented in a regular college classroom (see Saville et al., 2006). If researchers obtain similar results in a regular college classroom, the results from the first study would have high external validity; if not, the study would have low external validity.

After discussing exactly what external validity is, I have found it effective to discuss with my students how psychological researchers typically design their studies in hopes that their results will generalize to other participants, settings, and times. Most often, psychological researchers use random sampling and large sample sizes to increase the likelihood that their studies will have high external validity (although see Chapter 8 for further discussion). Although the definition of random sampling seems relatively straightforward, you may have found, as I have, that students sometimes have more trouble understanding exactly *how* random sampling affects external validity. If this is the case, a simple activity by R. A. Smith (1999) may be just the solution to this problem.

Hands-on Tip

Smith first randomly distributed "fun-size" packs of M&Ms to his students and asked them to examine the distribution of each of the different colors in their "samples." Based on their samples, Smith asked his students to make predictions regarding the distribution of colors in the greater "population" of M & Ms. Students then formed pairs—and, subsequently, larger groups—and once again generated hypotheses based on their new, larger samples. Ultimately, students were able to determine if their smaller samples were representative of the larger population of M & Ms; they were also able to see how larger, randomly selected samples tended to be more representative of the population from which they came. Using this, or a similar, activity will likely allow your students to see rather quickly how random sampling increases external validity. Moreover, you may find this to be a useful activity when first teaching students about inferential statistics and how they allow researchers to make inferences from samples to populations. Plus your students will enjoy eating the M&Ms.

When teaching your students about random sampling and external validity, one caveat is in order, however. Although some have argued that researchers should attempt to construct studies that contain high external validity (e.g., Campbell & Stanley, 1963; Cook & Campbell, 1979), other researchers have suggested that "External validity is not an automatic desideratum" (Mook, 1983, p. 379).

Rather, external validity is a type of assessment that simply asks a question: Do these results hold in other settings, with other participants, or at different times? Sometimes the answer to this question is "yes"; sometimes is it "no." Because students often believe that studies with low external validity are somehow inferior to studies whose results more easily generalize to other settings, participants, and times, it may be necessary to explain to students why "external validity is not an automatic desideratum" for all psychological researchers. To accomplish this task, I have found that discussing Mook's (1983) well-known article on external *in*validity provides students with useful information on why some researchers are little concerned with designing studies that have high external validity.

On the Relation between Reliability and Validity

Finally, it is important to discuss the general relation between reliability and validity. Because instructors often discuss reliability and validity together, students sometimes come to the mistaken conclusion that high (low) reliability denotes high (low) validity. To counteract this belief, it is important to explain to students that, although reliability is a necessary condition for validity, it is not sufficient (i.e., a measure can be reliable without being valid). To illustrate this point, I once again invoke the example on intelligence and foot size that I introduced earlier in the chapter. Imagine that a researcher has decided to study intelligence by measuring the size of students' feet. Although it is fairly obvious to students that our researcher will likely obtain the same average foot size today as in 2 weeks, I ask my students once again to consider the following question: Is foot size a valid, or accurate, measure of intelligence? In this case, students typically report that foot size does not accurately measure intelligence; they also quickly see that foot size is reliable but not valid and that the same may be true for other measures.

Once we have determined that a measure can be reliable but not valid, I ask students to identify a more valid measure of intelligence. Because of earlier class discussions, students often suggest college grade point average (GPA) or scores on an IQ test. I then ask students the following question: If our IQ test is a valid measure of intelligence—in other words, if it accurately measures what it is supposed to measure—do you think researchers would get approximately the same results if they gave someone the IQ test today and again in 2 weeks? Most often, students answer in the affirmative, and we spend some time discussing why a valid measure is likely a reliable measure as well. You might also wish to incorporate the preceding activity by Camac and Camac (1993) when discussing the relation between reliability and validity.

Conclusion

Teaching the concepts of reliability and validity, along with their subtypes, is arguably one of the most important, and difficult, tasks for any research methods instructor. The importance of these two concepts in psychological research is evidenced by examining any research methods textbook, in which authors typically spend a relatively large amount of time discussing these two central ideas, often devoting a chapter or more to each. For this very reason— that reliability and validity are two of the most important concepts in psychological research methods—you should devote significant amounts of time to discussing these concepts with your students. Only with extensive discussion and repeated exposure to the ideas contained in this chapter will your students come to understand why psychological researchers spend so much of their time assessing reliability and validity in their studies.

References

Bain, K. (2004). *What the best college teachers do*. Cambridge, MA: Harvard University Press.

Becker, A. H. (1999). Discovering the relationship between operational definitions and interobserver reliability. In L. T. Benjamin, B. F. Nodine, R. M. Ernst, & C. B. Broeker (Eds.), *Activities handbook for the teaching of psychology, Vol. 4* (pp. 57–63). Washington, DC: American Psychological Association.

Brown, H. (1963). *d*-amphetamine-chlorpromazine antagonism in a food reinforced operant. *Journal of the Experimental Analysis of Behavior, 6*, 395–398.

Camac, C. R., & Camac, M. K. (1993). A laboratory project in scale design: Teaching reliability and validity. *Teaching of Psychology, 20*, 102–104.

Campbell, D., & Stanley, J. (1963). *Experimental and quasi-experimental designs for research*. Chicago: Rand-McNally.

Carr, J. E., Taylor, S. L., & Austin, J. (1995). A classroom demonstration of self-monitoring, reactivity, and interobserver agreement. *The Behavior Analyst, 18*, 141–146.

Chew, S. L. (2005). Student misperceptions in the psychology classroom. In B. K. Saville, T. E. Zinn, & V. W. Hevern (Eds.), *Essays from e-xcellence in teaching, 2004* (Chap. 3). Retrieved March 13, 2006, from the Society for the Teaching of Psychology Web site: http://teachpsych.org/resources/e-books/eit2004/eit04-03.pdf

Cook, T. D., & Campbell, D. T. (1979). *Quasi-experimentation: Design and analysis issues for field settings.* Chicago: Rand-McNally.

Cooper, J. O., Heron, T. E., & Heward, W. L. (1987). *Applied behavior analysis.* Columbus, OH: Merrill.

Crocker, J., & Wolfe, C. T. (2001). Contingencies of self-worth. *Psychological Review, 108,* 593–623.

Cronbach, L. J. (1951). Coefficient alpha and the internal structure of tests. *Psychometrika, 16,* 297–334.

Cronbach, L. J., & Meehl, P. (1955). Construct validity in psychological tests. *Psychological Bulletin, 52,* 281–302.

Diener, E., & Seligman, M. E. P. (2002). Very happy people. *Psychological Science, 13,* 81–84.

Fitterling, J. M., Martin, J. E., Gramling, S., Cole, P., & Milan, M. A. (1988). Behavioral management of exercise training in vascular headache patients: An investigation of exercise adherence and headache activity. *Journal of Applied Behavior Analysis, 21,* 9–19.

Halpern, D. F., & Hakel, M. D. (2003). Applying the science of learning to the university and beyond. *Change, 35*(4), 36–42.

Herringer, L. G. (2000). The two captains: A research exercise using *Star Trek. Teaching of Psychology, 27,* 50–51.

Johnston, J. M., & Pennypacker, H. S. (1993). *Strategies and tactics of behavioral research* (2nd ed.). Hillsdale, NJ: Erlbaum.

Kantowitz, B. H., Roediger, H. L., III, & Elmes, D. G. (1997). *Experimental psychology: Understanding psychological research* (6th ed.). St. Paul, MN: West.

Kerlinger, F. N., & Lee, H. B. (2000). *Foundations of behavioral research* (4th ed.). Orlando, FL: Harcourt.

Lilienfeld, S. O., Wood, J. M., & Garb, H. N. (2000). The scientific status of projective techniques. *Psychological Science in the Public Interest, 1,* 27–66.

Lord, F. (1953). On the statistical treatment of football numbers. *American Psychologist, 8,* 750–751.

Meyer, G. J., & Archer, R. P. (2001). The hard science of Rorschach research: What do we know and where do we go? *Psychological Assessment, 13,* 486–502.

Milgram, S. (1963). Behavioral study of obedience. *Journal of Abnormal and Social Psychology, 67,* 371–378.

Milgram, S. (1974). *Obedience to authority.* New York: Harper.

Mitchell, M. L., & Jolley, J. M. (2004). *Research design explained.* Belmont, CA: Thomson Wadsworth.

Mook, D. G. (1983). In defense of external invalidity. *American Psychologist, 38,* 379–389.

Rauscher, F. H., Shaw, G. L., & Ky, K. N. (1993). Music and spatial task performance. *Nature, 365,* 611.

Rauscher, F. H., Shaw, G. L., & Ky, K. N. (1995). Listening to Mozart enhances spatial-temporal reasoning: Towards a neurophysiological basis. *Neuroscience Letters, 185,* 44–47.

Richter, P., Werner, J., Bastine, R., Heerlien, A., Kick, H., & Sauer, H. (1997). Measuring treatment outcome by the Beck Depression Inventory. *Psychopathology, 30,* 234–240.

Roediger, H. L., III, & McDermott, K. B. (1995). Creating false memories: Remembering words not presented in lists. *Journal of Experimental Psychology: Learning, Memory, and Cognition, 21,* 804–814.

Rosenberg, M. (1965). *Society and the adolescent self-image.* Princeton, NJ: Princeton University Press.

Rosenthal, R., & Jacobson, L. (1966). Teachers' expectancies: Determinants of pupils' IQ gains. *Psychological Reports, 19,* 115–118.

Ruscio, J. (2006). *Critical thinking in psychology: Separating sense from nonsense* (2nd ed.). Belmont, CA: Thomson Wadsworth.

Saville, B. K., Zinn, T. E., & Elliott, M. P. (2005). Interteaching vs. traditional methods of instruction: A preliminary analysis. *Teaching of Psychology, 32,* 161–163.

Saville, B. K., Zinn, T. E., Neef, N. A., Van Norman, R., & Ferreri, S. J. (2006). A comparison of interteaching and lecture in the college classroom. *Journal of Applied Behavior Analysis, 39,* 49–61.

Schotte, C. K. W., Maes, M., Cluydts, R., de Doncker, D., & Cosyns, P. (1997). Construct validity of the Beck Depression Inventory in a depressive population. *Journal of Affective Disorders, 46,* 115–125.

Seligman, M. E. P., & Maier, S. F. (1967). Failure to escape traumatic shock. *Journal of Experimental Psychology, 74,* 1–9.

Sherman, K. J., Cherkin, D. C., Erro, J., Miglioretti, D. L., & Deyo, R. A. (2005). Comparing yoga, exercise, and a self-care book for chronic low back pain. *Annals of Internal Medicine, 143,* 849–856.

Smith, R. A. (1999). A tasty sample(r): Teaching about sampling using M & Ms. In L. T. Benjamin, B. F. Nodine, R. M. Ernst, & C. B. Broeker (Eds.), *Activities handbook for the teaching of psychology, Vol. 4* (pp. 66–67). Washington, DC: American Psychological Association.

Smith, R. A., & Davis, S. F. (2007). *The psychologist as detective: An introduction to conducting research in psychology* (4th ed.). Upper Saddle River, NJ: Prentice Hall.

Steele, K. M., Bass, K. E., & Crook, M. D. (1999). The mystery of the Mozart effect: Failure to replicate. *Psychological Science, 10,* 366–369.

Steer, R. A., Rissmiller, D. J., & Beck, A. T. (2000) Use of the Beck Depression Inventory-11 with depressed geriatric patients. *Behaviour Research and Therapy*, *38*, 311–318.

Stevens, S. S. (1935). The operational definition of psychological concepts. *Psychological Review*, *42*, 517–527.

Steven S. S. (1946). On the theory of scales of measurement. *Science*, *103*, 677–680.

Vandervert, L. R. (1988). Operational definitions made simple, lasting, and useful. In M. E. Ware & C. L. Brewer (Eds.), *Handbook for teaching statistics and research methods* (pp. 132–134). Hillsdale, NJ: Erlbaum.

Velleman, P. F., & Wilkinson, L. (1993). Nominal, ordinal, interval, and ratio typologies are misleading. *The American Statistician*, *47*, 65–72.

Wood, J. M., Nezworski, M. T., Lilienfeld, S. O., & Garb, H. N. (2003). *What's wrong with the Rorschach? Science confronts the controversial inkblot test*. New York: Jossey-Bass.

Zuckerman, M., Eysenck, S., & Eysenck, H. J. (1978). Sensation seeking in England and America: Cross-cultural, age, and sex comparisons. *Journal of Consulting and Clinical Psychology*, *28*, 477–482.

Chapter 6

Teaching the Distinction between Experimental and Nonexperimental Research Methods

"Soda causes obesity, researchers assert." So declared the headline in a recent newspaper article (Marchione, 2006), just one of numerous reports in the media that has discussed the purported link between obesity and consumption of soda and other sugar-laden beverages. Although the headline of the article is unequivocal in its assertion—soda consumption, in fact, *causes* obesity—further inspection of the article paints a less certain picture of the causal relation between these two variables. In fact, that soda directly causes obesity is called into question early in the article when the author states, "Not that these drinks are the only cause—genetics, exercise and other factors are involved—but that they are one cause, perhaps the leading cause." The certainty of the headline is further weakened later in the article when the author *correctly* asserts how difficult studying dietary influences on obesity can be:

> Diet is hard to study. Most people drink at least some sweetened beverages and also get calories from other drinks like milk and orange juice, diluting the strength of any observations about excess weight from soda alone . . . [Also] Children are growing and gaining weight naturally . . .

By the end of the article, the direct cause-and-effect relation between consumption of soda and obesity is not as clear as the headline so vigorously reports. Fortunately, though, the author spends a good amount of time discussing evidence that questions the bold assertion made in the headline and how such evidence *might* point to a causal relation between soda consumption and obesity. Unfortunately, however, a quick glance at the morning headlines while on the way to work might lead some readers to conclude—maybe incorrectly—that soda and other sugary drinks are in fact the sole cause of obesity.

One might like to believe that such distortions of research findings only occur when media writers, some of whom may not be adroit at interpreting the scientific literature, attempt to condense verbose scientific prose into a few short paragraphs that their readers, some of whom may not be scientifically literate, can easily grasp. As I discuss later in the chapter, however, there seem to be many sources of inaccurate scientific information. As a result, misunderstandings regarding the scientific method, as well as skepticism regarding the ability of science to improve people's lives, abound. Such misunderstandings only amplify the confusion many people feel when they attempt to interpret scientific research; and skepticism regarding the utility of science may lead members of the lay public to avoid learning more—if anything at all—about the ways that researchers attempt to learn about and improve the world in which we live.

Presumably, most students do not enter our classrooms as "blank slates," completely devoid of any knowledge regarding the scientific method. In fact, a few might even state with some certainty that they know a lot about research. Unfortunately, though, much of what our students know about research is wrong. Consequently, as we teach about the methods that researchers use to acquire knowledge, we often have to spend a good bit of time disabusing our students of certain misconceptions they have about the scientific method. One of the most prevalent of these misconceptions relates to the process by which one can scientifically state that something *causes* something else—for example, that soda causes obesity. In other words, our students often fail to recognize that "correlation does not equal causation." To help expunge this and other important misconceptions about research methods, it is vital that we spend time discussing the distinction between experimental and nonexperimental research designs and the kinds of conclusions that can properly flow from different kinds of designs. In the pages that follow, I first present some history on the distinction between experimental and nonexperimental research designs, history that your students might find interesting. Next, I briefly discuss the distinction between experimental and nonexperimental methods, along with ways you can increase the likelihood your students will learn this important distinction. I conclude the chapter with a discussion of criteria that researchers sometimes use to make causal inferences from data they collected using nonexperimental research methods.

Psychology's Early Years and the (Non)Distinction between Experimental and Nonexperimental Methods

Most likely, students in your research methods course are familiar with the oft-stated notion, "correlation does not equal causation." And most likely, you will spend a good amount of time repeating this well-known mantra, at least until your students really understand that a relation between variables does not necessarily imply that one causes changes in the other. In fact, by the time students leave your methods course, they may be so familiar with the idea that correlation does not equal causation that they may find it hard to believe that early psychologists, in fact, did not make the distinction between experimental and nonexperimental research methods— a distinction that has come to hold a venerated place in science in general and in research methods courses in particular. That early psychologists did not make this distinction is an interesting aspect of experimental psychology's history, one that you may wish to spend some time discussing with your students.

Woodworth and the Distinction between Experimental and Correlational Methods

In the late 1800s and early 1900s, psychology *was* experimental psychology (rather than one of several subdisciplines such as clinical or social psychology), providing a home for early researchers studying everything from maze learning in rats to intelligence in humans. Some of this research was experimental in nature, whereas some was purely observational. Consequently, the name "experimental" psychology was sometimes a misnomer, because many of the psychological phenomena studied by early "experimental" psychologists were, in fact, examined using nonexperimental research designs. Robert S. Woodworth (1938) alluded to this fact in his classic textbook *Experimental Psychology*, stating: "Today we are inclined to claim for experimental psychology a scope as wide as that of psychology itself, while admitting that we do not yet know exactly how to subject some of the biggest problems to a rigorous experiment" (p. 1).

Woodworth, however, believed it important to distinguish between the two general categories of designs, devoting the first few pages of his book to delineating the difference between "the experimental method" and "the comparative and correlational method" (p. 3). In doing so, Woodworth became the first psychologist to make this distinction—at least in writing (see Goodwin, 2005).

In addition to drawing a distinction between experimental and nonexperimental (i.e., correlational) research methods, Woodworth also introduced the terms "independent variable" and "dependent variable" into the psychology vernacular and noted the importance of controlling extraneous factors that could confound the results of an experiment. Whereas an experiment includes independent and dependent variables, Woodworth (1938) noted that a correlational study "does not introduce an 'experimental factor'; it has no 'independent variable' but treats all the measured variables alike. It does not directly study cause and effect" (p. 3).

Although Woodworth seemed to endorse the superiority of experimental methods early on in his textbook, stating that "Until [some of psychology's biggest problems] are attacked experimentally, they probably will not be solved" (p. 1), he subsequently suggested that experimental and nonexperimental research methods should hold equal footing in psychological research. He also urged researchers who use the two different approaches to work together: "Contact between the two should remain close. The experimentalist needs to use the statistical techniques devised by the correlationist . . . and the correlationist often bases his tests on laboratory experiments" (p. 3). Nevertheless, debate regarding the relative importance of experimental and nonexperimental research methods in the field of psychology continued unabated for years following Woodworth's early adjuration (e.g., Boring, 1957; Cronbach, 1957; Eysenck, 1995).

Teaching the Distinction between Experimental and Nonexperimental Methods

After you have given your students some historical background, you can more easily turn your attention to teaching them to identify the difference between experimental and nonexperimental research designs. Do not be surprised, however, if it takes some time for them truly to understand the distinction. Subtle nuances often make it difficult for students new to the world of research methods to recognize the characteristics that demarcate a research design as experimental or nonexperimental. For example, although twin studies (e.g., Bouchard, Lykken, McGue, Segal, & Tellegen, 1990) do not entail the manipulation of an independent variable in the traditional sense —a researcher does not determine whether twins are identical or fraternal or whether they are raised together or apart—some researchers consider twin studies to be exemplars of "natural" or "social" experiments and thus open to the same types of inference made in more traditional, laboratory-based experiments (see, e.g., Bouchard & Pedersen, 1999). The fuzzy borders between different experimental and nonexperimental designs have led some researchers even to suggest that research designs actually lie on a continuum, with pure experiments and pure correlational studies serving as anchors, and other designs, such as those used in twin studies, falling somewhere in between (e.g., Boring, 1957; Eysenck, 1995). Nevertheless, although one could argue for the existence of a continuum of research designs, your students will likely obtain a better understanding of research designs in general if you first present them as falling into dichotomous categories, distinguishable by the presence or absence of an explicitly manipulated independent variable.

Experiment or Nonexperiment?
Factors that Impede Learning

There are at least three other factors that may impede your students' ability to make the initial distinction between experimental and nonexperimental designs, and to apply this distinction on a continuing basis. These factors include the influence of media portrayals of research, faulty assertions by researchers, and inconsistencies in the use of terms.

Misinterpretations of research in the media. As I mentioned earlier in the chapter, widespread miscommunications and misinterpretations of research in the media exacerbate the general public's misunderstanding of research findings. For example, a recent report on a well-known news Web site contained the following headline: "Breast-feeding *lowers* anxiety, says study" (http://www.guardian.co.

uk/medicine/story/0,,1836028,00.html, my italics). The report subsequently informed readers that "Breast-feeding's calming *effects* seem to be long-lasting" (my italics). Unfortunately, further examination of the story calls into questions these conclusions. The longitudinal study, which followed nearly 9,000 British children for a decade, was observational in nature and did not include the manipulation of an independent variable. Although the article later qualified its earlier cause-and-effect statements ("The researchers do not know why breast-fed babies were less anxious. They suggested breast-feeding could be an indicator of other parental factors or the physical contact between the mother and the child may have helped to reduce anxiety"), it is possible, or even highly likely, that readers of the article—many of whom presumably do not have a solid understanding of research methods—may be left with one conclusion: Breast-feeding *causes* a reduction in childhood anxiety.

Faulty assertions by psychological researchers. A second reason why our students may have trouble distinguishing between experimental and nonexperimental designs is that they often see and hear trusted authorities—including well-known researchers—making faulty assertions regarding research findings. Sadly, it is quite common for psychological researchers either to imply, or even boldly assert, that there are causal relations between variables in their studies, even if the nonexperimental nature of their research designs often does not warrant such conclusions.

For example, in one recent study, the researchers examined the relation between students' overall evaluations of their instructors (from "poor" to "excellent") and several other variables, including class size, instructor gender and rank, and average grade given by the instructor. The researchers collected archival data on these variables and used multiple regression analyses to examine the relations. They (correctly) observed that the average grade given and instructor rank *predicted* students' overall evaluations. However, the researchers concluded that average grade given by the instructor and instructor rank are among those variables that *affect* students' evaluations of their instructors.

Is this conclusion warranted based on the results of one study that utilized a relatively well-known statistical procedure? Or is it possible that even well-intentioned and statistically savvy researchers may not always remember to take into account every factor (e.g., student–instructor rapport) that could possibly affect student perceptions of teaching effectiveness? Even in experiments, in which researchers attempt to control as many outside influences as possible, eliminating all unwanted causes of variation in the dependent variable can be difficult. As Eysenck (1995) stated, "Physicists can eliminate experimentally all factors other than the independent variable; psychologists cannot. Whatever the experiment, it involves persons, with different IQs, different personalities, different motivations, different attitudes, different emotions" (p. 217).

Granted, the use of such statistical techniques may allow researchers to discount the likelihood of causal relations between certain variables. However, it is important for your students to understand that ruling out these and other relations does not, by default, allow one to conclude that there are necessarily causal relations between other variables of interest—even in the most elegantly designed nonexperimental studies. Although a strong relation between variables may be one marker of causation, only experimental designs—those in which a researcher manipulates an independent variable and controls for possible confounds—allow researchers the luxury of making causal inferences. Some researchers might turn to complex statistical analyses in their quest for the holy grail of causation, but the absence of true experimental designs should prompt your students to be wary of statements such as the following: "We examined whether men or women bought more shoes in 2004 and found that gender affected shoe-buying behavior." Although such a conclusion might be feasible if the researchers had, for example, systematically manipulated the gender of the person selling shoes, this is often not the case in nonexperimental studies that infer causation. As a colleague of mine is fond of stating, "Cause and effect lies in the research design, not in the statistical analyses."

Inconsistent use of terminology. A final reason that students sometimes continue to confuse experimental and nonexperimental research designs concerns the way some authors, instructors, and researchers use certain research terminology. Take, for example, the case of simple linear regression, a common statistical tool that students likely encounter both in their undergraduate statistics courses and when they peruse the psychology literature. Although simple regression analyses technically allow researchers only to make predictions about one variable, y (often called the *criterion variable*), based on what they know about another variable, x (often called the *predictor variable*), it is not uncommon for authors, instructors, and researchers (and even certain statistical software packages) to use the terms *dependent variable* and *independent variable* in place of criterion variable and predictor variable, respectively.

For instance, imagine the following scenario in which a researcher wants to study the relation between students' scores on Exam 1 and Exam 2 and decides to use simple linear regression to see if scores on Exam 1 predict scores on Exam 2. A common textbook description of linear regression might read something like this:

The equation for simple linear regression is:

$$y = mx + b$$

where y = scores of the dependent variable, m = the regression coefficient (or slope of the regression line), x = scores of the independent variable, and b = the intercept constant.

Although this study is clearly nonexperimental in nature—the researcher has not manipulated either set of exam scores—the use of the terms independent variable and dependent variable may give students the impression that researchers actually manipulated an independent variable and measured a dependent variable, and that all regression analyses examine data gathered using experimental research designs.

Also common is the practice of discussing outcomes in factorial designs in terms of main effects and interactions. Many such studies are clearly nonexperimental in nature, yet when researchers observe differences between men and women, for example, they often state that there was a main *effect* of sex, implying that simply being male or female *caused* the observed differences. Because "sex" is not a manipulated variable in these studies, one can only conclude that men and women *differed* on the dependent measure of interest. Again, because such usages of terminology are common in research vernacular, it may give our students the idea that cause-and-effect conclusions are warranted when, in fact, they may not be.

In short, if we want our students to understand the distinction between experimental and nonexperimental research designs—and consequently be better consumers of information, better critical thinkers, and maybe even better researchers—we need to take steps to teach them this distinction adequately. Let's consider some of these steps.

Variables and Manipulation: a Starting Point

Quite possibly the most effective way to teach the distinction between experiments, with their manipulated variables, and non-experiments, which feature no such manipulations, is to begin with the following questions: (a) What is a variable? and (b) What does manipulating a variable entail?

What is a variable? The characteristic that separates experimental from nonexperimental research designs is the explicit control or manipulation of an independent variable. However, before discussing what manipulating an independent variable entails, you would do well to spend some time first reviewing the concept of a *variable*, if you have not done so already.

In its most colloquial form, a variable is, to be redundant, something that varies. Therefore, because psychologists focus their efforts on studying observable behavior or products of observable behavior (some also make inferences about nonobservables based on their observations), a variable is simply a behavior or some other environmental event that can take on *at least* two different values. For example, the number of students yawning during my lectures on independent and dependent variables may change from day to day, as can the temperature in my office. In contrast, a *constant*, as your students will quickly tell you, does not vary. For example, my height, in contrast to my weight, does not change—at least not appreciably. Neither do the number of chairs in my office or the number of lazy cats that currently inhabit my household.

After introducing the concept of a variable to your students, you might also wish to inform them that variables can be either *continuous* or *discrete*. (Some of you might also wish to discuss other ways of categorizing variables: dichotomous vs. multivalued, qualitative vs. quantitative, and so on.) Continuous variables can theoretically take on any value within a certain range of values. For example, a person could be 45 inches tall, 57.2 inches tall, 78.25 inches tall, 80.245 inches tall, 95.2458 inches tall, or any other height within a feasible range of values. In contrast, discrete variables take on a limited number of values. A person might be a man or a woman; a voter might be Democrat, Republican, or Independent; a student might be a freshman, sophomore, junior, or senior; a Likert scale might have five points; and so on.

In addition, although many of the psychological phenomena that researchers study are continuous variables, common in psychological research is the practice of converting continuous variables into discrete variables (but not necessarily vice versa). For example, although "personality" is a continuous variable (i.e., personality varies infinitely, in theory), researchers often describe people instead in terms of discrete personality traits: "introverted" or "extroverted," "neurotic" or "emotionally stable," "cooperative" or "competitive." Your students should also know that although converting continuous variables into discrete variables is common in psychology, it sometimes results in a loss of potentially useful information. For instance, knowing that a person is "short" or "tall" provides less information than knowing that a person is 4 feet 7 inches tall or 7 feet 5 inches tall.

Once your students understand the distinction between continuous and discrete variables, you should also take time to distinguish *variables* from *levels of variables* (for variables that are discrete). For example, imagine that a researcher manipulated the amount of alcohol that participants drank, asking them to consume either 0 drinks or 3 drinks before measuring their performance on some task. Whereas some students might identify "alcohol" as the variable of interest, a more accurate descriptor would be "amount of alcohol consumed," with the levels being 0 and 3 drinks.

Teaching your students to focus on levels of variables, as well as asking them to describe their variables accurately, will likely keep from them from making mistakes such as thinking that "men" and "women" constitute two separate variables in a study of sex differences, or that there are three independent variables (lecture, discussion, or combination of lecture and discussion) in a study of teaching methods rather than one variable (teaching method) with three different levels. Learning this distinction, as well as whether a variable is continuous or discrete (along with the levels), will likely enhance your students' understanding of more complex ideas (e.g., factorial designs) later in the semester.

As you discuss the preceding topics, you may find it useful to provide your students with different scenarios (either self-constructed or excerpted from journal articles) and ask them to identify the variables, levels, types, and so forth, in each. You might even wish to construct different scenarios and allow your students to contemplate their answers in smaller groups before discussing the answers as a larger class. Regardless of which format you choose, you should provide your students with extensive feedback.

What does manipulating a variable entail? Once your students seem comfortable with the preceding information on variables, you can turn your attention to the second question that will help them learn the distinction between experimental and nonexperimental research designs: What does it mean to manipulate a variable? As you well know, researchers have made the distinction between experimental and nonexperimental research designs based on whether a study involved the explicit manipulation of a variable (e.g., Woodworth, 1938).

Experimental designs. In essence, a *manipulation* occurs when a researcher treats groups of participants differently in some way. Your students should know that this differential treatment constitutes the levels of the independent variable and that any changes a researcher observes depend on this differential treatment (hence, the name *dependent* variable). Moreover, you should also introduce at this time the concept of *extraneous* variables (i.e., confounds), which are unwanted factors that *affect groups differently* and make it difficult for researchers to know what caused changes in their dependent variable(s). To preclude extraneous variables from clouding their results, researchers usually attempt to remove or control as many of these variables as possible. They most often do so by treating groups similarly in all respects, except for any differential treatment that constitutes manipulation of the independent variable. Thus you would do well to remind your students continually that extraneous variables must affect groups differently; if not, they are constants and are not contributing to any observed differences.

To introduce these ideas, I typically discuss with my students several studies that included relatively straightforward experimental manipulations. For example, in her classic study on false memories, Loftus (1975) treated groups of participants differently by varying the questions they answered after viewing a videotaped event. In her third experiment, for example, Loftus showed participants a brief video of a car accident. She then asked half of the participants (Group 1), "How fast was the white sports car going when it passed the barn while traveling along the country road?"; she asked the remaining participants (Group 2),

"How fast was the white sports car going while traveling along the country road?" (p. 566). In fact, there was no barn in the video. One week later, Loftus asked participants from each group whether they remembered seeing a barn in the video. Loftus found that participants from Group 1 remembered a barn significantly more than participants in Group 2. She concluded that "leading" questions can alter a person's memory.

After reviewing this study, I typically ask students to identify whether Loftus treated her groups differently. From there, they can easily identify independent and dependent variables, discuss possible extraneous variables, and so on. Based on their answers, they usually correctly identify Loftus's classic study as experimental in nature.

Hands-on Tip

To further demonstrate the idea of manipulation, I have found useful the following activity, based on one described by Carr and Austin (1997; see Chapter 8). First, explain to your students that you need some of them to help you with a relatively innocuous activity: light exercise. Once you have obtained 20 students, randomly assign 10 of them to an "exercise" condition and 10 of them to a "no exercise" (control) condition. Ask students in the exercise condition to engage in some form of light exercise (e.g., walking in place) for 1 minute, while students in the control group simply stand still. After 1 minute, ask students in each group to measure their heart rates for 30 seconds. Obtain an average heart rate for each group and then examine whether there are differences between the groups. Finally, discuss the manipulation with your students and whether causal statements are appropriate based on the study you conducted. You might also wish at this time to discuss random assignment and how it controls for extraneous variables. Most likely, after this activity, your students will have a better understanding of what it means to manipulate a variable.

Although many experiments involve the differential treatment of groups, your students should also know that manipulations do not always entail a researcher treating *groups of participants* differently. Manipulations can also entail a researcher treating *single participants* differently at different times. Such manipulations typically occur in *small-N* or *single-subject* research designs (see Chapter 8).

Hands-on Tip

After discussing an example or two of studies that used small-N designs, you might wish to reintroduce Carr and Austin's (1997) activity, which should help your students further understand this type of manipulation. This time, however, ask a small number of students (e.g., 10 or fewer) to alternate between 1-minute intervals of exercise and no exercise and ask each to measure his or her heart rate for 30 seconds at the end of each interval (i.e., an A-B-A-B design; see Chapter 8). By keeping track of each subject's heart rate following intervals of exercise and no exercise, you will be able to determine if exercise had an effect on heart rate. Moreover, your students should easily see how manipulations in small-N designs differ from manipulations that entail treating groups differently.

Nonexperimental designs. Whereas an experiment involves the differential treatment of groups or the differential treatment of one participant at different times, nonexperimental research designs do not include such explicit manipulations, and therefore do not allow researchers to determine exactly how changes in one or more variables produce, or cause, changes in another variable. Rather, nonexperimental research designs simply allow researchers to *describe* what they have observed, without enabling them to identify causal relations.

Whereas some nonexperimental designs (e.g., naturalistic observations) simply allow researchers to describe their participants' behavior, other nonexperimental designs provide additional information, such as whether there are relations among variables (e.g., correlational designs) or whether certain groups differ on some measure— not because of differential treatment, but because the groups were different in some way prior to the start of the study (e.g., ex post facto designs).

Let's consider three such nonexperimental studies. You might want to discuss these or other similar studies with your students, so they can begin to see how the presence—or, in the following cases, the absence—of manipulation differentiates experimental and non-experimental research designs. Following my description of each study, I offer a variation of Carr and Austin's (1997) activity that you could include to solidify your students' understanding of these various research designs.

In Stanley Milgram's (1963) well-known obedience study, he simply measured the number of participants ("teachers") who were willing to deliver a fake shock to a "learner" (actually a confederate) when he made an error. Although Milgram subsequently conducted experiments to determine how certain variables caused changes in obedience (see Milgram, 1974), notice that his initial study did not involve the manipulation of an independent variable (Milgram, however, referred to his study as an "experiment" in the published article). Rather, Milgram simply noted how many participants behaved a certain way.

Hands-on Tip

After discussing Milgram's *observational study*, you could illustrate this type of nonexperimental design for your students by simply asking each to keep track of his or her heart rate for 30 seconds (see Carr & Austin, 1997). Then, ask them to raise their hands if they had heart rates under 50 beats per minute, 60 beats per minute, 70 beats per minute, and so on. After collecting the data, discuss the results with your students along with why these designs do not allow for cause-and-effect statements.

A second type of nonexperimental design, the *correlational design*, provides additional information regarding relations among variables. Most often, these designs result in a correlation coefficient, which provides specific information regarding the strength and direction of a relation between variables. For example, Griffore, Kallen, Popovich, and Powell (1990) examined the relations among level of self-esteem, as measured by the Rosenberg Self-Esteem Scale, and numerous other variables (e.g., amount of family income, grade point average). They observed that self-esteem was positively related to family income, locus of control, ratings of partner attractiveness, and ratings of self-attractiveness. Because Griffore et al. did not manipulate any variables in their study (i.e., they did not treat groups differently), any statements regarding causality are highly speculative at best. Although your students might argue that certain conclusions are more likely than others (e.g., simply having high self-esteem does not *cause* your family to be rich), the nonexperimental nature of this study makes it difficult to know what factors were ultimately responsible for changes in self-esteem and the other variables Griffore et al. measured.

Hands-on Tip

Subsequent to your discussion of correlational studies, you could further explain this type of design by once again asking your students to measure their heart rates for 30 seconds and to note the results on a sheet of paper (see Carr & Austin, 1997). Then choose another variable—preferably one that is continuous and will provide you with some variability (e.g., height)—and ask them to note it on the same sheet. Depending on how many students you have in class, you could either collect every sheet or randomly select a smaller number. If you have access to statistical software in your classroom, you could then quickly enter the data and analyze the results. Conversely, you could analyze the results outside of class and present them to your students the following day. Finally, discuss the results with your students and why "correlation does not equal causation."

One final type of nonexperimental research design that you are likely to cover in your research methods courses is the *ex post facto design*, a commonly used design in which researchers measure group differences. Although experiments also allow researchers to examine group differences, ex post facto designs, in contrast, do not include explicit manipulation of an independent variable, either because someone has already "manipulated" the variable (e.g., examining whether students who had class with Professor A or Professor B last semester received better grades) or because the variable is inherently nonmanipulable (e.g., measuring gender differences). Consequently, and as I discussed earlier in the chapter, you should inform your students that using the terms *independent* and *dependent* to describe their variables may be misleading. Instead, they should use *predictor* variable to refer to the different groups and *criterion* variable to refer to the measured variable. Doing so will likely help avoid confusion and make it clearer for your students to differentiate experiments and ex post facto studies, which share several common characteristics. In addition, because the purpose of ex post facto studies is not to identify causal relations, you should also inform your students that it is not necessary to identify extraneous variables—a mistake that students often make when attempting to interpret the results of these nonexperimental designs.

In one ex post facto study that I often discuss with my students, Robins, Trzesniewski, Tracy, Gosling, and Potter (2002) measured self-esteem (their criterion variable) in participants aged 9 to 90 years (several categories constituted their predictor variables). They observed that men typically had higher self-esteem than women, that children tended to have higher self-esteem than adolescents, and that younger adults had lower self-esteem than older adults (except for the elderly). Again, although your students might speculate on possible causal relations—for example, it seems logical to assume that the very process of growing old may lead to decreases in self-esteem but illogical to assume that having low self-esteem causes one to grow older—you would do well to remind your students that Robins et al.'s study, along with other studies of this nature, did not include any manipulations. So any differences in self-esteem Robins et al. observed were likely present before the study began and thus a function of one or more unknown variables.

Hands-on Tip

Again, a variation on Carr and Austin's (1997) activity will help hammer home an understanding of ex post facto designs. This time, ask your students to keep track of their heart rates for 30 seconds. Then randomly select a number of men and women and examine their heart rates for gender differences. Once you have analyzed the data for gender differences, you can further discuss ex post facto designs with your students. For example, because students sometimes confuse experiments with ex post facto designs, you would do well to mention how these designs differ (e.g., presence or absence of manipulation) and how they are similar (e.g., same statistical procedures used to analyze data). With any luck (and a bit of effective teaching), your students will see that ex post facto designs, although similar to experiments in many ways, do not allow researchers to infer causation.

Drawing Causal Inferences from Nonexperimental Research

After spending some time discussing the preceding designs, your students should be familiar with each and, ideally, can determine whether a particular study is experimental or nonexperimental in nature. Moreover, this knowledge should increase your students' ability to evaluate psychological research and come to their own conclusions regarding potential cause-and-effect relations. Before moving on to other material, however, you would do well to spend a bit of time discussing one other matter that I have found often plagues students in the research methods course, especially those who have learned and embraced the well-known mantra, "correlation does not equal causation."

Once students are able to distinguish the difference between experimental and nonexperimental research methods, they often fail to see how researchers can use the findings from nonexperimental studies to draw causal inferences. "The researchers didn't manipulate anything," the students protest, "so they can't conclude that smoking *causes* lung cancer," for example. What students often fail to see is that the combined findings from several different studies can provide convincing, maybe even conclusive, evidence that two or more variables are, in fact, causally related. Researchers sometimes refer to this as *triangulation of evidence.*

Although no research of which I am aware has randomly assigned participants to "smoking" and "no smoking" conditions and subsequently analyzed the incidence of lung cancer in the two groups, mounds of data gathered over many years provide fairly conclusive evidence that "Smoking is by far the leading risk factor for lung cancer" and that "Tobacco smoke causes more than 8 out of 10 cases of lung cancer" (http://www.cancer.org/docroot/CRI/content/CRI_2_2_2x_What_Causes_Non-small_Cell_Lung_Cancer.asp?sitearea=).

"If experimental designs are unparalleled in their ability to allow researchers to infer causation, how, then," one of your students might ask, "can findings from studies using nonexperimental designs allow researchers also to make causal statements? Didn't you say that experiments are the only type of research method that allows researchers to state that one variable *caused* changes in another?" More than 40 years ago, Sir Austin Bradford Hill (1965) published a highly influential paper that attempted to delineate how researchers might use findings from nonexperimental studies to make inferences regarding causation. Specifically, Hill asked, "What aspects of [an] association should we especially consider before deciding that the most likely interpretation of it is causation?" (p. 295). In response to students' questions regarding correlation and causation, you would do well to spend some time discussing Hill's ideas on the matter (see also Ruscio, 2006).

Hill suggested that researchers should consider the following criteria when attempting to determine if relations might be causal in nature (if your time in class is limited, you may want to discuss only a few of these):

1. *Strength.* A strong relation between two variables—caloric intake and obesity, for example—might point to a possible causal relation between the two. In contrast, a weak relation, although not necessarily precluding causation, would make such a conclusion considerably more tenuous.
2. *Consistency.* The relation between two causally linked variables should also be consistent. Whereas a small number of studies showing a relation between caloric intake and obesity may not allow researchers to conclude that the relation is "real," consistent findings across a larger number of studies—especially when the studies have used disparate methods—make it unlikely that the relation was simply due to chance and may even point to a causal relation between the two.
3. *Specificity.* Specificity refers to whether a variable is related only to one other variable (i.e., it is specific) or to many variables (i.e., it is not specific). For example, although caloric intake is linked to obesity, it is also linked to other types of disease, including Alzheimer's disease (e.g., Grant, Campbell, Itzhaki, & Savory, 2002). Thus the relation between caloric intake and obesity is not specific. The more specific a relation is, the more likely it is causal.
4. *Temporality.* If changes in one variable always precede changes in another, there is a chance the two are causally related. Because excessive caloric intake often precedes cases of obesity, there may be a causal link between the two. Importantly, however, this does not rule out *reciprocal causality* (see Ruscio, 2006). For example, although excessive caloric intake might lead to obesity, obesity may subsequently lead to excessive caloric intake, thus creating a vicious cycle. Myopic analysis might overlook the reciprocal causal relation between these two variables.
5. *Biological gradient* (or *dose–response relation*; Ruscio, 2006). In the case of caloric intake and obesity, biological gradient suggests that greater caloric intake should be linked with a greater incidence of obesity. Conversely, if the relation was more complex (e.g., as caloric intake increased, obesity first increased, then decreased), it might call into question the causal nature of the relation.

6. *Plausibility*. Plausibility asks if there is a reasonable explanation for why two variables *could* be causally related. In the case of caloric intake and obesity, researchers are well aware that weight loss and weight gain tend to be a function of overall calorie expenditure. Therefore, if caloric intake is excessive, weight gain seems a likely outcome, and the causal relation between caloric intake and obesity seems plausible.

7. *Coherence*. Although researchers may deduce a plausible explanation for a causal relation, what they observe should not be at odds with what they already know about some phenomenon. In other words, a cause-and-effect explanation is possible only insofar as it concurs with existing data. For example, the causal relation between caloric intake and obesity seems more likely given that obesity is much less prevalent in countries where famine is present.

8. *Experiment* (although *quasi-experiment* might be more appropriate). Does manipulation of the possible "cause" produce results consistent with a cause-and-effect hypothesis? For example, researchers might limit caloric intake in some individuals and observe whether obesity decreases. Although such a manipulation may not rule out other causal factors (especially when there is no control group comparison), it does provide evidence for causation.

Although the preceding criteria provide evidence for a possible causal relation between two variables, especially when several of the criteria are present, they by no means provide authoritative "proof" that causation exists. Rather, only through controlled experimentation can researchers be certain that changes in one variable caused changes in another variable. As Hill stated over 40 years ago:

> None of my . . . viewpoints can bring indisputable evidence for or against the cause-and-effect hypothesis and none can be required as a *sine qua non.* What they can do, with greater or less strength, is to help us to make up our minds on the fundamental question—is there any other way of explaining the set of facts before us, is there any other answer equally, or more, likely than cause and effect? (Hill, 1965, p. 299)

However, for ethical reasons or otherwise, experimental designs often are not possible or feasible. Thus your students should be familiar with Hill's criteria and understand that triangulation of evidence may provide strong support for a causal relation between two variables.

References

Boring, E. G. (1957). *A history of experimental psychology* (2nd ed.). Englewood Cliffs, NJ: Prentice-Hall.

Bouchard, T. J., Jr., Lykken, D. T., McGue, M., Segal, N. L., & Tellegen, A. (1990). Sources of human psychological differences: The Minnesota Study of Twins Reared Apart. *Science, 250,* 223–228.

Bouchard, T. J., Jr., & Pedersen, N. (1999). Twins reared apart: Nature's double experiment. In M. C. LaBuda & E. L. Grigorenko (Eds.), *On the way to individuality: Current methodological issues in behavioral genetics* (pp. 71–93). Commack, NY: Nova Scientific Publishers.

Carr, J. E., & Austin, J. (1997). A classroom demonstration of single-subject research designs. *Teaching of Psychology, 24,* 188–190.

Cronbach, L. J. (1957). The two disciplines of scientific psychology. *American Psychologist, 12,* 671–684.

Eysenck, H. J. (1995). Can we study intelligence using the experimental method? *Intelligence, 20,* 217–228.

Goodwin, C. J. (2005). *A history of modern psychology* (2nd ed.). Hoboken, NJ: Wiley.

Grant, W. B., Campbell, A., Itzhaki, R. F., & Savory, J. (2002). The significance of environmental factors in the etiology of Alzheimer's disease. *Journal of Alzheimer's Disease, 4,* 179–189.

Griffore, R., Kallen, D., Popovich, S., & Powell, V. (1990). Gender differences in correlates of college students' self-esteem. *College Student Journal, 24,* 287–291.

Hill, A. B. (1965). The environment and disease: Association or causation? *Proceedings of the Royal Society of Medicine, 58,* 295–300.

Loftus, E. F. (1975). Leading questions and the eyewitness report. *Cognitive Psychology, 7,* 560–572.

Marchione, M. (2006, March 5). Soda causes obesity, researchers assert. *The San Diego Union-Tribune.* Retrieved May 5, 2006, from http://www.signonsandiego.com/uniontrib/20060305/news_1n5soda.html

Milgram, S. (1963). Behavioral study of obedience. *Journal of Abnormal and Social Psychology, 67,* 371–378.

Milgram, S. (1974). *Obedience to authority.* New York: Harper.

Robins, R. W., Trzesniewski, K. H., Tracy, J. L., Gosling, S. D., & Potter, J. (2002). Global self-esteem across the lifespan. *Psychology and Aging, 17,* 423–434.

Ruscio, J. (2006). *Critical thinking in psychology: Separating sense from nonsense* (2nd ed.). Belmont, CA: Thomson Wadsworth.

Woodworth, R. S. (1938). *Experimental psychology.* New York: Holt.

Chapter 7

Teaching the Relation between Statistics and Research Methods

For many students, the prospect of taking research methods shortly after completing a statistics course does not exactly elicit thoughts of excitement. In fact, many psychology students may even try to motivate themselves by saying, "If only I can get through statistics and research methods, then I can get into some *real* psychology classes." Although many of our students tend not to be fond of statistics or research methods, my experience suggests that they often view research methods as the lesser of two evils. One possible reason for this belief may be that students often equate statistics with math, which many of them dislike, or even fear. So having completed their statistics courses, and assuming they won't have to do any further "math," our students are sometimes disappointed to find that statistics and research methods are so closely related that the latter cannot be discussed without reference to the former. True, many research methods instructors do not focus on "math" to the same extent that most statistics instructors do, but discussion of statistics is vital for understanding research methods or, more specifically, the inferences researchers can make based on the methods they use. Thus the purpose of this chapter is to discuss ways you can effectively teach students the relation between statistics and research methods. This may seem like a daunting task, but I have found that teaching this relation may in fact enhance students' interest in statistics, because they come to understand *how* researchers use statistics to learn more about the psychological phenomena they study.

The first step in teaching students the relation between statistics and research methods is simply to state that there is such a relation and that much of the research methods course will focus on two ways in which statistical analysis depends on research design. The first of these is that the type of research design one uses in a study determines which statistic is most appropriate for analyzing the resulting data. The second is that different types of research designs have a distinctive impact on between- and within-groups variability, which affects the likelihood that a statistically significant outcome will emerge.

One way to introduce your students to the relation between statistics and research methods is by presenting, comparing, and discussing the definitions of statistics and research design. Specifically, *statistics* is

> the theory and method of analyzing quantitative data obtained from samples of observations in order to study and compare sources of variance of phenomena, to help make decisions to accept or reject hypothesized relations between the phenomena, and to aid in drawing reliable inferences from empirical observations. (Kerlinger & Lee, 2000, p. 259)

In contrast, *research design* is

> the plan and structure of investigation, conceived so as to obtain answers to research questions. The plan is the overall scheme or program of the research. It includes an outline of what the investigator will do, from writing the hypotheses and the operational implications to the final analysis of data. (Kerlinger & Lee, 2000, p. 449)

In other words, research design defines a general strategy for conducting a study, and statistics refers generally to a method for analyzing and interpreting the data one has collected during a study. Without research design, statistics would have no data to analyze or interpret; without statistics, research design would outline a method for collecting data but, in most cases, provide no way to interpret those data (see Chapter 8 for a discussion of research methods that historically have not relied on statistical analysis for interpreting data). Hopefully, after discussing these topics, your students will begin to see that statistics and research design are inexorably linked.

Identifying Research Questions

Arguably, the most important step in the research process is identifying the right question to ask (Johnston & Pennypacker, 1993). Although the relation between statistics and research design is more evident at subsequent stages of the research process (e.g., when identifying which inferential statistic to use), the specific question that researchers attempt to answer by conducting a study and analyzing data sets the entire process in motion. Until researchers have identified the specific research question they hope to answer, they cannot operationally define their variables of interest (see Chapter 5). Moreover, the way in which researchers measure their variables depends on how they have chosen to operationally define them. Because both research design and statistical analysis depend on measurement, it becomes clear that teaching your students to identify appropriate research questions is vital to understanding the link between design and analysis.

Many research methods textbooks spend a good amount of time discussing possible sources of research ideas (see Smith & Davis, 2007), so I will not dwell on that information here. It is worth explaining to your students, though, that developing a research question is not as complicated as they might think. I have found that many students struggle to develop research questions because they mistakenly believe that interesting questions come only from experienced researchers. Clearly, researchers do get better at identifying useful questions as they gain familiarity with the existing literature, but identifying an interesting research question does not necessarily depend on a long, drawn-out relation with a monstrous stack of journal articles. Rather, it may arise after identifying a gap in the extant literature, or it may follow some observation made on the way to class. Regardless of the specific research question, though, your students should understand that, in order to be useful, the questions they identify *must* be testable (see Chapter 2).

Statistical Analysis and Research Design: Choosing the Appropriate Statistic

Once your students understand that identifying an appropriate research question initiates the entire research process, you can more meaningfully introduce the first important way in which statistics and research design are related, namely that the type of research design one uses determines which statistical analysis is most appropriate. I am not suggesting that statistical analysis and research design is always so simplistic. In fact, a brief perusal of recent discussions on statistics and research design makes it more than evident that these are complicated topics. Nevertheless, asking your students to think about (a) the number of independent variables (IVs) or predictor variables in a study, (b) how a researcher assigned participants to groups, and (c) scales of measurement will help them begin to see more clearly how statistics and research design are related.

Because of the complex nature of statistical analysis and research design, and because it would be impossible to cover these issues completely in a single chapter, I will not discuss in detail all of the criteria that ultimately determine which statistical analysis goes with which research design. Rather, my discussion will focus on the most elementary statistical analyses and research designs that students typically encounter in their introductory statistics and research methods courses.

Number of Predictor Variables and/or IVs (and Groups)

As you well know, studies that have no predictor variables or IVs are correlational in nature, a type of research design that "treats all the measured variables alike" (Woodworth, 1938, p. 3). The purpose of a correlational study is simply to measure the relation between two (or more) variables. In contrast, studies that contain one or more predictor variables—and consequently, at least two groups—are ex post facto studies, which, like correlational designs, are also nonexperimental in nature. Finally, studies that include the explicit manipulation of one or more IVs are experiments, a type of research design that, like ex post facto designs, also contains at least two groups. However, in contrast with ex post facto designs, researchers define their groups by exposing subsets of participants to different treatment conditions, not by identifying some preexisting characteristic such as sex or year in school. Ideally, by this point in the semester, your students will be able to differentiate these research designs.

Once your students have identified the number of predictor variables or IVs in a study, they can then determine *how many groups* are present in it. If a study contains *zero* predictor variables or IVs and, consequently, only one group of participants, and a researcher is simply attempting to identify a relation between variables in members of that group, then some type of correlational or regression analysis is most appropriate. If a study contains *one* predictor variable or IV and, consequently, *two or more groups*, then the statistic of choice would be one that analyzes group differences. Finally, if a study contains *two or more* predictor variables or IVs, and consequently *at least four groups*, then a fact-orial analysis is most appropriate. The specific statistical analysis, however, depends on additional factors.

Group Assignment

Once your students can identify how many groups are in a study, they will also need to determine how researchers assigned participants to those groups—if there are two or more groups. Specifically, they will need to know whether there are *independent* groups, *dependent* (or *correlated*) groups, or *mixed* groups (i.e., a combination of independent and dependent groups). Independent groups are those in which one participant's assignment to a group is completely independent of another participant's assignment to a group. For example, when conducting an ex post facto study on sex differences in self-esteem, one participant's assignment to the "male" condition is independent of whether the previous or subsequent participant is in the "male" or "female" condition. Rather, researchers place participants into a group based on the preexisting characteristic of sex. Similarly, the process of random assignment in experimental designs assures that the assignment of a participant to one treatment condition is completely independent of the condition to which researchers assign another participant.

In contrast, dependent-groups designs are those in which assignment of a participant to one group *depends* on the group to which researchers assign another participant. As you know, there are three specific types of dependent designs: (a) *matched pairs* or *matched sets*, in which researchers match participants on some variable other than the predictor variable or IV and then place them into different groups; (b) *natural pairs* or *natural sets*, in which researchers take advantage of some preexisting relationship between participants (e.g., twins) and place them into different groups; and (c) *repeated-measures* designs, in which researchers measure each participant's behavior under each treatment condition.

Finally, mixed designs are those in which there is some combination of independent and dependent groups. Probably the most common of these mixed designs is the *pretest–posttest control-group design* (Campbell & Stanley, 1963). Here, researchers randomly assign participants to two or more treatment conditions and then measure the dependent variable (DV) both before and after manipulation of the IV (i.e., pretest–posttest, or measurement at Time 1 and Time 2). The use of random assignment creates independent groups with regard to the particular treatment conditions, and the use of pretest and posttest measures constitutes a form of dependent groups, specifically repeated-measures. A combination of independent and dependent groups is also possible with ex post facto designs and with research designs that incorporate aspects of both ex post facto and experimental designs. For example, Green, Fry, and Myerson (1994) examined how the delay to a hypothetical monetary reward ($1,000 or $10,000) reduced the subjective value of that reward in children, young adults, and older adults. Because their participants were of different ages, their group membership was independent (i.e., no participant's group membership depended on that of another participant). In addition, because Green et al. did not treat the groups differently (i.e., there was no manipulation of this variable), this part of the design was ex post facto in nature. However, because Green et al. exposed their participants to each of the different reward conditions ($1,000 and $10,000), this part of the design was dependent (repeated-measures) and experimental.

Research methods textbooks tend to spend a good amount of time discussing experimental research designs, so your students will probably have little trouble identifying different types of group assignment within the context of experiments. However, I have found that students often have trouble identifying different types of group assignment in ex post facto designs or in designs that integrate both ex post facto and experimental designs. In experiments, the use of random assignment often provides a cue to the researchers' use of independent groups, but students sometimes forget that "independent" technically means that one participant's assignment to a treatment condition is completely independent of another participant's assignment. So even though a study on sex differences, for example, constitutes an example of an independent-groups design, students may fail to recognize that this design entails independent groups. You would do well to remind your students that different types of group assignments can be present in both experiments and ex post facto designs and in research designs that incorporate aspects of both experimental and ex post facto designs.

Scales of Measurement

Once you have established the importance of identifying the number of predictor variables and IVs and the number of groups in a study, you should spend some time discussing how scales of measurement come into play with regard to statistical analysis and research design. This would be a good time for your students to review their notes and readings on scales of measurement and the specific characteristics that define nominal, ordinal, interval, and ratio scales (see Chapter 5).

Having reintroduced scales of measurement in this way, you now can tell your students that, generally speaking, data that are interval or ratio in nature typically require the use of *parametric* statistics, whereas data that are nominal or ordinal in nature require *nonparametric* statistical tests. Although most students will be familiar with some common parametric tests from their statistics courses, I have found that many of them are less familiar with nonparametric statistics, simply because their statistics instructors may not have had enough time to discuss them in any detail. In any case, you may wish to spend some time discussing the differences between parametric and nonparametric statistical analyses. Specifically, the use of parametric statistics requires making certain assumptions regarding the population from which researchers choose their participants (normally distributed observations, equal group variances, and interval or ratio data). In contrast, nonparametric, or "distribution-free," statistics are appropriate in situations in which one or more of these assumptions do not hold (Kerlinger & Lee, 2000).

Thus in correlational designs that measure variables on interval or ratio scales, a Pearson correlation coefficient is the most appropriate statistic; with at least one variable measured on an ordinal scale, which violates the assumption of equidistant intervals between adjacent observations, a Spearman correlation coefficient is the best choice. Similarly, whereas a two-group design that produces criterion- or dependent-variable measures on an interval scale would require the use of a *t* test (independent or dependent, depending on group assignment), the same two-group design with ordinal data would require a Mann–Whitney *U* (independent groups) or Wilcoxon Test (dependent groups); and a multiple-groups design with ratio data would typically require an analysis of variance (ANOVA), whereas a multiple-groups design with ordinal data would employ a Kruskal–Wallis test. Depending on the time available and your course objectives, you may wish to focus only on the most common parametric statistics in the hope that your students will learn additional statistical analyses in later courses. In any case, the main point is that your students should come away from your course with awareness that the scale of the measured variables affects the type of statistical analysis that is most appropriate.

As discussed elsewhere in this book, one useful way to improve your students' understanding of this information is to create scenarios or have them read journal articles in which they work their way through each of the questions listed above and determine the specific research design and which statistic they would use to analyze their data. After they have read a scenario, I ask the students to tell me how many groups are in the study, how researchers assigned the participants to different groups, and the scale of measurement for the DV. Based on this information, they can determine the most appropriate statistical analysis. With extensive practice, your students will likely become much more efficient at gleaning the information they need to make decisions regarding statistical analysis.

Finally, although you may be tempted to ask your students to memorize this information, they will likely be better off—and ultimately learn the material better—if you ask them to memorize the decision-making process I have outlined above. Teaching your students to follow this decision-making process, and urging them to consult a statistics book (or similar resource) for additional information on specific statistical analyses, will likely produce a deeper understanding of the relation between statistical analysis and research design.

Research Design and Statistical Analysis: The Impact of Between- and Within-Groups Variability

As your students should be able to see by now, the type of design that researchers choose to use in their studies directly affects the specific statistical tests they will use to analyze their data. However, research design and statistical analysis are related in yet another important way: The type of research design that researchers choose affects the amount of variability observed in a study. More specifically, research design affects both between- and within-groups variability, which then alters the probability that one will observe a statistically significant outcome. So as you discuss different research designs throughout the semester, remember to focus your students' attention on how different designs affect between- and within-groups variability.

Your students should remember between- and within-groups variability from their statistics courses, but if you find that they don't, you should spend a bit of time discussing them. Understanding these important ideas will likely enhance your students' comprehension of the relation between statistics and research design.

Variability

Before you introduce your students to the more specific notions of between- and within-groups variability, you might wish to back up one step and briefly discuss with them what *variability* means within the context of scientific discourse. Generally speaking, variability refers to "any differences among events" (Johnston & Pennypacker, 1993, p. 371). For example, students' interests within the field of psychology might be different, instructors' teaching styles might be different, and even the amount of information that readers of this book find useful might be different. Although this idea might seem exceedingly simple to your students, reviewing the definition of variability will help them better understand between- and within-groups variability when you discuss these ideas.

Hands-on Tip

Connor (2003) described a simple activity that might help your students better understand the concept of variability. Connor asked her students to imagine a line of numbers ranging from 0 (*absolutely do not like at all*) to 10 (*completely and totally like*) stretching across the front of the classroom. She then asked a group of volunteers to respond to a number of questions (e.g., "How much do you like chocolate?") by standing on the spot that would represent their particular response. Connor reported that students found the activity interesting and less aversive than other ways of teaching the same material. Using variations of this activity in which you construct questions designed to produce different types of variability (e.g., normal, bimodal, and skewed distributions) might help your students understand the concept of variability as well as the more specific concepts of between- and within-groups variability.

Between-groups Variability

In a research design that examines the differences between two or more groups, there are two types of variability that can affect researchers' ability to make accurate inferences based on their observations. The first is between-groups variability, which refers to systematic differences *between* groups on some criterion or dependent measure. When introducing the concept of between-groups variability to your students, it might be best to start off with the following question: "If a researcher observes that two or more groups are systematically different at the end of a study, what might be responsible for the observed differences?"

To help answer this question, discuss with your students some representative studies that might clarify their understanding of between-groups variability. Consider again, for example, Green et al.'s (1994) study on the discounting of hypothetical monetary rewards. Green et al. observed that older adults discounted, or devalued, delayed rewards to a lesser extent than younger adults or children. Because no experimental manipulation of age occurred in the study, one can assume that older adults discounted delayed rewards differently than younger adults and children prior to the start of the study. In other words, the between-groups variability that Green et al. observed in their study was not a function of any experimental manipulation. Rather, it was a function of differences in older and younger adults and children that already existed.

Just as preexisting differences can account for observed group differences, so too can differences produced by an explicit experimental manipulation. For example, imagine that a researcher wanted to know whether hearing a lecture or experiencing an alternative teaching method produced better exam scores in college students (e.g., Saville, Zinn, Neef, Van Norman, & Ferreri, 2006). At the end of the study, the researcher found that students who heard a lecture had an average exam score of 75%, whereas students who experienced the alternative teaching method had an average exam score of 90%. The difference in average exam scores between the groups in this study would represent variability produced by the researcher's experimental manipulation.

Hands-on Tip

To illustrate the idea of between-groups variability, you could incorporate Connor's (2003) activity into your classroom. A simple way to show between-groups variability without having to introduce a complicated experimental manipulation would be to separate your students into a group of men and a group of women and then examine if group differences emerge. A question like, "How do you feel about research methods?" might provide you with little between-groups variability, but a more gender-stereotypical question such as, "How much do you enjoy watching professional football on Sunday afternoons?" might produce interesting differences.

Ideally, your students will see that preexisting differences between groups, as well as differences produced by some experimental manipulation, may be responsible for between-groups variability observed in a study.

Within-groups Variability

Whereas between-groups variability obviously refers to systematic differences between groups, within-groups (or error) variability refers to differences *within* a group on some criterion or dependent measure. For example, although students who experience an alternative teaching method might earn better exam scores *on average* than students who hear a lecture, there might also be considerable variability in the exam scores within each group. In fact, some students in the lecture condition might actually earn better exam scores than some of the students who experienced the alternative teaching method. Regardless of whether there is overlap between the two groups, some scores in both conditions will fall above the group average just as some scores will fall below the group average. An appropriate question, then, to ask your students might be: "If students in the lecture or alternative method condition all experienced the same treatment (i.e., the same level of the IV), why didn't they all earn the same exam score?" Or put differently, "What might be responsible for differences observed *within* each of these groups?"

At this point, you should spend some time discussing two primary sources of within-groups variability: individual differences and measurement error (Smith & Davis, 2007). The first source of within-groups variability is *individual differences*. In a nutshell, the notion of individual differences points to a simple fact: People differ. Some people are taller than others, some people run faster than others, and some people are more intelligent than others. Consequently, when students listen to a lecture and subsequently take an exam, one can expect that their exam scores will vary, simply because the students are different in myriad ways that likely contribute, in one form or another, to how well they do on the exam.

Hands-on Tip

If you feel inclined to use an activity to help illustrate the idea of individual differences, Connor's (2003) class activity works well here, too. Your students will probably respond differently to almost any question you ask them.

A second source of within-groups variability is *measurement error*, which I discussed in some detail in Chapter 5. To provide a simple example to your students, assume once again that they have either heard a lecture or experienced an alternative teaching method and then took an exam. The way an instructor grades an exam might contribute to differences within groups. For example, imagine that one question on the exam is a rather complicated 10-point essay question. While grading each student's essay, it is possible that the instructor's grading criteria might change ever so slightly from student to student. Given the difficulty that sometimes comes with grading essay questions, this outcome is certainly a possibility. In this way, the presence of *random* measurement error (see Chapter 5) would contribute to differences observed within a group.

"Statistic" as "Between-groups Variability/ Within-groups Variability"

By this point, your students will ideally understand between- and within-groups variability as well as what produces each. They should now be ready to discuss how these measures ultimately affect the likelihood of obtaining statistically significant outcomes.

Ask your students to recall the specific equation for an independent-groups *t* test or a one-way ANOVA for independent groups, and many are likely to respond with a shrug of the shoulders. However, most will likely tell you that the equation for a *t* test was rather

complex, as was the series of calculations involved in finding the
F ratio for an ANOVA. So students tend to be surprised when they
find out that all statistics that examine group differences reduce, in
one form or another, to a relatively simple ratio:

$$\text{Statistic} = \frac{\text{Between-groups variability}}{\text{Within-groups variability}}$$

In other words, the statistical value that researchers obtain after
analyzing their data is a function of how much variability exists
between groups and how much variability exists within groups.

Hands-on Tip

To introduce your students to the idea of how between- and within-
groups variability affects the likelihood of obtaining a statistically
significant outcome, you may wish to include one or both of the
following activities in your class. The first of these involves manipulating numbers in a data set so students can see how the manipulations
affect an F ratio (you could easily use the same activity with a t test).
Specifically, Johnson (1989) introduced to his students several data
sets, each of which consisted of three groups of data (representing
three levels of an IV: A, B, & C) and contained five data points apiece.
The data for his first set consisted of the same numbers. For example:

A	B	C
10	10	10
10	10	10
10	10	10
10	10	10
10	10	10

Johnson then discussed with his students why this data set had no
between- or within-groups variability. He also showed them an ANOVA
source table and how these values produced an F ratio of zero. Next,
Johnson changed all of the values for one group (e.g., changing Group
C from 10 to 20) and again discussed between- and within-groups variability as well as how this change altered the F ratio. In short, by changing
the values both within and across groups, Johnson was able to show how
increased between- and within-groups variability affected the F ratio.
    Sciutto (2000) described a second activity that you may find useful
for teaching students about between- and within-groups variability

and how each affects the likelihood of obtaining a significant outcome. Following a discussion of between- and within-groups variability, Sciutto introduced objects that represented individual differences (small action figures), measurement error (stopwatches), and treatment effects (different size batteries). He then asked a student to volunteer to hold two boxes, into which Sciutto randomly placed the action figures and stopwatches. At this point, Sciutto asked the student to state whether he could tell the difference in weight between the two boxes and how sure (on a 100-point scale) he was of his statement. Sciutto then manipulated between-groups variability (i.e., "treatment") by systematically adding different size batteries to one of the boxes and reduced within-groups variability by removing action figures (individual differences) and stopwatches (measurement error) from each box. After each "manipulation," Sciutto asked the student to state whether there was a difference between boxes and to rate his certainty. Sciutto found that students' ratings of certainty were positively related to the presence of a treatment effect (i.e., a large battery in one of the boxes) and the absence of individual differences and measurement error (i.e., few action figures or watches in the boxes).

Now that your students are comfortable with the concepts of between- and within-groups variability and how they influence the statistical results one obtains in a study, it is time to discuss how research design affects between- and within-groups variability. Before doing so, however, you should reintroduce an earlier question: "If a researcher observes that two or more groups are systematically different at the end of a study, what might be responsible for the observed differences?"

As noted above, all statistics that examine group differences reduce to the following equation:

$$\text{Statistic} = \frac{\text{Between-groups variability}}{\text{Within-groups variability}}$$

Assuming your students now understand this equation and the concepts of between- and within-groups variability, you can alter the equation slightly, as described below, in hopes of helping students to understand more specifically what ultimately contributes to group differences. As you have already discussed with your students by now, between-groups variability refers to systematic differences between groups, and within-groups variability refers to differences within groups. You have also explained that a systematic difference between groups results when groups are different to begin with (as in ex post facto studies) or when an experimental manipulation produces group differences. Finally, you have introduced the idea that within-groups variability is a function of individual differences or measurement error. What your students may not realize, however, is that individual differences or measurement error may also contribute to differences *between* groups. To begin your discussion of the contribution of within-groups variability to overall between-groups variability, you should present a new version of our earlier equation:

$$\text{Statistic} = \frac{\text{Between-groups variability} + \text{Within-groups variability}}{\text{Within-groups variability}}$$

Now ask students to imagine that a researcher has randomly selected 100 participants from a larger population of 1000 individuals and then randomly assigned them to different treatment conditions. Because you will have likely discussed random selection and random assignment at this point in the semester, your students should understand how these processes will probably create groups that are *approximately* equal, but not *exactly* the same.

Hands-on Tip

To prove this point, you may want to include a simple activity such as the following. Randomly select and then assign a number of your students to one of two groups and then calculate their average height. Although the average height of the two groups may be comparable, it will likely not be identical. This simple activity quickly shows students that individual differences (and possibly measurement error, depending on how you decide to obtain each person's height) can contribute to a difference between groups. Depending on the extent of the individual differences or measurement error, the difference between groups can be exceedingly small or surprisingly large.

Just as Johnson (1989) used sample data sets to show how between- and within-groups variability contribute to the *F* ratio, so too can you use the same process to show students how within-groups variability, in the form of individual differences and measurement error, can contribute to overall between-groups variability.

Hands-on Tip

You could also use an example such as the following. I ask my students to imagine that a researcher is interested in examining the extent to which exercise improves self-esteem in college students. The researcher randomly selects students and then assigns them to either an exercise condition or a no-exercise condition. Prior to manipulating exercise, the researcher pretests each student and subsequently finds that there is a nonsignificant, half-point difference in average self-esteem between the two groups, presumably because of individual differences. Six weeks later, the researcher again measures the self-esteem of each student and now finds that there is a significant 11.5-point difference between the two groups. Assuming that the half-point difference has "carried over" to the posttest, our researcher can reasonably assume that individual differences or measurement error contributed one-half point to the overall difference at the end of the study and that exercise was responsible for the remaining 11 points.

Because within-groups variability contributes to the overall between-groups variability observed in a study, you may find it useful to finish your discussion of this topic by showing your students the following further modified version of our original equation:

$$\text{Statistic} = \frac{\text{(Preexisting differences or IV)} + \text{(Individual differences and measurement error)}}{\text{(Individual differences and measurement error)}}$$

How Research Design Affects Between- and Within-groups Variability

The final step in teaching students the relation between statistics and research design is discussing with students how different research designs affect between- and within-groups variability, which together determine the likelihood of obtaining a statistically significant outcome.

From the preceding equations, one can quickly see that maximizing between-groups variability (i.e., increasing the number in the numerator) and minimizing within-groups variability (i.e., decreasing the number in the denominator) is the fastest route to obtaining statistical significance. For example, when between-groups variability is reduced to 0—in other words, when there are no systematic differences between groups—the equation will reduce to

$$\text{Statistic} = \frac{\text{Within-groups variability}}{\text{Within-groups variability}}$$

and your statistic will approach 1.0, which typically signals a non-significant outcome. Conversely, if between-groups variability greatly exceeds within-groups variability, your statistic will be large, a sure sign that your results are "real" and not due to chance.

Maximizing Between-groups Variability

As your students might guess, researchers often attempt to maximize between-groups variability by designing studies in which the groups are as different as possible. More specifically, in an ex post facto study, in which no experimental manipulation occurs, a researcher is apt to obtain a significant outcome if the participants in different groups are considerably different, on average, to begin with. Take, for example, a study in which a researcher wants to know the extent to which self-esteem changes across the lifespan (e.g., Robins & Trzesniewski, 2005). Because 5-year-olds and 6-year-olds are similar in terms of psychological development, it probably wouldn't be a good idea to come to any conclusions based on the results of a study that compared the self-esteem of 5- and 6-year-olds. Comparing children, teenagers, and older adults is much more likely to produce an outcome that accurately describes age differences in self-esteem.

Similarly, in experimental designs, using meaningfully different levels of an IV will produce maximum between-groups variability (assuming the IV has an effect). To illustrate, imagine again that a researcher wants to know whether exercise has a positive effect, this time on blood pressure. As your students can probably surmise, the easiest way to test this would be to use a standard two-group design in which one group exercises and another group does not. However, to determine convincingly whether exercise affects blood pressure, it would probably not be a good idea to operationally define "exercise" as walking very slowly for 2 minutes every other day. Instead, our researcher would probably want to utilize two meaningfully different amounts of exercise, for example, 30 minutes of brisk walking every day versus no planned exercise. If exercise has an effect on blood pressure, significant differences are more likely to show up under these conditions.

Minimizing Within-groups Variability

Just as maximizing between-groups variability will increase the likelihood of obtaining a statistically significant outcome, so too will minimizing within-groups variability. There are two primary ways to decrease within-groups variability: use similar participants or use a larger number of participants.

As your students know by now, within-groups variability refers to how much participants in a group differ from one another. If participants are very different, within-groups variability will be large; if participants are more similar, within-groups variability will be smaller. Thus a simple way to reduce within-groups variability is to use participants who are similar in some way. Again, consider the example in which a researcher randomly assigns participants to exercise or no-exercise conditions. Prior to making group assignments, the researcher might wish to control within-groups variability by limiting eligible participants to those who are similar in some way, for example, women who fall within a certain weight range, who do not take any blood pressure medication, and who have agreed to consume no more than 2,000 calories per day.

Another way to capitalize on similarities among research participants—and thus reduce within-groups variability—is to use research designs that create an explicit relation between groups. Whereas random assignment creates equivalent groups by equally distributing extraneous sources of variation, the dependent-groups designs discussed earlier create equal groups by (a) matching participants on extraneous variables; (b) using participants who have naturally occurring relationships (e.g., twins) and, consequently, are similar in some important way; or (c) using the same participants in a repeated-measures design. With each of these designs, a researcher creates a relationship that ultimately serves to make participants more similar to one another. For example, when attempting to examine the effects of exercise on blood pressure, a researcher who uses random assignment is working on the assumption that this procedure will eventually create groups whose average weight, a possible extraneous variable, is approximately the same. However, random assignment does not assure that extraneous variables will be distributed equally (Smith & Davis, 2007). In contrast, using a repeated-measures design nearly assures our researcher that participants in the exercise and no-exercise conditions will have the same average weight—simply because each group consists of the same participants.

Once your students understand how using similar participants decreases within-groups variability, you can introduce a second way researchers attempt to minimize within-groups variability in their studies: by increasing the number of participants.

Hands-on Tip

Although some of your students may find this idea counterintuitive, a relatively simple activity may help them to understand the underlying rationale. First, randomly choose two or three students from your class and ask them to estimate how similar they are, on average, in terms of age, height, hair color, and so on, to the other students in the "sample." With a larger class, it is especially likely that the students will be more different than similar. Then, choose a few more students to add to the sample and ask the same question. After repeating this procedure a few more times, your students will likely find that there are more and more people in the sample who are similar to them in one way or another *and* that the people in the larger sample are much more alike, on average.

Finally, because measurement error can affect within-groups variability, your students should be aware that researchers typically take steps to measure their variables as accurately as possible. For example, if a researcher wants to measure how fast participants can run 100 meters, counting aloud (i.e., "1 one-thousand, 2 one-thousand, 3 one-thousand, 4 one-thousand . . .") would be much less accurate, and ultimately lead to greater measurement error, than using a stopwatch. Similarly, if researchers want to know whether lecture or an alternative teaching method produce better exam scores, they would take steps to assure that they graded the exams as carefully and accurately as possible (see Chapter 5 for a further discussion of measurement error).

Conclusion

Although your students may initially wince at the thought of having to learn the relation between statistics and research methods, they may be relieved, if not excited, to learn that this relation isn't too terribly complicated. Focusing on two primary topics—how different research designs require different statistical analyses and how different research designs affect the likelihood of obtaining statistical significance—will increase the chances that your students will learn about this relation and appreciate its importance.

References

Campbell, D., & Stanley, J. (1963). *Experimental and quasi-experimental designs for research*. Chicago: Rand-McNally.

Connor, J. M. (2003). Making statistics come alive: Using space and students' bodies to illustrate statistical concepts. *Teaching of Psychology*, *30*, 141–143.

Green, L., Fry, A. F., & Myerson, J. (1994). Discounting of delayed rewards: A lifespan comparison. *Psychological Science*, *5*, 33–36.

Johnson, D. E. (1989). An intuitive approach to teaching analysis of variance. *Teaching of Psychology*, *16*, 67–68.

Johnston, J. M., & Pennypacker, H. S. (1993). *Strategies and tactics of behavioral research* (2nd ed.). Hillsdale, NJ: Erlbaum.

Kerlinger, F. N., & Lee, H. B. (2000). *Foundations of behavioral research* (4th ed.). Orlando, FL: Harcourt.

Robins, R. W., & Trzesniewski, K. H. (2005). Self-esteem development across the lifespan. *Current Directions in Psychological Science*, *14*, 158–162.

Saville, B. K., Zinn, T. E., Neef, N. A., Van Norman, R., & Ferreri, S. J. (2006). A comparison of interteaching and lecture in the college classroom. *Journal of Applied Behavior Analysis*, *39*, 49–61.

Sciutto, M. J. (2000). Demonstration of factors affecting the *F* ratio. *Teaching of Psychology*, *27*, 52–53.

Smith, R. A., & Davis, S. F. (2007). *The psychologist as detective: An introduction to conducting research in psychology* (4th ed.). Upper Saddle River, NJ: Prentice Hall.

Woodworth, R. S. (1938). *Experimental psychology*. New York: Holt.

Chapter 8

Teaching the Distinction between Large-N and Small-N Research Designs

No doubt, those who teach psychological research methods spend a good amount of time discussing with their students different types of experimental designs and the proper way to examine potential cause-and-effect relations between independent and dependent variables. Moreover, it is likely that a good amount—if not most—of that time is spent discussing the most common type of research design in the psychological sciences: large-N designs. However, it is also likely that most students receive considerably less exposure—if any at all—to another type of research design used in the field of psychology: small-N designs. Yet small-N designs hold an important place in the history of psychology. In fact, before the advent of large-N designs in the early 1900s, small-N designs were the method of choice for psychological researchers. Given their storied place in the history of our discipline, as well as the fact that there has been a resurgence in the use of small-N designs over the last 30 to 40 years, it seems important for instructors to spend at least some time in their re-search methods courses discussing these important, but somewhat neglected, research designs.

Large-N Designs

As you know, large-N designs can take on three general forms: between-groups designs, within-groups designs, and mixed designs. In between-groups designs, researchers randomly assign large numbers of participants (i.e., 30 or more per group) either to an experimental condition (or one of several experimental conditions), which receives the treatment(s) under study, or a control condition, which does not receive the treatment. Researchers then compare the differences across groups to determine if the observed differences are meaningful. In within-groups designs, researchers observe a large group of participants both before and after the introduction of a treatment to see if there are meaningful differences in responding across conditions. In mixed designs, which include elements of both between- and within-groups designs, researchers randomly assign large numbers of participants to a control condition or one or more experimental conditions and then observe both groups before and after the introduction of the treatment to see if there are differences across groups and across time.

Regardless of the particular type of large-N design, researchers typically compare average group performances using inferential statistical analyses such as a t test or analysis of variance (ANOVA). If the differences between groups greatly exceed the differences within groups, the result is "statistically significant," and the researcher concludes that the independent variable, or treatment, and not some other random factor (i.e., "chance"), was likely responsible for the observed changes in the dependent variable. This type of experimentation is far and away the most common approach to examining causal relations in psychology (e.g., Baron & Perone, 1998; Blampied, 1999; Carr & Austin, 1997; Hubbard, Parsa, & Luthy, 1997). Moreover, the frequency with which researchers in psychology use large-N designs is evident by the amount of space these designs consume in undergraduate statistics or research methods textbooks.

A Brief History of Large-N Designs

William Sealy Gosset and Sir Ronald A. Fisher, whose seminal work on inferential statistics in the early 1900s paved the way for modern-day, group-based research designs, first introduced the concept of large-N designs into the psychological sciences. Gosset's derivation of the *t*-distribution (which he published under the pseudonym "Student") first appeared in 1908 in the journal *Biometrika* and was followed several years later by *Statistical Methods for Research Workers*, Sir Ronald A. Fisher's (1925) highly influential book, which introduced the ANOVA as a way for agriculturalists, and subsequently psychologists, to determine if there were meaningful between-groups differences in their dependent measures. By the mid-twentieth century, large-N designs had gained considerable popularity in psychology (Boring, 1954; Campbell & Stanley, 1963; Dukes, 1965), and by the late-twentieth century, most psychologists viewed large-N designs as a *sine qua non* for conducting sound experimental research (Campbell & Stanley, 1963; Saville & Buskist, 2003).

Small-N Designs

Unfortunately, because of the overwhelming emphasis on large-N designs in psychology, many undergraduates do not learn about small-N research designs, also known as single-subject experimental designs or single-case experimental designs. The latter titles, however, are misnomers, because small-N researchers rarely use a single participant (Saville & Buskist, 2003). As is true of large-N designs, the goals of small-N designs are to (a) identify cause-and-effect relations between independent and dependent variables and (b) rule out extraneous variables as potential causes of change in the dependent variable. In contrast to large-N designs, however, small-N designs typically analyze cause-and-effect relations using reversal designs and multiple-baseline designs (Baer, Wolf, & Risley, 1968). Examples of reversal designs include A-B-A and A-B-A-B designs, in which researchers investigate the effects of a single independent variable (B) by comparing the dependent variable of interest to the same dependent variable observed under baseline, or control, conditions (A); A-B-A-C designs, in which researchers compare the effects of two different independent variables (B and C) separately; and A-B-A-C-A-BC designs, in which researchers assess the effects of two (or more) independent variables (B and C), separately and then together, by measuring changes in the dependent variable relative to a baseline condition.

With all reversal designs, researchers typically alternate a baseline condition with one or more treatment conditions. For example, with the A-B-A design, researchers measure an individual participant's behavior first under a baseline, or control, condition and then under a treatment condition. To rule out extraneous factors as potential change agents (i.e., to assess internal validity), they reintroduce the baseline condition to see if behavior eventually reverts back to its pretreatment levels. With A-B-A-B or A-B-A-C designs, researchers reintroduce the treatment condition(s) yet again and observe changes in the dependent variable. With A-B-A-C-A-BC-A designs, researchers alternate two treatments, first separately and then together, with a baseline condition. This allows researchers to examine the interactive effects of two or more independent variables, just as one can do with large-N factorial designs.

With each of these designs, if behavior changes only with the introduction and removal of the treatment condition(s), the researcher can be relatively certain that the treatment(s), and not some extraneous factor, was the sole cause of these changes. Although practical matters such as time and money (if one is paying participants, for example) are important to consider, the more often researchers can introduce and remove the independent variable and produce contingent changes in the dependent variable, the more relatively certain they can be that there is a cause-and-effect relation between the two. Thus multiple introductions of the independent variable(s) constitute a form of replication and can help increase internal validity. Introducing the treatment condition a second time has at least one additional benefit: If the researcher is studying a behavior that is potentially harmful to the participants under study—for example, self-injurious behavior—using an A-B-A-B design allows the researcher to end the study under conditions in which the harmful behavior has been reduced or even eliminated.

A final type of small-N design is the multiple-baseline design (Baer et al., 1968), in which researchers establish two or more baselines before introducing a treatment condition. Depending on the purpose of the study, a small-N researcher may measure the same behavior across two or more participants, in the same setting (*multiple-baseline across participants*); different behaviors in the same participant, in the same setting (*multiple-baseline across behaviors*); or a single behavior in the same participant but in different settings (*multiple-baseline across settings*) (Saville & Buskist, 2003). Then, one by one, researchers introduce the treatment of interest for one participant (or one behavior or in one setting) while the other participants continue to respond under baseline conditions. If the dependent variable changes only with the introduction of the treatment, the researcher can be fairly confident that the treatment, and not some other extraneous variable, was responsible for any observed changes. Again, although practical issues are important to consider, the more participants, behaviors, or settings there are, the more likely one can conclude that changes in the independent variable produced changes in the dependent variable. Not only do multiple-baseline designs allow small-N researchers to assess the internal validity of their studies, they also are practical in situations where it might not be advantageous or ethical to remove an effective treatment (e.g., with self-injurious behavior).

All small-N designs share a number of common features: They use small numbers of participants (e.g., 10 or fewer); expose all participants to each level of the independent variable; repeatedly measure the dependent variable; rely on visual rather than statistical analysis to identify significant effects; and use direct and systematic replication, respectively, as means of testing internal validity and generalizing their results to other participants, behaviors, or settings (Saville & Buskist, 2003).

A Brief History of Small-N Designs

The history of psychology is replete with examples of classic studies that used small-N designs to examine their subject matter: Paul Broca's research on language centers in the brain, Gustav Fechner's early studies on the relation between physical stimuli and psychological experience, Hermann Ebbinghaus's seminal studies on memory and forgetting, Wilhelm Wundt's use of introspective techniques to study mind, Robert Yerkes' work in comparative psychology, Edward Thorndike's famous feline studies that resulted in the still-relevant law of effect, and Ivan Pavlov's early research on classical conditioning in dogs, to name but a few (Blampied, 1999; Saville & Buskist, 2003). However, quite possibly the most ardent proponent of small-N designs is also one of psychology's greatest historical figures: Burrhus Frederic (B. F.) Skinner. Starting with his seminal publication *Behavior of Organisms* in 1938, Skinner championed the use of single participants, suggesting that prolonged observation of one organism is more useful for obtaining information on the causes of behavior than brief observation of many organisms: "Operant methods make their own use of Grand Numbers: instead of studying a thousand rats for one hour each, or a hundred rats for ten hours each, the investigator is likely to study one rat for a thousand hours" (Skinner, 1966, p. 21). Just over 20 years after Skinner published *Behavior of Organisms*, Murray Sidman (1960), in his highly influential *Tactics of Scientific Research*, more clearly delineated the utility of the small-N approach to examining psychological phenomena. Since that time, numerous psychologists—including psychophysicists, educators, and clinicians, with whom small-N designs have become increasingly popular in recent years—have advocated the use of small-N designs for examining psychological phenomena in basic research settings (e.g., Johnston & Pennypacker, 1993) and for applying psychological principles in real world settings in an attempt to solve socially important problems (e.g., Baer et al., 1968, 1987). For the reasons listed above, it seems important to teach students in our research methods courses about the utility, practicality—and maybe even the history—of small-N designs.

Teaching the Distinction

Most likely, your discussion of small-N designs will come at a time in the course when students are familiar with many, if not most, of the important concepts associated with, and methodological issues pertaining to, large-N research designs. Consequently, one relatively easy way to discuss the particulars of small-N designs is by contrasting their important features with the features of large-N designs, which likely served as the basis for earlier discussions of experimentation. Comparing small-N and large-N designs allows students to build on an existing knowledge base while learning new information, an approach that seems to enhance learning (e.g., Bain, 2004).

Although there are some important similarities between small-N and large-N experimental designs, Saville and Buskist (2003) suggested that these designs differ along one or more of the following dimensions: (a) number of participants involved; (b) how many levels of the independent variable each participant experiences; (c) number of times researchers measure the dependent variable; (d) how researchers analyze their data; and (e) methods of generalizing the obtained results to other participants, times, or settings. It is important to inform students, however, that these are not completely independent dimensions, and that many of the issues pertaining to one dimension will be of importance on other dimensions as well. The following discussion reflects this overlap.

Number of Participants

Although there does not seem to be a specified rule for including a certain number of participants in small-N designs, tradition seems to suggest that 10 or fewer participants is typical (Saville & Buskist, 2003). For example, most studies reported in recent volumes of the *Journal of the Experimental Analysis of Behavior* (*JEAB*) and the *Journal of Applied Behavior Analysis* (*JABA*), two primary outlets for basic and applied research conducted in the small-N tradition, employed 2 to 12 participants, although some used as many as 30 or more. In contrast, large-N research designs typically use a minimum of 20 to 30 participants *per group*, which, in the case of multigroup experiments, may result in the participation of 100 or more participants per study.

It seems safe to assume that students can and will easily learn that "small-N designs use small numbers of participants" and "large-N designs use large numbers of participants," but it may take longer for them to appreciate the philosophical foundations for choosing either a small or large number of participants. Because of this, you may wish to spend some time explaining the rationale underlying these choices.

As mentioned earlier, B. F. Skinner believed that the intensive study of individual organisms across time—individuals responding under both baseline and treatment, or experimental, conditions—would yield more information regarding cause-and-effect relations than the study of the "average" performance of groups of participants responding under different treatment conditions. For Skinner and his followers, psychology is the science of behavior, and behavior is a phenomenon that occurs at the individual level (i.e., groups don't "behave").Therefore, "because behavior is a phenomenon that occurs only at the level of individual subjects, what the investigator observes with a single subject can be sufficient to make a defensible statement about the relation between the independent and dependent variables" (Johnston & Pennypacker, 1993, p. 250). For example, if you wanted to determine if exercise produced a change in heart rate (i.e., if the independent variable affected changes in the dependent variable), you could use an A-B-A-B design to test this relation (see Carr & Austin, 1997, for further details). First, you could introduce a "no-exercise" condition, in which one participant measured his or her heart rate every minute during a 10-minute period. This would yield 10 measures of the dependent variable, each of which the participant could plot on a graph (see below). Next, you could separate another 10-minute period into ten 1-minute intervals. During each interval, the participant might, for example, exercise for 30 seconds and then measure his or her heart rate for 30 seconds. Again, this would yield 10 measures of the dependent variable, which the participant could plot on the graph. Finally, you could repeat each condition an additional time, for a total of two no-exercise conditions alternated with two exercise conditions. If the participant's heart rate was elevated *only* during the treatment, or exercise, conditions, and not during the baseline, or no-exercise, conditions, then you could safely conclude that exercise, and not some other extraneous factor, was the cause of changes in heart rate. Although the observation of a single participant may not provide direct information regarding the typical response patterns of other participants, it nevertheless is more than adequate to identify changes in an individual participant's behavior that occur as a result of the manipulation of one or more independent variables (Johnston & Pennypacker, 1993).

In contrast, researchers who prefer large numbers of participants cite three primary reasons for their choice. First, as the number of participants in each group increases, so does the likelihood that any participant variables (e.g., differences in personality) will eventually "average out" across groups, making these variables less of a threat to internal validity (Campbell & Stanley, 1963). When discussing this concept with students, I typically pose the following question: "Imagine that I randomly chose several students (including you) from across campus to be in my study. Would you be more likely to meet someone similar to you if I chose a small number of participants or a large number of participants?" I will sometimes also randomly choose students from the class to be in one of two groups and measure the average height of each group. As the number of students in each group increases, the average height in each group tends to become approximately equal. With these examples, students quickly see that using large numbers of participants typically produces more homogeneous groups, or groups in which members are more likely to be similar to others in the same group.

The second reason for using large groups is purely statistical in nature. According to the central limit theorem, researchers need large numbers of participants to obtain the normally distributed, or bell-shaped, pattern of responses that is a prerequisite for many statistical procedures. As the sample size increases, so does the likelihood that the dependent measure of interest will approximate a normal distribution. Consequently, large-N researchers tend to rely on samples of 30 or more participants as a means of assuring that the statistical procedures they use to analyze their data (see below) produce the clearest information possible regarding potential cause-and-effect relations. Although nonparametric statistics allow research-ers to make comparisons when underlying assumptions regarding normality are not met, large-N researchers prefer normally distributed data because the associated statistics tend to be more powerful.

Finally, large-N researchers prefer large samples for reasons having to do with their ability to make generalizable statements about their findings (see below). Specifically, with large samples, researchers claim they can more easily make statements about the populations from which they chose their samples: The larger the sample, the more likely it represents the greater population from which it came, and the more likely such findings will hold with other participants who did not take part in the study (assuming, of course, the researchers randomly selected their participants).

Level of Independent Variable Experienced

Small-N designs require that all participants respond under each level of the independent variable. For example, imagine a researcher was interested in examining if teacher attention affected the likeli-hood that students would follow instructions (Schutte & Hopkins, 1970). To accomplish this, a researcher has decided to use an A-B-A reversal design. The researcher might first have each student respond under a "no attention," or baseline, condition in which the teacher gave instructions but did not reward the students with attention if they followed the instructions. Next, each student might respond under the "attention," or treatment, condition in which following instructions produced teacher attention. Finally, our researcher would reintroduce the "no attention" condition to see if the removal of contingent teacher attention affected instruction-following. In con-trast, with large-N designs, participants typically only experience one level of the independent variable. In the preceding example of teacher attention and instruction-following, a researcher would randomly assign some students to the "attention," or treatment, condition in which the teacher rewarded instruction-following with attention, and other students to the "no attention," or control, condition in which attention did not follow instruction-following.

It is important for students to understand that each type of design is functionally equivalent. Both measure the dependent variable under "normal" conditions in which the treatment is not present (i.e., baseline or control); and both measure changes in the dependent variable after the introduction of the treatment. However, whereas participants in small-N designs experience the control *and* treatment conditions, usually alternating with one another (e.g., A-B-A-B and A-B-A-C designs), participants in large-N designs typically experience either the treatment condition *or* the control condition, but not both.

One concern for any researcher attempting to analyze causal relations is the potential confounding effects of other factors that participants bring with them to the experimental setting. According to proponents of small-N designs (e.g., Johnston & Pennypacker, 1993; Sidman, 1960), these designs can reduce, or even eliminate, the effects of such participant variables because each participant serves as his or her own control. To illustrate, imagine once again that a researcher wants to examine if teacher attention affects instruction-following. Obviously, there are factors other than teacher attention that might affect the likelihood of following instructions. For example, different students might have different histories with regard to following instructions, and these histories may affect how quickly they initially respond to instructions, if attention will be an effective consequence, and so on. If at all possible, our researcher would like to reduce, if not eliminate, the effects of these extraneous variables. In small-N designs, where the same participant is responding repeatedly under both the "attention" and "no attention" conditions, it is unlikely that participant variables will differentially affect responding, simply because these variables are unlikely to change dramatically, if at all, within the same participant during the course of the experiment. Consequently, the absence of differences in instruction-following history will likely make it easier to identify if teacher attention affects instruction-following. As long as our researcher attempts to control other extraneous factors in the experimental setting, the only factor that could systematically effect a change in instruction-following is the presence or absence of teacher attention.

With large-N designs, researchers attempt to control these extraneous participant variables by, once again, using large numbers of participants and randomly assigning them to different conditions. The assumption is that random assignment will equally distribute any extraneous participant variables, such as different histories of instruction-following, which, given enough participants, will result in groups that are approximately equal on these variables prior to the start of the experiment. Therefore, participants in the different conditions will experience different levels of teacher attention for following instructions, but because extraneous participant variables, such as the "average" history of instruction-following, are approximately equal across groups, the difference in teacher attention ends up being the only variable that could differentially affect the extent to which students follow instructions.

Measurement of the Dependent Variable

With small-N designs, researchers measure the dependent variable of interest a minimum of three times (and typically often more) under each condition. For example, a researcher who wanted to determine if teacher attention affected instruction-following in students (Schutte & Hopkins, 1970), might, once again, use an A-B-A reversal design and simply measure the number of times that each student followed instructions. The researcher would likely do this first under a baseline condition in which contingent teacher attention did not follow instruction-following. Then, as mentioned previously, the researcher would introduce contingent teacher attention to see if it produced a change in the number of times each student followed instructions appropriately. Finally, the researcher would reintroduce the "no attention" condition by removing contingent attention and measure the resultant change in instruction-following. If, and only if, instruction-following changed with the introduction and removal of contingent attention could the researcher be relatively certain that changes in attention, and not some other unidentified factor, produced changes in instruction-following.

Under each condition, no attention and attention, the researcher would measure instruction-following a minimum of three times (e.g., for 3 days) or, more common, until there was stability in the number of times that each student followed instructions appropriately (i.e., until that number did not change appreciably over the last few days). Although there are no exact criteria for determining stability (see Johnston & Pennypacker, 1993, and Sidman, 1960, for more discussion of stability criteria), stability in instruction-following—or any dependent variable, for that matter—is more likely to represent the "real" effect of contingent teacher attention and not some ephemeral effect produced by carryover from a preceding condition or by the novelty of a new experimental condition, such as the excitement that might initially emerge when a teacher pays attention to students when they appropriately follow instructions. Moreover, repeated measurement of instruction-following allows small-N researchers to (a) observe how teacher attention affected moment-to-moment, session-to-session, or day-to-day changes in instruction-following; and (b) manipulate the independent variable—in this case, teacher attention—on a moment's notice to bring about desired changes in instruction-following if it is not having the desired or expected effect.

During your discussion of repeated measures and stability in data, it would probably be a good idea to reintroduce two concepts that you likely discussed with students earlier during the course: reactivity (also known as the *Hawthorne effect* or *reactance*) and counterbalancing. At this point in the course, students will (we hope) be familiar with the concept of reactivity and how reactive measures make it difficult to identify true cause-and-effect relations. Discussion of reactivity in the context of small-N designs will help students understand why it is important to measure the dependent variable a minimum of three times or until it stabilizes. Similarly, because all participants in small-N designs experience each level of the independent variable, there is the possibility that (a) the effects of one treatment condition might carry over into the next condition or (b) the order of the treatments might affect the way participants respond. To control for carryover and order effects, small-N researchers often use counterbalancing to tease apart changes in the dependent variable that are due to the treatment condition in effect and those that simply carry over from a previous condition or are a function of the order of treatments.

In contrast to small-N designs, large-N researchers typically measure the dependent variable only once or twice. After randomly assigning students either to a control ("no attention") or treatment ("attention") condition, large-N researchers would (a) introduce attention for one group and then measure instruction-following for both groups (a between-groups design); or (b) measure instruction-following first, introduce attention for one group next, and measure instruction-following again (a mixed design). It is the assumption of large-N researchers that any differences in reactivity or other potentially extraneous factors will, once again, "average out" across groups and that subsequent statistical analyses (see below) will identify which changes in instruction-following were due to "chance" (e.g., individual differences, measurement error) and which changes demonstrated the real effect of the independent variable, in this case, teacher attention. Because statistical analysis will help tease apart "true" effects from "chance" effects, researchers only need one or two measures of the dependent variable to identify cause-and-effect relations.

Data Analysis

Small-N researchers typically examine data using visual analysis of graphed data. To describe this practice, let us imagine once again that a researcher wants to examine if exercise leads to an increase in heart rate (Carr & Austin, 1997). After collecting data from a small number of participants under alternating "no exercise" and "exercise" conditions (e.g., an A-B-A reversal design), a researcher would first plot each participant's individual heart rate measures on a graph. Most likely, the graph would be a line graph that contained the dependent variable on the y axis, some measure of time (e.g., interval, session, day) on the x axis, and vertical bars representing changes in the treatment conditions (see Figure 8.1a). After plotting the data, the researcher would visually examine the results to see if there was a noticeable difference in individual heart rates under the two treatment conditions. If there was such a difference, and the researcher had ruled out other extraneous factors as possible causes of these changes, the researcher would likely conclude that exercise did, in fact, effect a change in heart rate.

Large-N researchers, in contrast, use inferential statistics to analyze their data. After randomly assigning a large number of participants to either a no-exercise or exercise condition, our large-N researcher would require participants in the exercise group to engage in some type of exercise, while participants in the no-exercise condition would not. The researcher would then measure heart rate for each participant and find an average heart rate for each group. Subsequently, the researcher would use an appropriate inferential statistic—in this case, either an independent-groups t test or a one-way ANOVA for independent groups—to determine if the ratio of between-groups variability (i.e., the difference between group means) to within-groups variability (i.e., the differences among participants *within* each group) was large enough to warrant the conclusion that the difference between groups was "statistically significant." If an "obtained" t or F value, for example, was larger than a "critical" t or F value, or if

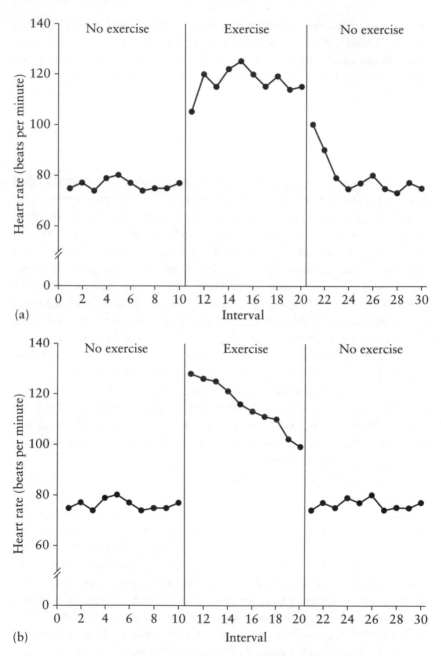

(a)

(b)

Figure 8.1 Shows a participant's hypothetical heart rate data (in beats per minute) under alternating "no exercise" and "exercise" conditions (i.e., an A-B-A reversal design). Each data point represents the participant's heart rate during a particular interval of time.

an obtained p-value was smaller than some predetermined alpha level (e.g., .05), then the researcher would reject the null hypothesis of no meaningful differences between groups and conclude that any difference in average heart rate between the two groups was due to the manipulation of the independent variable, exercise, and not some random factor, such as individual differences in the participants or minor errors in measurement.

Since the early 1900s, small-N designs and inferential statistics have had a rocky relation. Prior to the early 1900s, small-N researchers did not use inferential statistics for one simple reason: Gosset, Fisher, and others had yet to develop their soon to be popular statistical tools. However, even following the introduction of inferential statistics such as the t test and ANOVA in the early 1900s, proponents of small-N designs continued to avoid using inferential statistics for at least three reasons (e.g., Baer, 1977; Michael, 1974). First, although there may be a significant difference between groups, group averages may blur important information regarding individual behavior. For example, although heart rate in a group of 30 exercising participants may average 120 beats per minute, it is possible that not one participant in that group actually had a heart rate that equaled 120 beats per minute. Likewise, averaging data may blur important trends. Imagine once again that our researcher has collected the heart rate data shown in Figure 8.1b. Whereas heart rate under the no-exercise condition is relatively stable, heart rate under the exercise condition shows a decreasing trend. Although statistical analysis would find a significant difference, simply reporting the average heart rate under each condition would potentially obscure these important trends (e.g., Blampied, 1999; Johnston & Pennypacker, 1993). It has been over 50 years since Sidman (1952) showed that learning curves describing responding at the group level did not adequately describe responding at the individual level. Therefore, such "averaging" may lead to situations in which observations that obtain at the group level may not obtain at the individual level (Sidman, 1960). Stated another way, although inferential analyses may allow statements regarding the performance of the "average" respondent, they are less useful when it comes to making predictions about any individual respondent.

Second, small-N researchers have suggested that large-N designs, with their accompanying statistical analyses, isolate researchers from their data. Because large-N researchers typically only measure their dependent variables once or twice, usually some time after they have manipulated their independent variable(s), they miss out on the intense and repeated interactions with their data that allow for a more complete understanding of the relation between independent and dependent variables (Perone, 1999).

Finally, small-N researchers believe that it is better to exert strong experimental control over unwanted sources of variation than to use statistical techniques to "average out" these effects. For example, imagine once again that a researcher wants to know if teacher attention affects instruction-following (Schutte & Hopkins, 1970), but is concerned that students may differ in the extent to which they are affected by attention from their peers. Large-N researchers would randomly assign large numbers of students to each group, hoping that any differences in susceptibility to peer attention would average out across groups, and use statistical analysis to determine which differences were due to teacher attention and which were due to these uncontrolled factors (i.e., "chance"). Small-N researchers would attempt to gain control over the extraexperimental sources of variation in a way that would reduce their potential effects. For example, small-N researchers might isolate the sources of peer attention and remove those students from the experimental setting. If "chance" is nothing more than uncontrolled sources of variation, small-N researchers argue that it would be better to control those factors experimentally than simply to identify their effects using statistical procedures. Controlling these extraneous factors will ultimately result in a better understanding of how the independent variable affects the dependent variable. Because these extraneous factors may be subject to experimental control, then "chance in this sense is simply an excuse for sloppy experimentation" (Sidman, 1960, p. 45), and "the [use] of statistical analysis reduces the investigator's motivation to establish such control" (Perone, 1999, p. 112).

In contrast, large-N researchers feel that statistical analysis is the best way to identify cause-and-effect relations. To examine relations between variables, large-N researchers typically adopt an approach known as null hypothesis significance testing (NHST; e.g., Loftus, 1996). With NHST, the researcher starts off by stating two opposing hypotheses: (a) an alternative hypothesis, which states that, for example, some independent variable will affect some dependent variable, resulting in groups that are significantly different from one another; and (b) a null hypothesis, which states that the independent variable will not affect the dependent variable, resulting in groups that are not meaningfully different from one another (but not necessarily equal to one another as well). Next, the researcher randomly chooses participants for study, with the assumption that any groups created, typically through random assignment, are representative of the populations from which the researcher chose the samples. After manipulating the independent variable, the researcher gathers data and subsequently examines an obtained p value, which establishes the likelihood of observing those data if the null hypothesis were actually true. If the obtained p value is less than some predetermined alpha level, the researcher rejects the null hypothesis and concludes that the independent variable had a significant effect on the dependent variable; if the obtained value is greater than some predetermined alpha level, the researcher concludes that any differences were likely due to "chance" and that the independent variable did not have a significant effect on the dependent variable. The large-N researcher might also examine additional statistical information (e.g., effect size, power, confidence intervals) to gain further understanding of the extent to which the independent variable affected the dependent variable. Although some researchers have argued that NHST is fundamentally flawed (e.g., Loftus, 1996; Meehl, 1967), it remains the method of choice for most psychological researchers.

Generalizability

Small-N researchers utilize direct and systematic replication of previous studies as means for generalizing their results. Direct replication refers to those studies that (a) use new participants but otherwise simply repeat a previous experiment or (b) use the same participants but observe them under each of several different experimental conditions. In the preceding teacher attention and instruction-following example (Schutte & Hopkins, 1970), a direct replication might consist of conducting the same study with different students of approximately the same age and in a similar setting, or by repeatedly observing students' behavior under baseline and treatment conditions (e.g., an A-B-A-B reversal design). Systematic replications, in contrast, are those studies that vary in some meaningful way from the original study. For example, to establish if contingent teacher attention affects instruction-following both in younger and older students, a researcher might first conduct this study with 4th-graders and then systematically replicate the study with 12th-graders. Similarly, one might wish to examine if instruction-following persisted when parents, as well as teachers, give the instructions and provide contingent attention for compliance. By systematically manipulating the parameters of previous experiments, small-N researchers are able to determine the extent to which prior observations hold with new participants and under new conditions.

Large-N researchers, in contrast, use random sampling as a way to make statements about the generalizability of their findings. By using a truly random sample, one in which all members of a certain population have the same likelihood of being chosen for the study, and a large enough number of participants, large-N researchers believe that the average response of participants from the sample will approximate the average response that unstudied members of the population would make if they responded under similar conditions.

Commonalities between Large-N and Small-N Designs

Although the preceding discussion—along with arguments made by proponents of both large-N and small-N designs—might imply that large-N and small-N designs are dichotomous designs that have little in common, it is important to inform students that these designs have more in common than one might think. For example, many researchers use aspects of both large-N and small-N designs when studying various psychological phenomena. In a recent study published in the *Journal of the Experimental Analysis of Behavior*, Yi and Rachlin (2004) used certain aspects of both large-N and small-N designs to examine how participants played the Prisoner's Dilemma Game (PDG), a non-zero-sum game that has its roots in economic game theory (e.g., Luce & Raiffa, 1957; Poundstone, 1992). In the PDG, players can either cooperate with, or compete against, another player. In this particular study, participants played repeated trials of the PDG against five computers, each programmed to follow either a purely random (RAN) strategy or a tit-for-tat (TFT) strategy (i.e., cooperate on the first trial and then do on trial n what the other participant did on trial $n - 1$). As is common with large-N designs, Yi and Rachlin assigned 30 participants to the RAN condition and 30 participants to the TFT condition. All participants then played 50 trials of the PDG (measured in 5-trial blocks), which allowed Yi and Rachlin to observe how their behavior changed not only across conditions, but also within each condition, a characteristic of small-N designs. Furthermore, when reporting the number of trials on which their participants cooperated, Yi and Rachlin presented group data—specifically, the average number of cooperative responses in 5-trial blocks—and statistically analyzed their results using a mixed ANOVA, a characteristic of large-N designs. They also presented graphed data representing the cumulative frequency of cooperative choices across all 50 trials for each participant, a characteristic of small-N designs.

Similarly, several researchers have argued that statistical analyses can be appropriate, and even useful, when examining data collected using small-N designs. For example, Davison (1999) suggested that using nonparametric analyses on small-N data may improve communication with researchers who are not as familiar with the visual analyses small-N researchers typically use. Likewise, Crosbie (1999) argued that visual and statistical analyses are logically similar in that each attempts to identify situations where there is minimal overlap in distributions of responses across treatment conditions. Moreover, Crosbie asserted that having knowledge of inferential statistics might make small-N researchers "more methodologically sophisticated" (p. 105).

As a result, the similarities between large-N designs and small-N designs have led some researchers to assert that these designs do not, in fact, belong in separate categories, as some like to believe: "Like most dichotomies, this one is—especially for psychologists—a false one" (Harris, 2003, p. 41). "Rather," as Saville and Buskist (2003) stated, "these designs may be seen as lying on opposing ends of a continuum, where characteristics of each design may merge if the experimental question requires some combination of small-N and large-N methodology" (p. 73). Ultimately, it is important to tell students that one type of design is not necessarily better than another. Each type of design may be more or less appropriate depending on the purpose of a given study.

References

Baer, D. M. (1977). Perhaps it would be better not to know everything. *Journal of Applied Behavior Analysis, 10,* 167–172.

Baer, D. M., Wolf, M. M., & Risley, T. R. (1968). Some current dimensions of applied behavior analysis. *Journal of Applied Behavior Analysis, 1,* 91–97.

Baer, D. M., Wolf, M. M., & Risley, T. R. (1987). Some still current dimensions of applied behavior analysis. *Journal of Applied Behavior Analysis, 20,* 313–327.

Bain, K. (2004). *What the best college teachers do.* Cambridge, MA: Harvard University.

Baron, A., & Perone, M. (1998). Experimental design and analysis in the laboratory study of human operant behavior. In K. A. Lattal & M. Perone (Eds.), *Handbook of research methods in human operant behavior* (pp. 45–91). New York: Plenum Press.

Blampied, N. M. (1999). A legacy neglected: Restating the case for single-case research in cognitive-behaviour therapy. *Behaviour Change, 16,* 89–104.

Boring, E. G. (1954). The nature and history of experimental control. *American Journal of Psychology, 67,* 573–589.

Campbell, D., & Stanley, J. (1963). *Experimental and quasi-experimental designs for research.* Chicago: Rand-McNally.

Carr, J. E., & Austin, J. (1997). A classroom demonstration of single-participant research designs. *Teaching of Psychology, 24,* 188–190.

Crosbie, J. (1999). Statistical inference in behavior analysis: Useful friend. *The Behavior Analyst, 22,* 105–108.

Davison, M. (1999). Statistical inference in behavior analysis: Having my cake and eating it? *The Behavior Analyst, 22,* 99–103.

Dukes, W. F. (1965). N = 1. *Psychological Bulletin, 64,* 74–79.

Fisher, R. A. (1925). *Statistical methods for research workers.* Edinburgh: Oliver & Boyd.

Harris, R. J. (2003). Traditional nomothetic approaches. In S. F. Davis (Ed.), *Handbook of research methods in experimental psychology* (pp. 41–65). Malden, MA: Blackwell.

Hubbard, R., Parsa, R. A., & Luthy, M. R. (1997). The spread of statistical testing in psychology. *Theory and Psychology, 7,* 545–554.

Johnston, J. M., & Pennypacker, H. S. (1993). *Strategies and tactics of behavioral research* (2nd ed.). Hillsdale, NJ: Erlbaum.

Loftus, G. R. (1996). Psychology will be a much better science when we change the way we analyze data. *Current Directions in Psychological Science, 5,* 161–171.

Luce, R. D., & Raiffa, H. (1957). *Games and decisions.* New York: Wiley.

Meehl, P. E. (1967). Theory-testing in psychology and physics: A methodological paradox. *Philosophy of Science, 34,* 103–115.

Michael, J. (1974). Statistical inference for individual organism research: Mixed blessing or curse? *Journal of Applied Behavior Analysis, 7,* 647–653.

Perone, M. (1999). Statistical inference in behavior analysis: Experimental control is better. *The Behavior Analyst, 22,* 109–116.

Poundstone, W. (1992). *Prisoner's dilemma.* New York: Doubleday.

Saville, B. K., & Buskist, W. (2003). Traditional idiographic approaches: Small-N research designs. In S. F. Davis (Ed.), *Handbook of research methods in experimental psychology* (pp. 66–82). Malden, MA: Blackwell.

Schutte, R. C., & Hopkins, B. L. (1970). The effects of teacher attention on following instructions in a kindergarten class. *Journal of Applied Behavior Analysis, 3*, 117–122.

Sidman, M. (1952). A note on functional relations obtained from group data. *Psychological Bulletin, 49*, 263–269.

Sidman, M. (1960). *Tactics of scientific research: Evaluating experimental data in psychology.* Boston, MA: Authors Cooperative.

Skinner, B. F. (1938). *The behavior of organisms: An experimental analysis.* New York: Appleton-Century-Crofts.

Skinner, B. F. (1966). Operant behavior. In W. K. Honig (Ed.), *Operant behavior: Areas of research and application* (pp. 12–32). Englewood Cliffs, NJ: Prentice Hall.

Student. (1908). The probable error of a mean. *Biometrika, 6*, 1–25.

Yi, R., & Rachlin, H. (2004). Contingencies of reinforcement in a five-person prisoner's dilemma. *Journal of the Experimental Analysis of Behavior, 82*, 161–176.

Chapter 9

The Laboratory as Teaching Tool

There are many ways to structure the laboratory aspect of your research methods course, but regardless of how you choose to do this, keep in mind that "the fundamental goal of education in psychology, from which all others follow, is to teach students to think as scientists about behavior" (Brewer et al., 1993, p. 169). With regard to your research methods lab in particular, you would do well to keep in mind McKeachie and Milholland's (1961) suggestion that the goals for any exceptional laboratory experience should include (a) an appreciation of why science is an important endeavor, (b) general knowledge of research methods, (c) acquisition of specific research skills, and (d) the ability to think critically about the research process. Providing your students with the opportunity to "do science" by conducting a study and teaching them to communicate their findings via APA-style papers will go a long way toward accomplishing these goals. Specifically, giving your students a chance to conduct research will likely solidify their understanding of important course concepts and give them the hands-on experience they need truly to understand psychology as science. In addition, such an opportunity will hopefully provide your students with a deeper understanding of the importance of science in general and of research methods in particular; why research methods serve as a starting point for everything else they have learned, or will eventually learn, in their other psychology courses; and why research methods are, and will continue to be, vital to the advancement of our field. Moreover, by writing one (or preferably several) APA-style papers based on the outcomes of these studies, your students will learn *how* psychological researchers communicate their results and *why* effective communication is important in scientific endeavors. With a bit of luck and some effective teaching, a few of your students (and maybe more) might actually find that they enjoy conducting research and that communicating their results through APA-style papers can, in fact, be enjoyable.

Learning Science by "Doing Science"

There seem to be two general formats that most instructors use when structuring their research methods labs (Yoder, 1979). The first format consists of giving students "canned" or "cookbook" studies to perform; the second format allows students to develop their own studies.

"Canned" or "Cookbook" Studies

One approach to teaching your students about research methods is to incorporate "canned" or "cookbook" studies into your labs. In essence, this approach consists of having your students conduct studies that you or other researchers have already developed and for which the outcomes are fairly predictable.

Kerber (1983), for example, provided a list of four studies that instructors could use in a research methods lab to teach students about various research designs (see also Clary, Sherman, Olson, & Thorsheim, 2005, for more examples of canned studies). Similarly, Koschmann and Wesp (2001) described how students could conduct simple studies in a college dining facility. For example, they described (a) an observational study in which students counted the number of diners who went back for seconds, (b) a correlational study in which students examined the relation between a student's height and the amount of food he or she ate, and (c) an experiment in which students assessed whether handing out napkins (versus having students take them on their own) increased napkin usage.

In addition to the aforementioned studies, you could also turn to "classic" psychology studies that yield predictable results. These include, for example, Stroop's (1935) well-known study on selective attention; Peterson and Peterson's (1959) study on the duration of short-term memory; Dion, Berscheid, and Walster's (1972) analysis of "what is beautiful is good"; or any other well-known, easy-to-implement studies (see Suter & Frank, 1986, for more examples). Finally, articles in journals such as *Teaching of Psychology* contain many examples of studies that instructors have successfully incorporated into their courses.

When deciding whether you should incorporate canned studies in your research methods labs, there are some issues you should consider. On the plus side, the nature of canned studies may simplify the process of getting them passed by your institution's research review board. Many instructors have used these studies time and again. Consequently, their procedures are well known, their outcomes are fairly predictable, and their risks tend to be minimal, which may, in fact, exempt them from full IRB review. Further, because you can anticipate problems that may arise during the course of these studies, you will be able to inform your institution's review board of possible risks and what steps you and your students will take beforehand to reduce these risks as much as possible.

In addition, as you continue to use these studies semester after semester, you will become more familiar with problems that might arise during the course of a study, such as how many participants you will need to recruit, how long it takes them to complete a task, and so on. Given that research review boards can be notoriously slow and that data collection always seems to take longer than expected, being intimately familiar with the studies you use can be a tremendous time-saver.

Another potential advantage to using canned studies is that you can weave a common theme throughout each of them, which may have a positive effect on your students' learning. For example, Marek, Christopher, and Walker (2004) described a course in which they implemented a theme-based approach to teaching research methods. Using the topic of academic ethics as a guide, students discussed survey construction, ethics, research design, statistical analysis, and writing APA-style papers, among other topics. Marek et al. found that students rated the theme-based approach highly and performed well under this framework. Incorporating a theme-based approach into your lab (or even throughout your entire course) may provide your students with a sense of continuity as they discuss research methods. This may help them see the relations among important course concepts and better understand course material as you progress from simpler to more complex ideas.

Just as using canned studies has its advantages, there are potential disadvantages to consider when developing or modifying your lab. One of these is that your students will have little say in the studies they will be conducting. Ryan and Deci (2000) suggested that motivation is enhanced when people are able to set their own goals rather than having those goals imposed by someone else. Indeed, forcing your students to conduct canned studies, which they did not choose and in which some may have little interest, could possibly undermine their motivation to pursue additional research opportunities in the future. One way to overcome this hurdle, while still retaining some control over the studies your students conduct, would be to assemble a list of topics, each with an accompanying study, and allow your students to choose which of them they would like to examine (Yoder, 1979).

A second, and possibly more important, potential disadvantage of using canned studies is that students do not actively apply the information they learn in class (Yoder, 1979). So even if students happen to enjoy the topic you give them to study and may be actively involved in data collection and analysis and subsequently communicating their results in an APA-style paper, they will not have had the experience of identifying a research question, developing a study to test that question, and grappling with the subtle nuances of research that are often not apparent until students have had the chance to collect their own data.

Student-developed Studies

Arguably, the only way for students truly to understand the research *process* is by designing a study, carrying out that study from start to finish, and communicating the results via an APA-style paper. If you concur, you may wish to give your students the opportunity to develop studies of their own, examining topics in which they are truly interested. This might consist of having your students develop one or a few group studies (e.g., Meyers, 1997), or it might consist of having every student develop and carry out his or her own study (e.g., Underwood, 1975). Regardless of how you incorporate student-developed studies into your lab, remember that there are both advantages and disadvantages to consider.

On the plus side, allowing students the autonomy to make their own decisions regarding the studies they conduct will likely have a positive influence on their interest in research (Ryan & Deci, 2000). Not only might your students learn that research is not necessarily as complex as some make it out to be, they might also learn that examining psychological phenomena and learning how nature "works" can be enlightening and enjoyable.

In addition, giving your students the opportunity to develop and conduct their own studies will likely help them understand how using research methods gives psychologists a more thorough understanding of the phenomena they study. Hands-on experience will give them more intimate knowledge of research methods, help them acquire important research skills, and become more critical thinkers —especially when they are confronted with data that do not conform to their preconceived notions about reality.

Still, because your students may be interested in studying topics that are not easily amenable to study in a college or university setting (e.g., child development), you may have difficulty obtaining the resources or participants that your students will need to conduct studies of their own creation (Yoder, 1979). Consequently, modifications may be necessary that preclude your students from studying a topic in which they are truly interested. Hopefully, in these situations, you can find middle ground, settling on a study that will be easy to carry out and that will pique the interest of your students as well.

Another potential problem associated with student-developed studies concerns difficulties that often arise when submitting research for IRB approval (e.g., Yoder, 1979). To illustrate, if I submit a research proposal to my institution's IRB and they identify potential problems, I have the flexibility to revise and resubmit the proposal, knowing that a brief delay in the start of data collection will probably not affect the study to any great extent. In contrast, because the length of the semester constrains what we can accomplish in our courses, any delays that occur during the IRB review process can greatly affect the studies our students wish to conduct. This may be especially true when your students design a relatively novel study. Although you may be able to predict with some certainty how your IRB may respond to such a proposal, there is always the chance that the IRB will ask your students to revise and resubmit their proposal. Ultimately, this may make it impossible for your students to conduct the study according to their planned schedule and perhaps lead them to believe that research consists of working as quickly as possible, even if it results in a shoddy study. If you think this may be a problem in your course, you would do well to begin the IRB approval process early and make sure your students submit their proposals well in advance of when they will begin collecting data. Although there are clearly benefits to having students go through the IRB process (Kallgren & Tauber, 1996), you must remain aware of that fact that various aspects of IRB processes can create problems that may delay and ultimately derail your students' research plans, either temporarily or permanently.

A Combined Alternative

Is it possible to gain the advantages of both canned and student-developed studies while minimizing their disadvantages? Perhaps not entirely, but one alternative would be to construct a lab in which students first carry out one or more short canned studies, each of which would serve as the basis for part or all of an APA-style paper, and then develop a study (or studies) of their own, which would culminate in a final APA-style paper. I have used this combined format and have found it to be a "best of both worlds" solution to some of the problems identified earlier. For example, one canned study I have used frequently examines gender differences in self-esteem. Students either fill out, or ask their friends to fill out, the 10-question Rosenberg Self-Esteem Scale (Rosenberg, 1965), and I add the data to an archived database I have built over the years (see Brinthaupt & Pennington, 2005). Students then use the data to write three drafts of an APA-style paper, only the last of which includes all sections. Although students often do not yet have the requisite knowledge to understand every piece of information they include in these early papers, exposure to APA style early in the semester facilitates their writing of subsequent papers. Later in the semester, students work in groups to develop several smaller research projects, for which they submit an IRB proposal and collect data using our department's undergraduate participant pool. Finally, they write one more APA-style paper based on their studies.

By incorporating both canned and student-developed studies in lab, my students first have the opportunity to focus on data collection and analysis and on communicating their results effectively as they learn to write APA-style papers. As they subsequently learn more about research design, they acquire the knowledge needed to conduct their own studies, which ultimately serves to solidify their understanding of research design and increases their interest in using the scientific method to answer questions about various psychological phenomena.

Writing APA-Style Papers: Teaching Students the Importance of Effective Communication

"I don't understand why we spend so much time worrying about writing style and grammar. This is a research methods class, not an English class." Perhaps you have heard similar comments from your students. Unfortunately, some of our students fail to comprehend the reasons why we spend so much time trying to improve their writing skills. As research methods instructors, shouldn't we just teach them how to "do research" and let their English instructors teach them how to write effectively? If it were only that easy.

Although many of our students view "research" as consisting of research design and data collection and analysis, the research process, in fact, consists of additional steps, one of the most important of which is effectively communicating the findings of a study. Only when a researcher has done so can those results have an impact on the subsequent activities of other researchers and practitioners (Sternberg, 2004). Thus it is in the best interests of our students— even if they do not initially agree with us—that we spend a good amount of time discussing with them the importance of learning to communicate effectively through the writing of APA-style papers. Below I provide suggestions for improving your students' writing and teaching them to communicate effectively.

Start Early

Although some instructors believe that students should write their APA-style papers toward the end of the semester, after they have acquired the requisite knowledge needed to communicate their ideas most effectively, I believe you would do well to start your students writing early in the semester. Doing so will give them multiple opportunities to learn from their mistakes and become more adept at communicating their results. In addition, students will have more time to work on their papers and, consequently, may experience less stress toward the end of the semester.

Allow Multiple Drafts

Starting the writing process early also will allow your students to write multiple drafts of their APA-style papers, a practice that tends to have great benefits in terms of writing improvement. If you do choose to have your students write multiple drafts, you would do well to structure your grading in such a way that early drafts are worth considerably fewer points than later drafts. This will send the message to your students that you are more concerned about them learning to write high-quality papers—papers that may at first be filled with numerous mistakes, but after several revisions, evolve into well-written pieces—than you are about just giving them a grade (e.g., Yoder, 1979).

For example, you may require that your students' first drafts consist of a title page and method section. Because these sections of an APA-style paper tend to be easier to write than other sections, you can ease students into the writing process by having them focus on these sections first. Once students have turned in their first drafts, you (or a teaching assistant) can provide them with extensive, written feedback. The next draft might consist of a title page and method section (both revised, if necessary), along with results, tables, figures, and figure captions. After receiving further feedback and revising their papers again, students might add an introduction and reference section. Finally, students can add a discussion and abstract, thus completing a full APA-style paper. At this point, you might incorporate peer reviews (see below), so that students have the opportunity to receive additional feedback before turning in their papers for a final grade. Depending on your course objectives and how much time you have available in your lab, you may need to modify the process a bit. Nevertheless, asking students to write papers in this manner will help them to learn that writing a well-constructed paper is not a "one-shot" deal, but rather a process that consists of multiple rewrites and revisions.

Finally, as you plan your own system, remember that writing the introduction and discussion sections may take students considerably more time than writing the method and results sections, for example. (These sections will also require more of your time when you provide feedback.) Be sure to inform your students of this well in advance.

Include Peer Reviews

Just as psychologists (typically) benefit considerably from the peer review process when submitting their research for publication, so too will your students likely benefit from receiving feedback from, and providing feedback to, other students.

Hands-on Tip

White and Kirby (2005) described a peer review activity they used in their undergraduate research methods courses to improve the quality of their students' writing. First, students read an article by Sternberg (2002) on the importance of providing fair reviews and useful criticism. Then, after they had completed a class project and written an APA-style paper based on their results, students submitted three copies of their papers, two of which did not contain any identifying information. White and Kirby then randomly distributed the students' "blank" copies to their classmates for blind review and kept the third copy for themselves. Students read the papers they had received, responded to a short questionnaire (e.g., "Did the author review the literature well?" "Were the results accurately presented?"), wrote comments on the papers, and completed a two-page blind review. Before handing the reviews back to the students, the instructor examined them for quality, errors, and so on. Finally, after receiving three reviews, two from classmates and one from the instructor, students revised their papers and resubmitted them for a final grade. Although there was significant variability in the quality of the reviews, students reported that reviewing another student's paper improved their own quality. They also reported that they preferred revising and resubmitting their papers to handing in only a single draft. Regardless of how many APA-style papers you ask your students to write in your labs, you can incorporate the peer review process with relative ease.

Other Suggestions

As your students work on their APA-style papers—especially their first drafts—you may need to spend some additional time addressing three other matters that may arise: (a) plagiarism, (b) reading and interpreting empirical research, and (c) general writing skills.

Plagiarism. As I discussed in Chapter 4, plagiarism is a topic about which many students likely have misconceptions. Although we would like to think that our students know what it means to plagiarize, they may not really understand what does and does not constitute plagiarism (e.g., Roig, 1997). So you would do well to spend some time in your lab discussing plagiarism with your students.

Hands-on Tip

You might also wish to incorporate an antiplagiarism activity (e.g., Landau, Druen, & Arcuri, 2002; see Chapter 4 for a description).

Reading and interpreting empirical research. Although there is variability across psychology departments as to when students typically take their first research methods course, students frequently do so some time during their sophomore or junior years. As a result, the majority of them has had only one or two previous psychology courses (e.g., introductory psychology and statistics) and may have little to no experience reading empirical research reports. If their first opportunity to do so comes during our research methods courses, they may perceive journal articles to be a compilation of gibberish, foreign language, and impenetrable mathematical symbols, and they may experience considerable anxiety and apprehension—especially when we require them to "review the literature" for their APA-style papers. In this case, student-oriented journals such as the *Psi Chi Journal of Undergraduate Research* and the *Journal of Psychological Inquiry* may provide a nice—and possibly easier to understand—introduction to psychological research for your students. Even so, many of them may still feel uncomfortable when trying to incorporate material from journal articles in their research reports. You may need to spend some time addressing these aspects of the writing process.

Hands-on Tip

Varnhagen and Digdon (2002) described an activity, titled "Reading the Research," that you can incorporate into your labs to help your students begin to read and interpret empirical research. Although this activity was Web-based (see http://www.psych.ualberta.ca/~varn/Kenrick/Reading.htm), transforming it into a paper-based format should be relatively painless. The activity proceeds as follows. Students first preview a set of questions that will guide them through various sections of an empirical research report (see Varnhagen & Digdon, 2002, for a complete list). For example, you might ask your students to address the following:

Who conducted the research?
What questions were the researchers attempting to answer?
What research design did the researchers use?
What were the main results of the study?
Why is the research important?
Are the participants appropriate for this study?
Do the researchers use appropriate dependent measures?
Do the results help to answer the research questions?

Regardless of which questions you choose to include, you would do well to utilize both factual and critical thinking questions.

Next, students read summaries of various sections of the research report and answer the preceding questions. (Varnhagen and Digdon suggested that instructors write summaries of each section, which allows them to tailor the questions for their students. Depending on your course objectives and your students' abilities, you may wish instead to have them read the actual report rather than summaries of each section. Alternatively, you could have them start with summaries and eventually work their way to complete research reports.) Varnhagen and Digdon also suggested that instructors using a Web-based format might provide links to other related Web sites (e.g., sites with pictures of apparatus, etc.) at various points in the activity.

Finally, students answer additional questions (e.g., multiple-choice) that assess their understanding of the research report. For instructors interested in other assessment formats, Varnhagen and Digdon suggested the use of Web-based discussion boards on which students can provide comments and discuss the report.

Varnhagen and Digdon found that students in an experimental psychology course reported an improved ability to read and evaluate empirical research as a result of participating in this activity. Considering that students in research methods often find empirical research less than entertaining, the preceding activity may be a welcome tool in your laboratory teaching arsenal.

General writing skills. Our students may eventually understand APA style and have the ability to interpret empirical research, but if they are not able to express their ideas clearly, they will not be seen as effective communicators. They also need to learn to write with "clarity, conciseness, and felicity of expression" (Brewer, 2002, p. 504) if they are to communicate their ideas effectively. Therefore, it is part of our job as research methods instructors to spend some lab time attempting to improve students' general writing skills.

Hands-on Tip

Fortunately, recent research provides a useful framework that instructors can use to do so. Fallahi, Wood, Austad, and Fallahi (2006) described a program in which they taught students to focus on grammar, writing style, writing mechanics, and other issues related to APA style (e.g., proper citations, developing a reference list). At the beginning of the semester, students received a rubric that outlined grading criteria for their writing assignments and contained additional information on key writing skills. Before writing their first paper, students heard a short lecture on common writing errors along with ways to avoid these errors. Then, after completing their first drafts, students exchanged papers and participated in peer review, using as a guide the same grading criteria they had discussed at the beginning of the semester. After making revisions, they turned in a completed paper. No more than 1 week later, students received their graded papers, along with extensive written feedback from the instructor. Students also heard another brief lecture on common writing errors, this time tailored to emphasize mistakes that occurred frequently on the first paper. Finally, students received their second writing assignment, and the process began anew.

Fallahi et al. observed that following this process over the course of several writing assignments significantly improved their students' general writing skills. Importantly, though, they also found that some specific improvements (e.g., in the clarity of writing) did not improve considerably until the fourth or fifth writing assignment. These results support my earlier suggestion that you allow your students the opportunity to write several drafts of their APA-style papers. Only with repeated practice will your students have the chance to revise their papers and receive the feedback necessary to improve their writing skills.

Finally, based on their observations, Fallahi et al. made the following specific recommendations for helping students become better writers:

1. Obtain writing samples at the beginning of the semester, so you can assess your students' existing skills.

2. Prior to each writing assignment, discuss with your students common errors from previous papers.
3. Provide your students with a rubric containing grading criteria and information about general writing skills.
4. Make available to your students additional resources to which they can refer when they are writing their papers.

Conclusion

Students may not enter our labs with extensive research skills or the writing prowess of Robert Frost or Jane Austen, but with a little help and support, they have the opportunity to become more knowledgeable researchers and better writers. Although the thought of teaching students how to conduct research and write APA-style papers may seem discomfiting to some, the laboratory can be a useful tool in combating students' negativity about the research process.

References

Brewer, C. L. (2002). Reflections on an academic career: From which side of the looking glass? In S. F. Davis & W. Buskist (Eds.), *The teaching of psychology: Essays in honor of Wilbert J. McKeachie and Charles L. Brewer* (pp. 499–507). Mahwah, NJ: Erlbaum.

Brewer, C. L., Hopkins, J. R., Kimble, G. A., Matlin, M. W., McCann, L. I., McNeil, O. V., et al. (1993). Curriculum. In T. V. McGovern (Ed.), *Handbook for enhancing undergraduate education in psychology* (pp. 161–182). Washington, DC: American Psychological Association.

Brinthaupt, T. M., & Pennington, J. T. (2005). Developmental of a departmental data archive for teaching and research. *Teaching of Psychology, 32*, 257–259.

Clary, G., Sherman, B., Olson, A., & Thorsheim, H. (2005). General psychology laboratories. In B. K. Saville, T. E. Zinn, & V. W. Hevern (Eds.), *Essays from e-xcellence in teaching, 2004* (Chap. 1). Retrieved September 25, 2006, from the Society for the Teaching of Psychology Web site: http://teachpsych.org/resources/e-books/eit2004/eit04-01.pdf

Dion, K., Berscheid, E., & Walster, E. (1972). What is beautiful is good. *Journal of Personality and Social Psychology, 24*, 285–290.

Fallahi, C. R., Wood, R. M., Austad, C. S., & Fallahi, H. (2006). A program for improving undergraduate psychology students' basic writing skills. *Teaching of Psychology, 33*, 171–175.

Kallgren, C. A., & Tauber, R. T. (1996). Undergraduate research and the institutional review board: A mismatch or happy marriage? *Teaching of Psychology*, 23, 20–25.

Kerber, K. W. (1983). Beyond experimentation: Research projects for a laboratory course in psychology. *Teaching of Psychology*, 10, 236–239.

Koschmann, N., & Wesp, R. (2001). Using a dining facility as an introductory psychology research laboratory. *Teaching of Psychology*, 28, 105–108.

Landau, J. D., Druen, P. B., & Arcuri, J. A. (2002). Methods for helping students avoid plagiarism. *Teaching of Psychology*, 29, 112–115.

Marek, P., Christopher, A. N., & Walker, B. J. (2004). Learning by doing: Research methods with a theme. *Teaching of Psychology*, 31, 128–131.

McKeachie, W. J., & Milholland, J. E. (1961). *Undergraduate curricula in psychology*. Chicago: Scott, Foresman.

Meyers, S. A. (1997). Increasing student participation and productivity in small-group activities for psychology classes. *Teaching of Psychology*, 24, 105–115.

Peterson, L. R., & Peterson, M. J. (1959). Short-term retention of individual verbal items. *Journal of Experimental Psychology*, 58, 193–198.

Roig, M. (1997). Can undergraduate students determine whether text has been plagiarized? *The Psychological Record*, 47, 113–122.

Rosenberg, M. (1965). *Society and the adolescent self-image*. Princeton, NJ: Princeton University Press.

Ryan, R. M., & Deci, E. L. (2000). Self-determination theory and the facilitation of intrinsic motivation, social development, and well-being. *American Psychologist*, 55, 68–78.

Sternberg, R. J. (2002). On civility in reviewing. *APS Observer*, 15(1), 3, 34.

Sternberg, R. J. (2004). *Psychology 101½: The unspoken rules for success in academia*. Washington, DC: American Psychological Association.

Stroop, J. R. (1935). Studies of interference in serial verbal reactions. *Journal of Experimental Psychology*, 18, 643–662.

Suter, W. N., & Frank, P. (1986). Using scholarly journals in undergraduate experimental methodology courses. *Teaching of Psychology*, 13, 219–221.

Underwood, B. J. (1975). The first course in experimental psychology: Goals and methods. *Teaching of Psychology*, 2, 163–165.

Varnhagen, C. K., & Digdon, N. (2002). Helping students read reports of empirical research. *Teaching of Psychology*, 29, 160–164.

White, T. L., & Kirby, B. J. (2005). 'Tis better to give than to receive: An undergraduate peer review project. *Teaching of Psychology*, 32, 259–261.

Yoder, J. (1979). Teaching students to do research. *Teaching of Psychology*, 6, 85–88.

Chapter 10

Innovative Approaches to Teaching Research Methods

For the past few years, Amanda, a third-year assistant professor, has spent considerable time honing her lecture skills and revising her notes for research methods, a course she has taught off and on since she was a second-year graduate student. More often than not, she receives decent student evaluations in the course, although if truth be told, it is fairly common for students to mention that Amanda's lectures can be "a little boring at times" and that the material is "not the most exciting stuff in the world." Amanda has noticed that her enthusiasm for teaching research methods has been waning recently—maybe because her students' enthusiasm seems to be waning as well, which, of course, only detracts from her enthusiasm to teach the course. Although she has not yet made any changes to her course, Amanda has been looking for some alternatives to the standard lecture format with which she and her students are so familiar. What exactly can Amanda do to inject a little spice into her teaching, to create an atmosphere in which she is excited to teach about—and her students are excited to learn about—research methods?

Lecturing as Teaching, Teaching as Lecturing

"Teaching," as most of us know it, is synonymous with "lecturing"—it is the telling of stories, the transmission of information from the instructor to the students, who are like empty receptacles, waiting to be filled with important facts, new and interesting concepts, and practical tidbits of applicable information (Bain, 2004). As it is with Amanda, lecture is the method of choice for a large majority of college instructors. And why shouldn't it be? Lectures can be stimulating, informative, even highly entertaining and down-right inspirational. In fact, well constructed lectures have numerous pedagogical advantages: Instructors who lecture can (a) impart large amounts of information to many students in a relatively short time, (b) present recent information that may not yet be available in textbooks, (c) summarize and integrate material that comes from many different sources, (d) mold or adapt their lectures to fit the specific interests of a particular audience, (e) help students become better readers and thinkers by providing a conceptual framework within which students can evaluate assigned readings, and (f) use their lectures to motivate students to pursue further learning (McKeachie, 2002). Moreover, lectures typically give instructors full control over the delivery and explanation of the course material, which may result in a more structured classroom experience for students. Finally, one might simply argue the following regarding lecture-based methods: Lecture was the method used by most of our favorite psychology instructors, and we didn't turn out so badly, did we?

Ways to Make Research Methods Lectures More Effective

If you feel inclined to lecture in your research methods course, there are several ways to make those lectures more effective (for further suggestions, see Bain, 2004; Davis, 1993; McKeachie, 2002). First, be enthusiastic about the material. The one element that seems to pervade all discussions of exceptional teaching is enthusiasm or passion for the subject matter and for teaching in general (Buskist, Sikorski, Buckley, & Saville, 2002). If you do not show enthusiasm for research methods, how are your students going to find interest in a topic that many assume will be boring, even before they enter our classrooms? Second, try to relate the course material to the interests of your students. For example, you probably have several students interested in clinical psychology, so include examples that elucidate how clinical psychologists use various research methods to determine the efficacy of their therapies. Regardless of the specifics, if you can relate the material to various aspects of your students' lives, they will find the course more enjoyable. Third, get your students involved: Ask them questions about specific concepts, but be sure to ask questions that are unambiguous in nature (see Zinn & Saville, 2005); ask them to identify ways they might answer a specific research question; ask them how the course material relates to their lives; and use hands-on activities that require them to apply the concepts they learn in class. Regardless of the approach you take, get your students involved—active students understand, retain, and enjoy the material more than passive students. Finally, break up your lectures with demonstrations, problem-solving activities, and the like (e.g., Bernstein, 2006). Because students' attention spans are relatively short (McKeachie, 2002), a good way to maintain their attention is by breaking up the session into 10- to 15-minute chunks of lecture followed by a brief activity designed to get them actively engaged in the material. Although this list is not exhaustive, it can serve as a starting point for injecting a little spice into your lectures.

Undoubtedly, lecture can be a useful approach for teaching research methods. With a little work, you can transform your research methods lectures from something that students dread into something that students look forward to hearing.

Why not to Lecture in Research Methods

Although Amanda, our aspiring research methods instructor, could simply incorporate many of the preceding suggestions into her classes to make her lectures more effective, you might also ask whether there are reasons why instructors might *not* want to use primarily lecture-based instruction in research methods courses. If you think the answer is "yes," and maybe can even list some reasons why, then you too might be ready to consider implementing some non-lecture-based methods into your course.

There are numerous reasons why Amanda and other research methods instructors might want to think about moving away from the lecture-based methods with which students and instructors are so familiar. First, compared to other methods, lectures tend to promote passivity on the part of students, rendering our classes less effective than they might be otherwise. Common is the scenario in which an instructor asks students a question pertaining to the course material and is met by a sea of glazed looks and blank stares. Just as common is the scenario, especially in large classrooms, in which students who no longer want to attend to a less-than-stimulating lecture on internal validity, for example, close their eyes or even put their heads on their desks in hopes of catching a quick nap before lunch. In contrast, methods that require students to be active and engage the course material tend to produce more interest and better learning than methods that encourage passivity (e.g., Mathie et al., 1993; McKeachie, 2002; Miserandino, 1999; Yoder & Hochevar, 2005).

Second, because lectures tend to promote student passivity, instructors sometimes have trouble obtaining immediate feedback— and maybe more importantly, *realistic* feedback—regarding students' understanding of course material. Perhaps you have had the follow- ing experience: After lecturing over a certain piece of information, you queried your students to see if they had a decent understanding of the material. Most likely, many of them nodded their heads, affirming that they clearly understood everything. Only later— after the next exam, for example—did it become clear that your students did *not* understand everything you said. Teaching methods that promote active involvement on the part of students allow us to get a better idea about our students' understanding of course material.

Third, although lectures tend to enhance short-term memory, they do little to promote long-term retention of material (Halpern, 2004), which is one of the primary goals we often have for our students. In contrast to lecture-based methods, those that promote active learn- ing typically produce better long-term retention of course material (e.g., Halpern, 2004; Schwartz, Mennin, & Webb, 2001), thus saving a lot of class time. For example, in most research methods courses, instructors spend a good bit of time discussing the import- ant relation between statistics and research methods. Although students likely benefit from hearing information on statistics once again, such repetition may not be desirable if it takes time away from covering other information that is more central to learning research methods.

Fourth, numerous studies show that information learned via lectures does not transfer well to contexts outside the classroom (Halpern, 2004; Halpern & Hakel, 2003). Although our best stu- dents often show glimpses of an ability to apply course concepts across topics while in our classrooms, these students, whom William

Perry (1970) called "procedural knowers," sometimes lose this ability when confronted with related information beyond the class-room setting. For example, students in many different courses hear again and again that correlational studies do not allow researchers to make causal statements, and these students make clear to us in exams and during in-class discussions that they seem to understand this important idea. Nevertheless, those same students may make inappropriate causal inferences about information they encounter through the media, from friends, or elsewhere, even though they seemingly understand the mantra that "correlation does not equal causation." Given that research methods serve as a common denominator for the many diverse areas of psychology (Stanovich, 2001), we need to be sure that our students can apply what they learn in our research methods courses in later courses and in other areas of their lives.

Fifth, because lectures often lead to decreased student–instructor interaction, they may not be the best way to build rapport in the classroom, a factor that is important for maximizing student interest and learning (Astin, 1993). Joseph Lowman (1995) suggested that exceptional instructors acquire the ability to pique their students' interest in a topic by reaching out to them intellectually *and* emo-tionally. One way exceptional instructors do this is by focusing on the interpersonal factors that seem to have a powerful effect on students' willingness to "go the extra mile" for their instructors. Simple gestures such as learning your students' names and getting to know a little bit about them—gestures that often result from increased student–instructor interactions—go a long way in creating a classroom environment that enhances learning (Buskist & Saville, 2004). In short, methods that increase student involvement and maximize the amount of interaction between you and your students are likely to have a positive effect on the learning process (e.g., Barron, Benedict, Saville, Serdikoff, & Zinn, 2007; Saville, Zinn, Neef, Van Norman, & Ferreri, 2006).

Finally, non-lecture-based methods may simply provide you with a welcome change of pace, a new way to inject some fun and excitement into your research methods course. Regardless of which new pedagogical strategy you choose to incorporate into your courses, trying something different in your research methods courses may be one way to avoid becoming "lecture-weary instructors" (Halpern, 2004, p. 173) and a way of "maintaining vitality in the classroom" (Lloyd, 1999, p. 7).

Innovative Approaches to Teaching Research Methods

So, what alternatives are there for an instructor like Amanda, who wishes to move away from the lecture-based approaches that tend to dominate our research methods classrooms? Three factors seem to be especially important for maximizing student learning: time-on-task, student–student interaction, and student–instructor interaction (Astin, 1993; Barron et al., 2007). Any method that capitalizes on these factors is likely to have a positive effect on various measures of student learning and student interest. Let's consider three relatively new approaches to classroom instruction that seem especially effective at producing the positive changes in learning that we hope to see from our students in research methods: Just-in-Time Teaching, problem-based learning, and interteaching.

Just-in-Time Teaching

"Just-in-Time Teaching (JiTT) is a teaching and learning strategy comprised of two elements: classroom activities that promote active learning and World Wide Web resources that are used to enhance the classroom component" (Novak, Patterson, Gavrin, & Christian, 1999, p. 3). Though JiTT was developed initially to teach undergraduate physics, instructors have incorporated it into a wide variety of courses, including art history, biology, chemistry, geology, calculus, music, and psychology, to name but a few (www.jitt.org). Psychology instructors have also used JiTT to teach numerous courses, including general psychology, introductory and advanced statistics, and research methods (Barron et al., 2007; Benedict & Anderton, 2004). Regardless of the particular course in which instructors use it, JiTT has the following benefits: (a) it creates a student-centered course, (b) it increases the likelihood that students will study the course material before class, (c) it provides students and instructors with prompt feedback regarding students' understanding of course material, (d) it promotes increased interaction between students as well as between students and instructors, and (e) it creates a dynamic and interactive classroom environment (Barron et al., 2007).

Instructors typically implement JiTT in the following fashion. First, the instructor identifies course objectives (typically two or three) for discussion in class on a given day and then writes questions—called

PreClass Questions (or PCQs), PreFlight Questions, or WarmUps (Barron et al., 2007)—to address those objectives. For example, suppose that Amanda has decided she would like to focus on the following objectives during her next class period: identifying independent variables and dependent variables, and differentiating independent variables from confounding variables. She would then write a set of questions that focus on those objectives. For example:

1. Define the following concepts: independent variable, dependent variable, and confounding variable.
2. In order to study the effects of loud noise on worker productivity, Dr. Decibel had one group of research participants work in a noisy room and a second group work in a quiet room. She then measured which group produced the most widgets, on average. In this example, the noise level of the room would be the _____ and the number of widgets produced would be the _____.
   A) independent variable; confounding variable.
   B) dependent variable; independent variable.
   C) confounding variable; dependent variable.
   D) independent variable; dependent variable.
3. The term that most accurately describes the scientific method is *control*. When conducting an experiment, what are two ways that a researcher exerts control? How does this practice allow the researcher to be confident that any changes in the dependent variable were caused by changes in the independent variable and not by some other confounding variable?

Although the number of questions may vary from three to five, depending on the instructor's goals for the day and the difficulty of the material, there is typically one question per objective (Novak et al., 1999). The questions should take students 15 to 30 minutes to complete and should focus on course concepts and solving problems related to the course material (Barron et al., 2007). The questions typically contain one or more short-answer or essay questions and at least one difficult multiple-choice question.

After writing questions that focus on the previously identified objectives, the instructor then posts the questions online (e.g., on a course Web page, Blackboard, WebCT). Students then have several days to study the course material and submit their answers electronically no later than 2 to 3 hours before class is scheduled to begin. Depending on the instructor's goals for the course, he or she may require students to work alone or as part of a small group when answering the questions, which ultimately count for a small portion (e.g., 5% to 10%) of the students' course grades.

Upon receiving students' submissions, the instructor reviews the answers, identifies which of them would be good to discuss, and constructs a lecture "just in time" for class. During the lecture, the instructor reviews each question and its accompanying objective, elaborates on the course material, and attempts to stimulate student discussion by showing some sample answers that indicate good understanding of the material, as well as some answers that demonstrate confusions or misunderstandings. During this discussion, the instructor does not reveal the identity of students who wrote each answer. These discussions seem to result in better understanding of the material (e.g., Chew, 2005; Mazur, 1997) and give students prompt feedback regarding their understanding of course material. Specifically, the discussions allow students to identify answers that are similar to their own and to compare their answers to those the instructor has identified as representative of good understanding of the course material. This discussion-based format also allows the instructor and students to engage in a dialog and to collaborate with one another in an attempt to maximize students' understanding of the course material.

Several studies suggest that JiTT is an effective way to teach physics (Novak et al., 1999), but the evaluation of JiTT's effectiveness in teaching psychology courses is only recently emerging. The results, however, are promising (see Benedict & Anderton, 2004).

Problem-based Learning

Problem-based learning (PBL) is a pedagogical method that seeks to maximize student learning by requiring students to work cooperatively in small groups to solve ill-defined, complex "real-world" problems that usually have more than one possible solution. One of the primary assumptions behind PBL is that humans are in essence "built" to solve problems and that encountering problems will ultimately motivate people to learn whatever is necessary to solve them (McKeachie, 2002). This student-centered approach emerged more than 30 years ago at McMaster University, where medical students learned by reviewing actual clinical case studies and providing solutions to the problems contained within them. PBL subsequently found its way into numerous other disciplines, including psychology (see Connor-Greene, 2005). Considerable research suggests that PBL is an effective method of instruction (e.g., Dochy, Segers, Van de Bossche, & Gijbels, 2002; Duch, Groh, & Allen, 2001). McKeachie (2002) has gone so far as to suggest that, "*Problem-based learning is . . .* one of the most important developments in contemporary higher education" (p. 196, italics in original). There are many potential benefits to such an approach; some of the most important include: improved creative and critical thinking; extensive collaboration and teamwork, both with other students and with an instructor; improved leadership skills; self-directed learning; effective communication skills; appreciation of diversity; and increased transfer of knowledge to novel situations (Barrows & Tamblyn, 1980; Engel, 1997).

Although there is some variability in how instructors implement PBL in their classrooms (Rhem, 1998), in typical PBL-based courses, the structure is fairly consistent. First, instructors create ill-defined problems. These problems are usually quite difficult and require students to learn and apply important course concepts on their way to a solution. Moreover, because problems precede the learning of course material, and not vice versa (as is often the case with traditional methods), instructors must take care to write good problems. Duch (2001) delineated five steps involved in writing good PBL problems (see also Connor-Greene, 2005):

1. Identify important concepts that students should learn during the course,
2. Identify "real-world" problems in which students can recognize or apply those concepts,
3. Identify pragmatic issues involved in solving the problem, for example, how long will it likely take students to solve the problem?
4. Construct a schedule that clearly defines what will occur in class (e.g., group discussions, mini-lectures, presentations), and
5. Identify potential resources that students can use to get started.

A sample problem for a research methods course might be the following: John, a graduate student in clinical psychology, is in the process of starting his dissertation. Because John is interested in self-injurious behavior (a psychological disorder in which individuals inflict bodily harm on themselves), he wants to design a study that will (a) identify what variables might be functioning to maintain self-injurious behavior and (b) determine if a form of therapy known as applied behavior analysis might be effective in reducing the rate of self-injurious behavior. Explain how John could design a study to answer these questions.

Because students may have only limited knowledge of research methods, self-injurious behavior, applied behavior analysis, and so on, they may have to investigate each of these topics before they can start to identify a potential solution to this problem. As a result, students will have to delve into topics that instructors might not typically cover in their research methods courses.

Once an instructor has created several problems, he or she distributes one of them to each group of students (e.g., 5 to 10 students per group). Before doing so, however, the instructor may wish to spend some time explaining the benefits of PBL and presenting some guidelines for how students should approach the problems. Students then examine the problem without the benefit of any preparation or previous study of relevant material. This requires them to assess the problem within the confines of their existing knowledge base. After identifying what they know—and do not know—about the problem, students discuss what they need to learn, as well as potential methods they might use, to find a solution. Once they have discussed some ways they might go about identifying a potential solution, group members allocate responsibilities among themselves and identify what information they will need in order to produce a good solution.

After allocating responsibilities, students work individually to obtain different pieces of information that they bring back to the group. Although students work individually to acquire information, the tasks should be interrelated so that collaboration is necessary. After reuniting, students integrate the new information and knowledge they have acquired, apply it to the problem at hand, and weigh alternative solutions. If this new knowledge leads to a reasonable solution and members of the group are in agreement with one another, students reflect on the process as well as on the course content they have learned while finding a solution. If, however, this new knowledge does not lead to a solution, students continue to acquire information until they have reached a consensus and successfully identified a solution. Because each problem can have multiple solutions, students must defend the process they used in finding a solution as well as the solution itself.

Throughout a PBL course, the instructor serves as a facilitator or tutor, meeting frequently with each group to assess its progress and help students if they encounter difficulties. The instructor does not, however, serve as a direct source of information. Finally, after the groups have identified their solutions, class discussion focuses on the solutions as well as the course material that students have learned during the problem-solving process. Although it may come in many different forms (e.g., traditional exams, final papers, course portfolios, class presentations), assessment focuses on students' ability to apply acquired knowledge in different problem-solving contexts.

Considerable evidence from other disciplines suggests that PBL is an effective way for students to learn course content as well as other important skills (e.g., Albanese & Mitchell, 1993; Antepohl & Herzig, 1999; Duch et al., 2001). Although PBL students tend not to perform any better on short-term assessments of basic content than students who learned via traditional lecture-based methods, PBL students typically perform better on tests of long-term retention, conceptual analysis, motivation for learning, use of relevant resources, and application of course material. They also report more positive emotions regarding, and less stress during, their education than their non-PBL counterparts (Schwartz et al., 2001). In addition, instructors typically report enjoying PBL more than traditional methods of instruction.

As with JiTT, however, researchers have not examined extensively the efficacy of PBL within traditional psychology courses. However, the results reported so far have been promising (see Connor-Greene, 2002; Hays & Vincent, 2004). Although psychology instructors would do well to compare the efficacy of PBL to traditional methods of instruction, this approach seems well suited to research methods, a course in which instructors already incorporate various problem-based activities and assignments.

Interteaching

Interteaching (IT) is a relatively new behavioral approach to classroom instruction that contains remnants of earlier behavior-analytic teaching methods (e.g., Personalized System of Instruction, Keller, 1968; Direct Instruction, Engelmann & Carnine, 1982) as well as elements similar to those in JiTT and PBL. IT offers instructors considerably more flexibility than its behavioral predecessors, and it attempts to resolve some of the problems found in earlier behaviorally based methods of instruction (Boyce & Hineline, 2002; Saville, Zinn, & Elliott, 2005). Although early behavioral teaching methods have proven themselves superior to traditional forms of classroom instruction (Moran & Malott, 2004), they have fallen out of favor with instructors in the last 20 years or so (e.g., Buskist, Cush, & DeGrandpre, 1991; Fox, 2004).

The general procedure for IT is as follows. First, the instructor constructs a preparation (prep) guide, the purpose of which is to guide students through the assigned readings. The instructor then distributes the prep guide in class or via a course Web site (e.g., Blackboard, WebCT) several days before a specified class period. Typically, each prep guide contains approximately 10 items, some of which may contain multiple questions reviewing various aspects of course material. The following are examples of typical prep guide items over course material on independent, dependent, and extraneous variables:

1. Stacy is a graduate student in social psychology and is interested in determining how time of day affects prosocial, or "helping," behavior. To examine this, she will have her research assistant pose in the morning and at night as someone who is in need of a helping hand. Stacy strongly suspects that more people will stop to help during the morning than at night. What is Stacy's independent variable? What is her dependent variable? What are some extraneous variables that could influence her results? Finally, what are Stacy's experimental hypotheses, and are they directional or nondirectional?

2. Discuss the following statement: Extraneous variables influence the difference between (but not within) groups. With regard to extraneous variables, what does it mean when we say that an experiment is confounded? If you determine that your experiment is confounded, what is the best course of action to take?

Each prep guide typically covers 10 to 20 pages of reading, depending on the difficulty of the material. Items on the prep guide usually require students to define, comprehend, apply, and evaluate course material (Bloom, 1956). Moreover, like problem-based learning, the prep guide items typically require students to solve one or more problems, such as the following:

Jason and John both want to determine if exercise reduces stress in college students. Whereas Jason wants to use a small-N design to examine the effects of exercise on stress, John has decided to use a large-N design. Briefly explain how each might go about conducting his experiment.

Students then use the prep guide to prepare for class. As with JiTT, students attempt to answer each prep guide item to the best of their ability before returning to the next class session. Once in class, students get into pairs and review the material contained on the prep guides. During this time, students discuss the prep guide items, clarifying any topics that are confusing and helping each other learn the pertinent information. The instructor moves around the room, answering questions, prompting students when they get stuck, and in general facilitating discussion of the material on the prep guides. Although the length of the discussions may vary depending on the material, a good rule of thumb is that the discussions should account for roughly two-thirds of the class time (e.g., 35 minutes in a 50-minute period, 50 minutes in a 75-minute period). If students consistently finish early or have few questions over the prep guide items, they probably are not discussing the material as deeply as they should. Also, to motivate students to attend class and engage in the pair discussions, they receive a small amount of course credit for each discussion they complete (e.g., 5% to 10% of their course grade).

Once students have finished discussing the prep guide items, they fill out an interteaching record, the purpose of which is to obtain information regarding their understanding of course material. On this form, students list (a) their name and their partner's name; (b) how long their discussion lasted and if there was sufficient time to get through the prep guide questions in detail; (c) how well the discussion went and what factors contributed to its quality; (d) which items, if any, were especially difficult to answer and why; (e) which topics, if any, the instructor should review or discuss in more detail (see below); and (f) any other information that might help the instructor evaluate the extent to which students understand the prep guide material. Based on this information, the instructor constructs a short lecture to present at the beginning of the next class period, just before the pair discussion for that day. During this lecture, the instructor typically reviews any prep guide questions that were difficult for the students to understand as well as those questions that students did not specifically request but that the instructor thinks are worthy of discussion. The instructor may also include in the lecture any supplemental material that may help clarify the information or motivate students to delve into the material further.

In addition to this general procedure, there are two other components that may contribute to the efficacy of IT. First, exams are frequent (i.e., at least five per semester), which seems to improve performance and reduce anxiety (e.g., Fulkerson & Martin, 1981). The exams contain items that are similar, but not identical, to items found on the prep guides. Specifically, exams contain two or three essay questions, most often taken *directly* from the prep guides, and a number of other objective questions (e.g., multiple choice, short answer), designed to test students' understanding of, and ability to apply, key concepts contained on the prep guide items. Although some might question the value of having prep guide items and test items that are similar, this similarity might lead to greater transfer of training (Halpern & Hakel, 2003; Moore, 2001).

Second, students receive a small number of points based on the quality of their pair discussions. Instructors can distribute these "quality" points in several different ways. They may simply distribute points to students during the pair discussions if the instructor thinks the students' discussion is "on target" and relevant to the material at hand (Saville et al., 2006). Alternatively, instructors may wish to award points for students' descriptions of the quality of their pair discussions, which they state briefly on the interteaching records (Boyce & Hineline, 2002). For example, if both students state that the discussion went well, the instructor may wish to award a small number of points to those students; if, however, one or both students state that the discussion did not go well, for whatever reason, the instructor may choose not to award the points. Finally, instructors may award points for exam performance, an indirect indicator of the quality of student discussions. Consider the following example. Last Tuesday, Tracy and Bill were partners and spent a good amount of time discussing the items on a particular prep guide. The next week, one of the essay questions on the exam, which was worth five points, came from the prep guide that Tracy and Bill discussed the preceding week. If both Tracy and Bill earn either an A or B (i.e., four or five points) on that particular essay question, they each receive a small number of points toward their course grades; if, however, either Tracy or Bill does not earn an A or B, neither receives these points. Regardless of how one awards quality points, each of these methods introduces a positive interdependency (i.e., cooperation) into IT, which previous research (e.g., Johnson, Maruyama, Johnson, Nelson, & Skon, 1981) suggests should have a positive effect on performance.

If after reading these descriptions of quality points you are hesitant to implement this component of IT, you may have good reason to be skeptical. First, anecdotal evidence suggests that students tend not to like this aspect of IT; they think it is unfair for part of their course grades to depend on the performance of others. Considerable research suggests that some type of positive interdependency tends to improve overall performance (Johnson et al., 1981), but students are often quick to voice their opposition to this component. Although our students' attitudes should not be the sole determinant of whether we introduce new features into our courses, we may wish to consider the effects that these features might have on our students' motivation, interest, and willingness to go the extra mile. Second, and perhaps more important, some research suggests that certain methods of awarding quality points may not contribute to the overall effectiveness of IT. In a recent unpublished study, Zinn et al. (2006) awarded quality points by having students' exam scores partially dependent on the essay question performances of their partners. They found no difference between students in a "quality points" condition and students in a "no quality points" condition. Zinn et al. suggested that the addition of quality points to exam scores, which often occurred more than 1 week after students' discussions, was delayed too long to be an effective consequence for engaging in quality discussion. Although distributing quality points in other ways (see above) may affect learning, instructors may wish to weigh the pros and cons of awarding quality points in their classes. If instructors choose to include quality points, they should account for approximately 10% of students' overall course grades (Boyce & Hineline, 2002).

In a series of studies, Saville and his colleagues (Saville et al., 2005; Saville et al., 2006; Zinn et al., 2006) observed that IT resulted in better learning than other methods of classroom instruction. However, as with JiTT and PBL, researchers will need to conduct further studies on IT to help determine if it is more effective than other teaching methods and, if so, which component(s) contribute to its effectiveness. Nevertheless, based on early studies, IT seems to be an effective method of instruction, as well as an enjoyable way for students to learn about research methods.

Caveats

Although JiTT, PBL, and IT all provide novel and potentially effective ways to teach research methods, there are certain caveats of which you should be aware before implementing any of these pedagogical methods. First, each requires a considerable amount of preparation time. For example, constructing problems for PBL, questions for JiTT, and prep guides for IT, although thought-provoking, is also time-consuming, a factor that you must consider given the ever-increasing demands on your time (Milem, Berger, and Dey, 2000; Wright et al., 2004). If you plan to use any of these methods, you may want to introduce them slowly, using them initially for bits and pieces of your courses and adding more content across one or more semesters.

Second, these methods can be initially anxiety-provoking and sometimes unpopular with students who are accustomed to more traditional lecture-based methods of instruction (e.g., McBurney, 1995). Students who are not used to preparing for class every day, or are used to being passive in class, may initially be uncomfortable with methods that require them to consistently and actively engage the course material. Similarly, students who are exceptional stenographers and who can memorize for exams the information contained in their books and notes are often nonplussed by the notion that the onus is now on them to identify relevant course material and actively manage their own learning. In other words, students are sometimes uncomfortable with a situation in which they must "learn how to learn" rather than simply learn how to take notes and regurgitate information on exams. As with most new experiences, students usually get comfortable with these new approaches. In fact, students often report that they were initially hesitant about using these methods but realized how useful they are. Other students may not appreciate the efficacy of these approaches until several semesters later when they realize that they still remember information from their nontraditionally organized courses and that they have in fact learned how to learn by themselves.

Finally, if you, like most instructors, are used to having total control in your courses, adopting one of these new methods may be anxiety-provoking because they all require you to turn some control over to your students. However, remember that your students will rise to the level at which you expect them to perform (Bain, 2004).

In conclusion, the positive aspects of adopting JiTT, PBL, or IT will likely greatly outweigh the negative aspects that may come with incorporating one of these methods into your research methods courses. There is good evidence that these methods result in better in-class performance as well as better ability to carry those newly acquired skills to other aspects of our students' lives. If our goal as instructors is to increase students' performance in our classrooms as well as increase the likelihood that new knowledge gained in our courses transfers to other areas of their lives, JiTT, PBL, and IT provide potentially effective and enjoyable alternatives to traditional lecture-based methods of classroom instruction to which we and our students have grown so accustomed.

References

Albanese, M. A., & Mitchell, S. (1993). Problem-based learning: A review of literature on its outcomes and implementation issues. *Academic Medicine, 68,* 52–81.

Antepohl, W., & Herzig, S. (1999). Problem-based learning versus lecture-based learning in a course of basic pharmacology: A controlled, randomized study. *Medical Education, 33,* 106–113.

Astin, A. W. (1993). *What matters in college?: Four critical years revisited.* San Francisco: Jossey-Bass.

Bain, K. (2004). *What the best college teachers do.* Cambridge, MA: Harvard University Press.

Barron, K. E., Benedict, J. O., Saville, B. K., Serdikoff, S. L., & Zinn, T. E. (2007). Innovative approaches to teaching statistics and research methods: Just-in-Time Teaching, Interteaching, and Learning Communities. In D. S. Dunn, R. A. Smith, & B. C. Beins (Eds.), *Best practices for teaching statistics and research methods in the behavioral sciences* (pp. 143–158). Mahwah, NJ: Erlbaum.

Barrows, H. S., & Tamblyn, R. N. (1980). *Problem-Based Learning: An approach to medical education.* New York: Springer.

Benedict, J. O., & Anderton, J. B. (2004). Applying the Just-in-Time Teaching approach to teaching statistics. *Teaching of Psychology, 31,* 197–199.

Bernstein, D. A. (2006). Building a repertoire of effective classroom demonstrations. In W. Buskist & S. F. Davis (Eds.), *The handbook of the teaching of psychology* (pp. 90–93). Malden, MA: Blackwell.

Bloom, B. S. (Ed.). (1956). *Taxonomy of educational objectives, Vol. 1: Cognitive domain.* New York: Longmans, Green.

Boyce, T. E., & Hineline, P. N. (2002). Interteaching: A strategy for enhancing the user-friendliness of behavioral arrangements in the college classroom. *The Behavior Analyst, 25,* 215–226.

Buskist, W., Cush, D., & DeGrandpre, R. J. (1991). The life and times of PSI. *Journal of Behavioral Education, 1,* 215–234.

Buskist, W., & Saville, B. K. (2004). Rapport-building: Creating positive emotional contexts for enhancing teaching and learning. In B. Perlman, L. I. McCann, & S. H. McFadden (Eds.), *Lessons learned, Vol. 2: Practical advice for the teaching of psychology* (pp. 149–155). Washington, DC: American Psychological Society.

Buskist, W., Sikorski, J., Buckley, T., & Saville, B. K. (2002). Elements of master teaching. In S. F. Davis & W. Buskist (Eds.), *The teaching of psychology: Essays in honor of Wilbert J. McKeachie and Charles L. Brewer* (pp. 27–39). Mahwah, NJ: Erlbaum.

Chew, S. L. (2005). Student misperceptions in the psychology classroom. In B. K. Saville, T. E. Zinn, & V. W. Hevern (Eds.), *Essays from e-xcellence in teaching, 2004* (Chap. 3). Retrieved March 13, 2006, from the Society for the Teaching of Psychology Web site: http://teachpsych.org/resources/e-books/eit2004/eit04-03.pdf

Connor-Greene, P. A. (2002). Problem-based service learning: The evolution of a team project. *Teaching of Psychology, 29,* 193–197.

Connor-Greene, P. A. (2005). Problem-based learning. In W. Buskist & S. F. Davis (Eds.), *The handbook of the teaching of psychology* (pp. 70–77). Malden, MA: Blackwell.

Davis, B. G. (1993). *Tools for teaching.* San Francisco: Jossey-Bass.

Dochy, F., Segers, M., Van de Bossche, P., & Gijbels, D. (2002). Effects of problem-based learning: A meta-analysis. *Learning and Instruction, 13,* 533–568.

Duch, B. J. (2001). Models for problem-based instruction in undergraduate courses. In B. J. Duch, S. E. Groh, & D. E. Allen (Eds.), *The power of problem-based learning: A practical "how to" for teaching undergraduate courses in any discipline* (pp. 39–45). Sterling, VA: Stylus.

Duch, B. J., Groh, S. E., & Allen, D. E. (Eds.). (2001). *The power of problem-based learning: A practical "how to" for teaching undergraduate courses in any discipline.* Sterling, VA: Stylus.

Engel, C. E. (1997). Not just a method but a way of learning. In D. Boud & G. Feletti (Eds.), *The challenge of problem-based learning* (2nd ed., pp. 17–27). London: Kogan Page.

Engelmann, S., & Carnine, D. W. (1982). *Theory of instruction: Principles and application.* New York: Irvington.

Fox, E. J. (2004). The Personalized System of Instruction: A flexible and effective approach to mastery learning. In D. J. Moran & R. W. Malott (Eds.), *Evidence-based educational methods: Advances from the behavioral sciences* (pp. 201–221). New York: Academic Press.

Fulkerson, F. E., & Martin, G. (1981). Effects of exam frequency on student performance, evaluations of instructor, and test anxiety. *Teaching of Psychology, 8,* 90–93.

Halpern, D. F. (2004). Creating cooperative learning environments. In B. Perlman, L. I. McCann, & S. H. McFadden (Eds.), *Lessons learned: Practical advice for the teaching of psychology, Vol. 2* (pp. 165–173). Washington, DC: American Psychological Society.

Halpern, D. F., & Hakel, M. D. (2003). Applying the science of learning to the university and beyond. *Change, 35*(4), 36–42.

Hays, J. R., & Vincent, J. P. (2004). Students' evaluation of problem-based learning in graduate psychology courses. *Teaching of Psychology, 31*, 124–126.

Johnson, D. W., Maruyama, G., Johnson, R., Nelson, D., & Skon, L. (1981). Effects of cooperative, competitive, and individualistic goals structures on achievement. *Psychological Bulletin, 89*, 47–62.

Keller, F. S. (1968). Good-bye teacher . . . *Journal of Applied Behavior Analysis, 1*, 79–89.

Lloyd, M. A. (1999). As time goes by: Maintaining vitality in the classroom. In B. Perlman, L. I. McCann, & S. H. McFadden (Eds.), *Lessons learned: Practical advice for the teaching of psychology* (pp. 7–10). Washington, DC: American Psychological Society.

Lowman, J. (1995). *Mastering the techniques of teaching* (2nd ed.). San Francisco: Jossey-Bass.

Mathie, V. A., Beins, B., Benjamin, L. T., Jr., Ewing, M. M., Hall, C. C. I., Henderson, B., et al. (1993). Promoting active learning in psychology courses. In T. V. McGovern (Ed.), *Handbook for enhancing undergraduate education in psychology* (pp. 183–214). Washington, DC: American Psychological Association.

McBurney, D. H. (1995). The problem method of teaching research methods. *Teaching of Psychology, 22*, 36–38.

Mazur, E. (1997). *Peer instruction: A user's manual.* New Jersey: Prentice Hall.

McKeachie, W. J. (2002). *McKeachie's teaching tips: Strategies, research, and theory for college and university teachers* (11th ed.). Boston: Houghton Mifflin.

Milem, J. F., Berger, J. B., & Dey, E. L. (2000). Faculty time allocation: A study of change over twenty years. *The Journal of Higher Education, 71*, 454–475.

Miserandino, M. (1999). Those who can do: Implementing active learning. In B. Perlman, L. I. McCann, & S. H. McFadden (Eds.), *Lessons learned: Practical advice for the teaching of psychology* (pp. 109–114). Washington, DC: American Psychological Society.

Moore, J. (2001). On certain assumptions underlying contemporary educational practices. *Behavior and Social Issues, 11*, 49–64.

Moran, D. J., & Malott, R. W. (Eds.). (2004). *Evidence-based educational methods: Advances from the behavioral sciences.* New York: Academic Press.

Novak. G. M., Patterson, E. T., Gavrin, A. D., & Christian, W. (1999). *Just-in-Time Teaching: Blending active learning with Web technology.* Upper Saddle River, NJ: Prentice-Hall.

Perry, W. G. (1970). *Forms of intellectual and ethical development in the college years: A scheme.* New York: Holt, Rinehart & Winston.

Rhem. J. (1998). Problem-based learning: An introduction. *The National Teaching and Learning Forum, 8*(1), 1–4.

Saville, B. K., Zinn, T. E., & Elliott, M. P. (2005). Interteaching vs. traditional methods of instruction: A preliminary analysis. *Teaching of Psychology, 32,* 161–163.

Saville, B. K., Zinn, T. E., Neef, N. A., Van Norman, R., & Ferreri, S. J. (2006). A comparison of interteaching and lecture in the college classroom. *Journal of Applied Behavior Analysis, 39,* 49–61.

Schwartz, P., Mennin, S., & Webb, G. (Eds.). (2001). *Problem-based learning: Case studies, experience, and practice.* London: Kogan Page.

Stanovich, K. E. (2001). *How to think straight about psychology* (6th ed.). Boston: Allyn & Bacon.

Wright, M. C., Assar, N., Kain, E. L., Kramer, L., Howery, C. B., McKinney, K. et al. (2004). Greedy institutions: The importance of institutional context for teaching in higher education. *Teaching Sociology, 32,* 144–159.

Yoder, J. D., & Hochevar, C. M. (2005). Encouraging active learning can improve students' performance on examinations. *Teaching of Psychology, 32,* 91–95.

Zinn, T. E., & Saville, B. K. (2005). Leading discussions and asking questions. In W. Buskist & S. F. Davis (Eds.), *The handbook of the teaching of psychology* (pp. 85–89). Malden, MA: Blackwell.

Zinn, T. E., Saville, B. K., Burnett, J., Cordon, S., Kincheloe, B., & Noll, N. (2006, May). *Interteaching: A component analysis.* Poster presented at the 18th annual Association for Psychological Science conference. New York.

Chapter 11

Reflection and Revision

Well, you've done it! You've just finished another (or maybe your first) semester teaching psychological research methods. There may have been numerous bumps along the way, especially if you were teaching the course for the first time, but there were surely some rewarding moments, too—quite a few of them, in fact. The student who confessed on the first day of class that he was petrified about failing the course actually ended up doing quite well; in fact, he received one of the highest grades in the class. And now that you think about it, your students' writing really did improve over the semester—maybe they really did look at the extensive comments you wrote on their papers! Perhaps most surprisingly, a student who had told you that she had absolutely no interest in research methods because she was going to be a school counselor approached you during the last week of class to ask about research opportunities that might be available in the department.

So, all in all, it probably turned out to be a pretty good semester. But you're exhausted, and because you won't be teaching research methods next semester, it's time to put your course materials away and not think about the class for a while. Or is it? In reality, this is actually a very good time to reflect on the course and spend some time revising, or at least making notes about revising, the course and its materials while the just completed semester is still fresh in your mind.

The Importance of Reflection

As Socrates avowed over 24 centuries ago, "An unexamined life is not worth living." To some extent, one might say the same about our teaching lives. Regardless of which classes you typically teach, taking time to reflect on them, and on your overall teaching approach and results, can have numerous benefits both for you and your students. Buskist and Davis (2006) put it this way:

> An often overlooked aspect of authentic teaching assessment is stepping back from both classroom teaching and its assessment and looking at them from afar—that is, reflecting over what it is that you do as teacher and how effective it may or may not be in benefiting your students' learning. (pp. 8–9)

Allowing yourself to "step back" every once in a while can provide insight into your teaching that may not be immediately obvious when you are "in the trenches," dealing with some of the day-to-day minutiae that can so easily come to dominate our academic lives (Forsyth, 2003).

"So," you might be asking yourself, "how can I initiate this process of reflection?" Ultimately, reflection is a personal matter (e.g., Palmer, 1998), and the process may differ considerably from one person to the next. However, there are two related activities that can be a great source of insight as you begin the process of reflecting on your teaching: writing a statement of your teaching philosophy and constructing a teaching portfolio. Because the focus of this book is on teaching research methods and because there are many excellent resources for learning more about these activities, I will mention each very briefly.

One way to initiate the process of reflection is by writing a statement of your teaching philosophy, or reviewing it if you already have written one. A statement of your teaching philosophy contains your personal beliefs about the process of teaching—in essence, the "whats," "whys," and "hows" of your approach to teaching. Because your overall teaching philosophy sets the stage for everything else you do in the classroom (Korn, 2002), simply taking the time to recognize and set down on paper your personal beliefs about teaching may help you pinpoint general, as well as more specific, ways in which you can improve your classroom performance and, consequently, have a greater impact on your students' learning (see

Chism, 1998 and Forsyth, 2003 for discussions on constructing a statement of teaching philosophy).

A second, and more in-depth, way to reflect on your overall teaching performance is to construct (or review, if you already have one) a teaching portfolio, which is "an organized collection of material that reflects your ideas about teaching, your performance as a teacher, and how your teaching has changed over time" (Korn, 2002, p. 203). Although there are many ways to construct a teaching portfolio, most versions will contain at least several of the following items: your curriculum vita; your statement of teaching philosophy (which should serve as the centerpiece of your portfolio; Korn, 2002); sample teaching materials (including, for example, course notes, syllabi, exams, and students' writing assignments); student and peer evaluations; and supplemental materials such as videos of yourself in the classroom and any teaching-related papers you may have published (Forsyth, 2003; Korn, 2002; Rasmussen, 2006; Seldin, 2004). In other words, a teaching portfolio includes materials that, together, highlight your personal teaching philosophy and history. Whether you are relatively new to teaching or a practiced veteran, revisiting these materials periodically can provide new ideas and, sometimes, a valuable stimulus for change.

Once you have had an opportunity to reflect on your teaching performance in general, you should take some time to think about your research methods course in particular. Here are some questions you may want to ask yourself as you reflect on the course you just completed.

1. Overall, how did the course go? Although there are many ways to evaluate the course (e.g., students' exam scores, course evaluations), it may be better to answer this question first on the basis of your "gut reaction." In general, did your students seem to struggle with the material, or did they seem to "get it"? Were they typically talkative in class, or did they just sit there, unresponsive, disinterested, struggling to stay awake? Did your students approach you regularly to ask questions, or did they seem to avoid you? Similarly, how did *you* feel about the course in general? Did you enjoy going to class every day, or did you find yourself bemoaning the thought of spending another minute discussing independent variables or internal validity? Did you enjoy grading exams (relatively speaking, of course) because you wanted to know how your students performed, or were you

convinced that each exam was just going to be "another bad one"? Your visceral responses to these questions and others like them may provide an overall context in which you can address the following, more specific questions.

2. Did you and your students meet your course objectives? You may have broadly defined objectives, but your assessments over the course of the semester should provide some insight into whether you met the objectives. For example, if one of your objectives was to teach your students to write APA-style papers, do you feel that their writing and understanding of APA style improved? If you wanted to spend more time discussing ethical considerations, were you able to integrate more of this information in your class sessions? By evaluating your students' performance in light of your course objectives and goals, you will gain a better understanding of how you might restructure your course in the future in order to meet the goals you set for yourself and your students. If you find it difficult to determine whether you met your course objectives, you may need to spend some time reviewing what you are trying to accomplish, consider better ways to link your assignments and activities back to your objectives, or maybe even revise your course objectives altogether.

3. How did your students perform relative to students in other research methods courses you've taught? Comparing students' performance across semesters can provide useful information about the course as well as your teaching performance. For example, were grades on the APA-style papers higher or lower than they were in previous semesters? Were grades on exams and other assignments comparable to previous semesters? If so, was it because you changed the assignments or structured your course differently? Although it may be difficult to identify the factors that accounted for across-semester differences, such comparisons may be useful when attempting to pinpoint means for improving your course.

4. How did your students perform on specific assignments? For example, did they do well on the exams that covered two-group and factorial designs? Or when you asked them to read journal articles and identify information you had discussed in lecture, were they able to do so with relative ease? Similarly, were there any assignments on which your students performed poorly? For

example, when you asked them to peruse an incorrectly formatted APA-style paper and identify errors, did they struggle to identify even the most blatant errors? Again, although your students' performance may be a function of many factors, some of which may be beyond your control, examining how they performed on specific assignments may provide information regarding which topics you should spend more time reviewing the next time around.

5. How were your student evaluations? Although several researchers have questioned the validity of student evaluations, looking for trends in ratings—or better yet, trends in written comments you received as part of your evaluations—can help you identify which parts of your course seemed to facilitate learning, which activities your students enjoyed, how your students felt about the course overall, and so on.

6. Are there other indicators that your course had a positive effect on students' interest in course-related material? For example, did students approach you during or after the semester and ask to get involved in your research, or did they inquire about other research opportunities that might be available to them? Such incidents are valuable indicators of the effect your course had on students' attitudes toward psychological research.

There are also other questions you may wish to ask yourself at the end of the semester. For example, how likely is it that your students will retain what they learned in your course? To answer this question, it may be useful to talk to other instructors in your department about their perceptions of your students' retention of research methods material. When these instructors discuss research methods in their courses, do students seem to remember the information, or do they sit with blank stares on their faces? Regardless of how you choose to reflect on your teaching, contemplating these and other questions will likely provide you with important insight regarding the overall conduct of your course as well as ways to improve your course the next time you teach it. A final word of caution: If you decide to make changes to your course, it may be a good idea to make small modifications initially rather than changing everything at once. Making major changes, especially when you are pressed for time (i.e., every semester), can be overwhelming and may result in a course that may be new, but not necessarily improved.

Maintaining Vitality While Teaching
Research Methods

As mentioned throughout this book, the research methods course can be one of the most difficult courses in the psychology curriculum to teach, and those who do not step back and reflect every so often may find themselves getting burned out and jaded, dreading the day they have to teach it again. More importantly, they may fail to identify those important rewards that can profoundly affect one's motivation to teach such a course. There are, however, ways to maintain vitality while teaching this important but difficult course (see Bernstein, 2005; Lloyd, 1999; McCann & Perlman, 2006). Although the following tips may apply to any course, they seem to be especially pertinent to those who teach research methods.

1. Try a new teaching approach. Adopting a new teaching method, such as the alternative teaching methods I discussed in the previous chapter, may be just what you (and your students) need to inject some much-needed energy into the course.
2. Change your course assignments. Because time is a scarce commodity for most of us, we may find ourselves incorporating the same assignments into our courses several semesters in a row. Whether you simply change a small activity here and there or opt completely to overhaul your course assignments, thinking of new ways to challenge your students may produce benefits for all involved.
3. Incorporate technology into your presentations. If you usually make "low-tech" classroom presentations, adding some "high-tech" features may provide a much-needed spark to your teaching. For example, simply providing your students with visuals in the form of overheads or PowerPoint slides might be a welcome supplement to your lectures and may even improve your students' understanding of important course concepts. If you choose to add technology to your classroom presentations, however, it is important that you do not "let the technology take over." Technology should complement your lectures, not replace them (see Beins, 2002; Daniel, 2005, 2006; Huelsman, 2006; Lutsky, 2002; McKeachie, 2002; for discussions on implementing technology into your classrooms).

4. Incorporate demonstrations and activities into your classroom presentations. As I have stated elsewhere in this book, the concepts we teach in research methods are often foreign to many, if not most, of our students. Thus demonstrations might be an effective way not only to improve your students' understanding of important course material, but also a way to inject some fun into the classroom and maybe even increase your students' motivation to learn more about research methods (Bernstein, 1999, 2006). Although I have described many classroom activities and demonstrations throughout this book, I urge interested readers to consult other sources, including the following: (a) *Teaching of Psychology*, a journal that provides a good range of effective teaching demonstrations for research methods; (b) teaching of psychology activities handbooks (e.g., Benjamin & Lowman, 1981; Benjamin, Nodine, Ernst, & Blair-Broeker, 1999; Hartley & McKeachie, 1990; Makosky, Whittemore, & Rogers, 1987; Ware & Brewer, 1988; Ware & Johnson, 1996), which contain useful activities for research methods courses; (c) *Teaching Tips*, a teaching column that appears monthly in the Association for Psychological Science's *Observer* and often contains information on unique classroom activities; (d) teaching of psychology discussion lists, including *PsychTeacher* (http://teachpsych.org/news/psychteacher.php) and *TIPS* (Teaching in the Psychological Sciences, http://faculty.frostburg.edu/psyc/southerly/tips), which often contain threads on effective teaching demonstrations; and (e) *OTRP Online* (Office of Teaching Resources in Psychology; http://teachpsych.org/otrp/index.php, a valuable resource for all psychology instructors. Not only are effective demonstrations useful for teaching difficult material, they may also be "just what the doctor ordered" to liven up your classroom presentations.

5. Talk to other research methods instructors. Sometimes a good way to maintain vitality when teaching research methods is simply to talk to others who have "walked a mile in your shoes." Not only might they be a welcome source of empathy when you need to discuss your successes and failures, many of which they may have also experienced, they might also be a useful resource when you are looking for new demonstrations, ways to structure your course, and the like. You might also take this a step further by asking your colleagues to allow you to observe them in action in their classrooms. Even if their teaching styles differ

from yours, you will most likely take away something of value that you can then try out in your own courses.

Conclusion

As I said at the beginning of this book, research methods have played, and will continue to play, an important role in our ever-evolving discipline. From the very beginning—from Hermann Ebbinghaus's early "forgetting curves" to the ebb and flow of John B. Watson's methodological behaviorism to the recent ascent of cognitive neuroscience—research methods have remained a constant in a discipline that has seen more change than a piggy bank. In much the same way, the research methods course has held, and will continue to hold, a respected place in the psychology curriculum. It is in the research methods course that our students receive their first comprehensive introduction to psychology as science and to the empirical tools that allow researchers to learn more about basic psychological phenomena and how we can use knowledge of those phenomena to improve the human condition. Hence those of us teaching psychological research methods have an important role to play, one that is vital to the advancement of our discipline; for it is the students of today who will go on to become the basic researchers and applied practitioners of tomorrow.

Although teaching research methods can be difficult and sometimes frustrating, it can also be a source of bountiful rewards. In fact, some of my most satisfying teaching moments have come in my methods course, when students, especially those who initially showed little interest in the course material, finally "saw the light" and realized why learning about research methods is so important. Granted, not every one of your students will go on to pursue careers conducting psychological research; in fact, most probably won't. However, your students *will* need to know something about science in general and about research methods in particular in order to function effectively in our rapidly changing world. Hopefully, the information contained in this book will help you teach your research methods course more efficiently and effectively, regardless of whether you are a graduate student who is teaching it for the first time, or a seasoned veteran who is teaching it for the thirty-first time.

References

Beins, B. C. (2002). Technology in the classroom: Traditions in psychology. In S. F. Davis & W. Buskist (Eds.), *The teaching of psychology: Essays in honor of William J. McKeachie and Charles L. Brewer* (pp. 307–321). Mahwah, NJ: Erlbaum.

Benjamin, L. T., Jr., & Lowman, K. D. (Eds.). (1981). *Activities handbook for the teaching of psychology.* Washington, DC: American Psychological Association.

Benjamin, L. T., Jr., Nodine, B. F., Ernst, R. M., & Blair-Broeker, C. (Eds.). (1999). *Activities handbook for the teaching of psychology, Vol. 4.* Washington, DC: American Psychological Association.

Bernstein, D. A. (1999). Tell and show: The merits of classroom demonstrations. In B. Perlman, L. I. McCann, & S. H. McFadden (Eds.), *Lessons learned: Practical advice for the teaching of psychology* (pp. 105–108). Washington, DC: American Psychological Society.

Bernstein, D. A. (2005). Was it good for you, too? In B. Perlman, L. I. McCann, & W. Buskist (Eds.), *Voices of experience: Memorable talks from the National Institute on the Teaching of Psychology, Vol. 1* (pp. 111–118). Washington, DC: American Psychological Society.

Bernstein, D. A. (2006). Building a repertoire of effective classroom demonstrations. In W. Buskist & S. F. Davis (Eds.), *The handbook of the teaching of psychology* (pp. 90–93). Malden, MA: Blackwell.

Buskist, W., & Davis, S. F. (Eds.). (2006). *The handbook of the teaching of psychology.* Malden, MA: Blackwell.

Chism, N. V. N. (1998). Developing a philosophy of teaching statement. *Essays on Teaching Excellence, 9*(3), 1–2.

Daniel, D. B. (2005). How to ruin a perfectly good lecture: Presentation software as a teaching tool. In B. Perlman, L. I. McCann, & W. Buskist (Eds.), *Voices of experience: Memorable talks from the National Institute on the Teaching of Psychology, Vol. 1* (pp. 119–130). Washington, DC: American Psychological Society.

Daniel, D. B. (2006). Evil technology: Nature or nurture? In T. E. Zinn, B. K. Saville, & J. E. Williams (Eds.), *Essays from e-xcellence in teaching, 2005* (Chap. 10). Retrieved November 1, 2006, from the Society for the Teaching of Psychology Web site: http://teachpsych.org/resources/e books/ eit2005/eit05-10.pdf

Forsyth, D. R. (2003). *The professor's guide to teaching: Psychological principles and practices.* Washington, DC: American Psychological Association.

Hartley, J., & McKeachie, W. J. (Eds.). (1990). *Teaching psychology: A handbook.* Hillsdale, NJ: Erlbaum.

Huelsman, T. J. (2006). Lessons learned using PowerPoint in the classroom. In W. Buskist & S. F. Davis (Eds.), *The handbook of the teaching of psychology* (pp. 94–98). Malden, MA: Blackwell.

Korn, J. H. (2002). Beyond tenure: The teaching portfolio for reflection and change. In S. F. Davis & W. Buskist (Eds.), *The teaching of psychology: Essays in honor of Wilbert J. McKeachie and Charles L. Brewer* (pp. 203–213). Mahwah, NJ: Erlbaum.

Lloyd, M. A. (1999). As time goes by: Maintaining vitality in the classroom. In B. Perlman, L. I. McCann, & S. H. McFadden (Eds.), *Lessons learned: Practical advice for the teaching of psychology* (pp. 7–10). Washington, DC: American Psychological Society.

Lutsky, N. (2002). Come, putative ends of psychology's digital future. In S. F. Davis & W. Buskist (Eds.). *The teaching of psychology: Essays in honor of Wilbert J. McKeachie and Charles L. Brewer* (pp. 335–345). Mahwah, NJ: Erlbaum.

Makosky, V. P., Whittemore, L. G., & Rogers, A. M. (Eds.). (1987). *Activities handbook for the teaching of psychology, Vol. 2.* Washington, DC: American Psychological Association.

McCann, L. I., & Perlman, B. (2006). Making your teaching and your life more enjoyable. *APS Observer, 19*(6), 25–27.

McKeachie, W. J. (2002). *McKeachie's teaching tips: Strategies, research, and theory for college and university teachers* (11th ed.). Boston: Houghton Mifflin.

Palmer, P. J. (1998). *The courage to teach: Exploring the inner landscape of a teacher's life.* San Francisco: Jossey-Bass.

Rasmussen, E. B. (2006). Creating teaching portfolios. In W. Buskist & S. F. Davis (Eds.), *The handbook of the teaching of psychology* (pp. 301–306). Malden, MA: Blackwell.

Seldin, P. (2004). *The teaching portfolio: A practical guide to improved performance and promotion/tenure decisions* (3rd ed.). Bolton, MA: Anker.

Ware, M. E., & Brewer, C. L. (Eds.). (1988). *Handbook for teaching statistics and research methods.* Hillsdale, NJ: Erlbaum.

Ware, M. E., & Johnson, D. E. (Eds.). (1996). *Handbook of demonstrations and activities in the teaching of psychology: Introductory, statistics, research methods and history, Vol. 1.* Mahwah, NJ: Erlbaum.

Appendix: Professional Development Resources in the Teaching of Psychology

A wide range of useful resources is available to help high school, community college, and college and university faculty and graduate students become more effective teachers and to develop professionally as teacher-scholars. In particular, psychology has been at the forefront of all disciplines in promoting effective teaching. This appendix contains a listing and brief description of many of these resources. This listing is not intended to be exhaustive, but it is designed to offer you a solid picture of the many excellent sources to which you may turn to learn more about teaching well, to hone your teaching style, and to join with others who value teaching as much as you do. The listing below includes teaching organizations, teaching conferences, and books on teaching.

Teaching Organizations

Society for the Teaching of Psychology
(STP; Division 2 of the American Psychological Association) (http://teachpsych.org/)

STP promotes the effective teaching of psychology at all levels of education. Its Web site receives hundreds of thousands of hits each year, testifying to the usefulness of its electronic resources. In addition to these resources, many of which are available through its wildly popular Office of Teaching Resources in Psychology (OTRP; http://teachpsych.org/otrp/index.php), STP also publishes one of the premier disciplinary pedagogical journals, *Teaching of Psychology* (http://teachpsych.org/top/topindex.php), and electronic books, which are downloadable in several formats and are free of charge (http://teachpsych.org/resources/e-books/e-books.php).

Education Directorate of the American Psychological Association (http://www.apa.org/ed/)

This arm of the APA focuses on promoting education in psychology at all levels. It offers many programs and initiatives aimed at enhancing both faculty development and student learning.

Association for Psychological Science (http://www.psychologicalscience.org/)

APS is devoted to promoting psychology as a science, including promoting the teaching of psychological science. Part of its Web site is devoted to information on teaching (see http://www.psychologicalscience.org/teaching/). APS sponsors a preconference institute on the teaching of psychology (overseen by STP) at its annual convention and includes several hours of teaching-related programming within the convention itself. APS also publishes a regular column on teaching in its monthly magazine, *The Observer*. These columns have been bound into two volumes entitled *Lessons Learned: Practical Advice on the Teaching of Psychology*, which are edited by Barry Perlman, Lee McCann, and Susan McFadden (1999–2004). Finally, APS oversees the APS Fund for the Teaching and Public Understanding of Psychological Science, which provides small grants for local, regional, national, and international teaching-related initiatives and supports other worthy causes related to "giving psychology away."

Canadian Psychological Association Section of the Teaching of Psychology (http://www.cpa.ca/sections/teaching/)

The general aim of the Section on the Teaching of Psychology is to provide a forum for the exchange of information, ideas, and data concerning all aspects of teaching, including methods and styles of teaching, innovative pedagogical techniques, and aspects of student behavior and evaluation. To this end, each year at the Canadian Psychological Association Convention, the Section offers a teaching-related symposium, paper session or workshop, the ongoing general theme of which has been since 1989, "Improving the teaching of psychology."

British Psychological Society Division of Teachers and Researchers (http://www.bps.org.uk/dtrp/dtrp_home.cfm)

This division of the BPS aims to be the professional home for any psychologist whose principal activities are in research, in teaching, or in a combination of both. It was formed to address the professional issues which concern that significant proportion of the Society's membership who do not offer direct psychological services to client groups, but undertake academic duties in schools, colleges, universities, and research establishments or are undergoing training to equip themselves for careers in these settings.

Educational Psychology, Division 15 of the American Psychological Association (http://www.apa.org/about/division/div15.html)

Division 15 is dedicated to supporting research on teaching and other aspects of education at all levels. It publishes a quarterly journal, the *Educational Psychologist*.

PT@CC, or Psychology Teachers at Community Colleges (http://www.apa.org/ed/pt@cc_update.html)

PT@CC is an APA-supported organization dedicated to providing support for psychology faculty who teach at two-year schools. One of PT@CC's many goals is to stimulate research in teaching and learning at the community college level.

TOPSS, or Teachers of Psychology at Secondary Schools (http://www.apa.org/ed/topssinfo.html)

TOPPS is an APA-backed organization that provides support for high school teachers of psychology.

CTUP, or the Council of Teachers of Undergraduate
Psychology (http://www.am.org/ctup/)

CTUP is an independent organization that promotes the teaching of
psychology by sponsoring workshops, symposia, posters, and talks
at regional and national psychology conferences.

CUPP, or the Council of Undergraduate Psychology
Programs (http://www.am.org/cupp/)

CUPP is an independent organization that focuses on improving
teaching and learning in psychology at the program/departmental
level. CUPP sponsors events at regional and national psychology conferences and its members often serve in advocacy positions within
other teaching-related psychology organizations.

Higher Education Academy Psychology Network
(http://www.psychology.heacademy.ac.uk/)

This is a UK government-supported organization whose aim is to
promote excellence in the learning, teaching and assessment of
psychology across the full range of curricula and activities relevant
to UK higher education.

Conferences on the Teaching of Psychology

National Institute on the Teaching of Psychology
(NITOP; http://www.nitop.org/)

NITOP is considered to be the world's premier conference on the
teaching of psychology. Its annual meeting is held in early January
in St. Pete Beach, Florida. NITOP's venue includes plenary sessions,
concurrent sessions, workshops, poster sessions, and participant idea
exchanges. Many of the top names in both psychological research
and the teaching of psychology present their work at NITOP.

American Psychological Association
(APA; http://www.apa.org/)

The APA holds its annual meeting in August, but occasionally
in July. STP (Division 2 of the APA) sponsors the bulk of the

conference programming related specifically to the teaching of psychology.

Association for Psychological Science
(APS; http://www.psychologicalscience.org/)

APS sponsors a preconference workshop and a day-long Teaching Institute as part of its annual meeting, which is held each year in late May. In addition, sessions on the teaching of psychology are embedded within the regular conference programming. STP oversees the preconference workshop, the Teaching Institute, and all conference programming related to the teaching of psychology.

Best Practices (BP) Conference

This conference, which is sponsored by both STP and NITOP as well as by the Center for Teaching and Excellence at Kennesaw State University is held each year in October. The conference was originally held in Atlanta but will take place in various other locations in the future. The conference focuses on a different theme each year— so all plenary sessions, workshops, concurrent sessions, and poster sessions are related to that theme. The themes in years past have included such topics as teaching introductory psychology, teaching research methods and statistics, diversity issues, and starting and finishing the psychology major.

Regional Conferences on the Teaching of Psychology

Several independent regional and state conferences devoted to the teaching of psychology are held annually. For a listing of these conferences, their dates, and locations, go to http://teachpsych.org/conferences/conferences.php. This Web site also lists more general teaching-related conferences in addition to those meetings devoted to the teaching of psychology.

Books

The books referenced below represent a partial, but compelling, list of excellent texts on the teaching of psychology, teaching across higher education, and careers in teaching. Although most of the books are recent, those that are not represent what many consider to be classics in the area. They are well worth the time you might invest in reading them.

Bain, K. (2004). *What the best college teachers do*. Cambridge, MA: Harvard University Press.

Baiocco, S. A., & DeWaters, J. N. (1998). *Successful college teachers: Problem-solving strategies of distinguished professors*. Boston: Allyn and Bacon.

Boice, R. (2000). *Advice for new faculty members*. Boston: Allyn and Bacon.

Boyer, E. L. (1990). *Scholarship reconsidered: Priorities of the professoriate*. San Francisco: Jossey-Bass.

Brookfield, S. D. (1990). *The skillful teacher*. San Francisco: Jossey-Bass.

Brookfield, S. D. (1995). *Becoming a critically reflective teacher*. San Francisco: Jossey-Bass.

Buskist, W., & Davis, S. F. (Eds.). (2006). *Handbook of the teaching of psychology*. Malden, MA: Blackwell.

Darley, J. M., Zanna, M. P., & Roediger, H. L. (2004). *The compleat academic: A career guide* (2nd ed.). Washington, DC: American Psychological Association.

Davis, S. F., & Buskist, W. (Eds.). (2002). *The teaching of psychology: Essays in honor of Wilbert J. McKeachie and Charles L. Brewer*. Mahwah, NJ: Erlbaum.

Duffy, D. K., & Jones, J. W. (1995). *Teaching within the rhythms of the semester*. San Francisco: Jossey-Bass.

Dunn, D. S., & Chew, S. L. (Eds.). (2006). *Best practices for teaching introductory psychology*. Mahwah, NJ: Erlbaum.

Forsyth, D. R. (2003). *The professor's guide to teaching: Psychological principles and practices*. Washington, DC: American Psychological Association.

Fox, R. (2005). *Teaching & learning: Lessons from psychology*. Malden, MA: Blackwell.

Glassick, C. E., Huber, M. T., & Maeroff, G. I. (1997). *Scholarship assessed: Evaluation of the professoriate*. San Francisco: Jossey-Bass.

Goss Lucas, S., & Bernstein, D. A. (2005). *Teaching psychology: A step by step guide*. Mahwah, NJ: Erlbaum.

Huber, M. T. (2004). *Balancing acts: The scholarship of teaching and learning in academic careers*. Washington, DC: The Carnegie Foundation for the Advancement of Teaching and the American Association of Higher Education.

James, W. (1962). *Talks to teachers on psychology and to students on some of life's ideals*. Mineola, NY: Dover. (Original work published 1899)

Keith-Spiegel, P., Whitley, B. E., Balogh, D. W., Perkins, D. V., & Wittig, A. F. (2002). *The ethics of teaching: A casebook* (2nd ed,). Mahwah, NJ: Erlbaum.

Lowman, J. (1995). *Mastering the techniques of teaching* (2nd ed.). San Francisco: Jossey-Bass.

McKeachie, W. J., & Svinicki, M. (2006). *McKeachie's teaching tips: Strategies, research, and theory for college and university teachers.* Boston: Houghton Mifflin.

Palmer, P. J. (1998). *The courage to teach: Exploring the inner landscape of a teacher's life.* San Francisco: Jossey-Bass.

Perlman, B., McCann, L. I., & McFadden S. H. (1999). *Lessons learned: Practical advice for the teaching of psychology, Vol. 1.* Washington, DC: American Psychological Society.

Perlman, B., McCann, L. I., & McFadden S. H. (2004). *Lessons learned: Practical advice for the teaching of psychology, Vol. 2.* Washington, DC: American Psychological Society.

Perlman, B., McCann, L. I., & Buskist, W. (2005). *Voices of experience: Memorable talks from the National Institute on the Teaching of Psychology.* Washington, DC: American Psychological Society.

Puente, A. E., Matthews, J. R., & Brewer, C. L. (1992). *Teaching psychology in America: A history.* Washington, DC: American Psychological Association.

Sternberg, R. J. (Ed.). (1997). *Teaching introductory psychology: Survival tips from the experts.* Washington, DC: American Psychological Association.

Index